RESEARCH AND PRACTI

Wayne Jour

Developing Historical Thinkers: Suppo... Historical Inquiry for All Students
BRUCE A. LESH

Toward a Stranger and More Posthuman Social Studies
BRETTON A. VARGA, TIMOTHY MONREAL, & REBECCA C. CHRIST, EDS.

Critical Race Theory and Social Studies Futures:
From the Nightmare of Racial Realism to Dreaming Out Loud
AMANDA E. VICKERY & NOREEN NASEEM RODRÍGUEZ, EDS.

How to Confront Climate Denial: Literacy, Social Studies, and Climate Change
JAMES S. DAMICO & MARK C. BAILDON

Racial Literacies and Social Studies: Curriculum, Instruction, and Learning
LAGARRETT J. KING, ED.

Making Classroom Discussions Work:
Methods for Quality Dialogue in the Social Studies
JANE C. LO, ED.

Teaching Difficult Histories in Difficult Times: Stories of Practice
LAUREN MCARTHUR HARRIS, MAIA SHEPPARD, & SARA A. LEVY, EDS.

Post-Pandemic Social Studies:
How COVID-19 Has Changed the World and How We Teach
WAYNE JOURNELL, ED.

Teaching History for Justice: Centering Activism in Students' Study of the Past
CHRISTOPHER C. MARTELL & KAYLENE M. STEVENS

Developing Historical Thinkers

Supporting Historical Inquiry for All Students

Bruce A. Lesh

TEACHERS COLLEGE PRESS
TEACHERS COLLEGE | COLUMBIA UNIVERSITY
NEW YORK AND LONDON

Published by Teachers College Press,® 1234 Amsterdam Avenue, New York, NY 10027

Front cover design by Peter Donahue. Unless noted otherwise, inset art is courtesy of the Library of Congress. Left to right, top to bottom: (1) Jacob T. Lawrence, *During World War I There Was a Great Migration North by Southern African Americans*, 1942, The Jacob and Gwendolyn Knight Lawrence Foundation, Seattle / Artists Rights Society (ARS), New York. (2) W.A. Rogers, *King Debs*, 1894. (3) E.B. & E.C. Kellogg, *The drunkard's progress*, Kelloggs & Thayer, ca. 1846. (4) Richard Newton, *Buonaparte Establishing French Quarters in Italy*. 1797, The Trustees of the British Museum. (5) John Zukowsky, *Berlin Wall with Tower and Souvenir Hunters*. (6) Charlotte Brooks, *Male Couples*. (7) Dorothea Lange, *Destitute pea pickers in California*. (8) Herman Hiller, *Malcolm X at Queens Court*. (9) Le Petit Journal, *The Lynchings in the United States: The Massacre of Negroes in Atlanta*, 1906, Wikimedia Commons. (10) Photographer unknown, *Marcus Garvey, 1924*. (11) "Demonstration, with Gay Liberation Front Banner," 1972, Wikimedia Commons. (12) P-2H Neptune over Soviet ship, 1962, Wikimedia Commons. (13) Jack Delano, *Group of Florida Migrants on Their Way to Cranberry, New Jersey, to Pick Potatoes*, 1970. (14) Arthur Rothstein, *Farmer and Sons Walking in the Face of a Dust Storm, Cimarron County, Oklahoma*, 1936. (15) *Names Project AIDS Memorial Quilt*, Wikipedia. (16) A. M. Byers, *Abraham Lincoln*, 1858, National Portrait Gallery. (17) Nathaniel Currier, *The drunkards progress. From the first glass to the grave*, 1846. (18) G.W. Peters, *The Statue Erected in Haymarket Square to the Murdered Policemen*, Undated. (19) Peter Leibing, *Leap Into Freedom*, 1961, Berlin, Germany. (20) French soldiers in trench with machine-gun, World War I. (21) Photographer unknown, *For the Freedom of the World*. 1917.

Library of Congress Cataloging-in-Publication Data is available at loc.gov

ISBN 978-0-8077-6876-1 (paper)
ISBN 978-0-8077-6877-8 (hardcover)
ISBN 978-0-8077-8193-7 (ebook)

Printed on acid-free paper
Manufactured in the United States of America

Contents

Preface

It was Philadelphia in the summer. It was hot, and the air conditioning was not functioning as well as one would hope on a steamy July day. No, it was not 1787—I am not that old!—but instead 2004. There were almost 100 teachers in the auditorium. We had been working together for the better part of a week under the auspices of a federally funded Teaching American History grant program. We read common texts, heard from noted historians, visited historical sites, and explored various pedagogies related to teaching history. It was our last day and people were hot and tired, and their brains were full.

My presentation that day focused on the abolitionist movement. One of the historical sources that participants reviewed made the argument that the North was as culpable in supporting slavery as the South because Northern insurance companies, banks, factories, and universities had funded, invested, and profited from the institution. Immediately, a teacher shot up and said, "Do you mean to tell me that you think the North supported slavery?" I quickly pivoted to the scholarship, linking the argument to historians and to the evidence they used to support their claim. Clearly unhappy with the answer and the historical argument, this gentleman proceeded to get up, gather his materials, shout an expletive, and leave the building. Yes, professional learning with teachers can be hard!

I used to think that working with students was challenging, and then I ventured into the world of professional development. How naive I was! Preservice and practicing teachers have a range of experiences, ingrained beliefs about teaching and learning (sometimes evidenced-based, but more often than not experiential), and papers to grade. Teachers also have an internal clock that gives people providing professional learning about 7 minutes to prove that the learning that is about to take place is more important that the papers that need grading. Over the years I have had teachers leave professional learning sessions because their principal called them back to the building, because they did not want to "change the way I do things," and because it was 3:00 P.M. and the union contract stipulated that they only worked until that time. Yes, professional learning with teachers can be tricky.

On the flip side, professional learning with teachers can be as, if not more, rewarding as working with students. The knowledge that preservice and practicing teachers possess, their passion for the profession, their desire to do what is best for students, and, in most instances, an interest in continual improvement makes teacher professional learning a rich field in which to garden.

DRIVE-BY PROFESSIONAL LEARNING

This book is framed around both classroom instruction and the professional development I provided for almost 30 years working with thousands of teachers in over 40 states. Starting in the late 1990s with John Jeffries, Dan Ritschel, and Rachel Brubaker at the Center for History Education at the University of Maryland, Baltimore County, to the Teaching American History grants in school districts partnering with the National Council for History Education, and finally to the opportunities to work with districts because of the publication of "*Why Won't You Just Tell Us the Answer*?" (Lesh, 2011), I was lucky enough to share my passion with thousands of teachers across 41 states. In particular, thanks to Shawn Owen, I was afforded the opportunity to work for 2 years with the Georgia State Department of Education. This allowed me to traverse from Camilla to Rome, Macon to Suwanee, and everywhere in between. These experiences working with teachers to develop their willingness and capacity to transition their instruction is the heart of this book.

In each instance, the professional learning I provided was conducted either solo or in partnership with a historian. When it was a partnership, the historian provided an overview of the content and guided discussions of key documents or monographs, and I provided the pedagogy. The majority of these experiences were between 3 and 5 days long. In a few rare instances, I had the occasion to work with a group of teachers over several years, but by and large, these were drive-bys. I came, I delivered, I left, never to return.

I loved the opportunity to engage with so many teachers and to move the teaching and learning of history in a positive direction. Loved it. But at the end of each professional development event, I always had a lingering feeling that I was leaving when the really hard work was about to begin. The professional learning I provided was not sustained, ongoing, or job-embedded. It was focused on student learning and teacher practice, grounded in research, and delivered with personality, but at the end of the day I was in my car headed home, and the teachers were headed back to the workplace without the sustainability they needed to turn the learning into changed practice. I had been present at the conception of this professional change, but not at the birth of the new practices. What always fueled my concern was the ubiquitous statement I heard at some point during my professional learning sessions: "My kids can't do this."

"MY KIDS CAN'T DO THIS"

Of the hundreds of times I presented to teachers, not a single presentation occurred without an audience member raising a hand and stating: "My kids can't do this." I have presented in wealthy suburban districts, impoverished rural and urban settings, and schools in the Northeast, South, Southwest, and three Hawaiian islands, and this question was always at the forefront of the pushback I received during my presentations. For over 2 decades, I sat through numerous professional development sessions as a teacher, and thus I was not shocked by this response. Every teacher worth their salt interprets professional development through several lenses: the availability of resources, the level of support they receive, the frequency of noninstructional interruptions, the poverty level of the community they serve, the needs of their students. These and numerous other factors are at the forefront of teachers' minds as they decide how to organize and implement their instruction. "My kids can't do this" is often more of a reactive response. Defensively, teachers are saying that I do not know their students, community, district, or instructional reality, and thus "My kids cannot do this" has a variety of meanings.

"My kids can't do this" means that the teacher is successful—or believes themself to be successful—and therefore the change being described by the professional development is simply superfluous. In that instance, "My kids can't do this" means that the teacher does not need to explore this approach because everything is working just fine. In some cases, the teacher isn't wrong; they are doing well, and their students are successful. In other, more frequent instances, the teacher is wrong and is thus expressing their inability to analyze their instruction critically.

Most frequently, I find that the response "My kids can't do this" really means that the teacher does not feel secure enough in their understanding of the approach or their ability to embrace and incorporate it in instruction. Instructional approaches that embrace inquiry, investigation, or really anything that is not textbook-centered and organized around teacher delivery stoke teachers' fears about losing control of the classroom and the inability to cover the content. Their statement begged for ongoing, continuous professional learning, not a drive-by.

The goal of this book is to examine ways to break through this statement and all of the real meanings behind it, and look for ways to promote teacher growth, at least as it pertains to teaching historical thinking. Transitioning away from history as intellectual bulimia to history as a process that engages students in investigating the past is difficult. Recognizing that all students can engage in these kinds of investigations is essential to ensuring this transition. The subsequent chapters encourage others to push past the perceived barrier that their students "cannot do this" and to embrace the idea that "Yes, your kids can do this!" My goal in writing *Developing Historical Thinkers: Supporting Historical Inquiry for All Students* is to mine the work from hundreds of professional development sessions and focus on gaps from my first book that were exposed while I made presentations to groups of educators. Chapters will focus on some changes to the approach that have occurred since the publication of "*Why Won't You Just Tell Us the Answer?*," as well as guidance focused on how to bring a large group of professionals to successful implementation of historical thinking in the classroom. Within this approach to promoting teacher growth, I also address aspects of my methodology that have evolved since my first book and address questions that arose consistently during my presentations.

Acknowledgments

This book was much more difficult to write than "*Why Won't You Just Tell Us the Answer?*" because 4 years after the publication of my first book, and after 22 years in the classroom, I left to take on a new position in public education. Although I started writing this book before leaving the classroom, my absence from the real frontlines of education—working directly with students, grading papers, talking with parents, chaperoning homecoming dances—made me feel that writing about teaching and learning was somehow fraudulent. How can I write about teaching students when I no longer do so?

My reticence was assuaged by some amazing colleagues who helped me understand that although I was no longer a teacher, 22 years in front of high school students, providing professional learning, overseeing state standards and frameworks, and delivering teacher development, combined with almost a decade as a state-level policymaker, does enable me to write about teaching and not to feel fraudulent. Struggling to overcome this conundrum, a colleague reminded me that teaching is a lot like riding a bike. Even if you stop for a while, you still have the muscle memory and experiences to guide you. Regaining confidence to move forward with the project, I shifted my focus slightly from classroom instruction with children exclusively, to teaching both children and adults.

No book is written on an island. I am grateful for the thoughtful, albeit at times painful, feedback I received from so many people. Special thinks go out to Sarah Drake Brown, Brigette Cascio, Debbie Daniel, Fritz Fischer, Catherine Holden, Adam Laye Leah Renzi, and Glenn Weibe, who supplied feedback on various versions of the book. This work is better because of their honesty, intellect, and time. A special shout-out goes to Jeff Nokes. Not only did he give multiple rounds of feedback, but he also volunteered to use one of the chapters with the students in his Fall 2022 methods course. I am grateful for his intellect, feedback, and friendship. Indirectly, but no less impactful, have been the thousands of teachers that I worked with during professional learning sessions. Teachers are brutally honest in their feedback—positive and negative—and I have benefited greatly from the kudos, compliments, criticisms, and questions from the teachers who attended my professional learning workshops. They made me better as a professional developer, teacher, and educator. Their questions are at the center of the book, and hopefully I have been able to honor and answer them in a way that continues to push teaching and learning in history in a better direction. Thanks also to the keen eye and endless red pen of the amazing Kathy Maher-Baker. Her edits ensured that I avoided numerous embarrassing spelling, grammar, and usage errors!

All the lessons I reflect on in the book were taught by me to high school students except the three on LGBTQ+ history. For the lessons highlighted in Chapter 6, I am grateful for the partnership with two teachers who were able to pilot new lessons that I had developed on LGBTQ+ and disability history. They are dedicated educators who rose to the challenges presented by COVID and remain committed to their students and teaching history in a thoughtful and engaging manner. It was amazing to see these instructional materials through their eyes and the eyes of their students. Thanks to them and their students for engaging in these lessons, sharing their work, and communicating insights into how these "hard histories" affected students.

For the past 30 years, so many people have impacted my development in positive ways that I fear I cannot recognize anyone without inadvertently leaving out someone important, so I am just going to say thank you to everyone I have taught with, been a colleague of, or touched my professional life in any way.

Thirty years in public education is a long time. In retrospect, I am struck at how much the profession has changed since the early 1990s. Sadly, many of these changes are not for the better, but I still believe that teaching—in the classroom, in front of students—is the most important, impactful, and honest element of the education infrastructure. Although it has been made harder in so many ways, the classroom is where the magic happens and where the rewards are tangible, lasting, and what we are all getting into the profession to obtain. There is a perversion in the profession where those who educate students do not receive the same renumeration, respect, resources, or recognition as those who create policy, legislate, or pontificate about what is best for education. I have enjoyed the new mental muscles developed as a state-level policymaker, but the cycle between action and outcome is so much slower than what happens in the classroom. Prone to political whims, promotion of silver bullets and panaceas, the policy realm is still in my mind significantly disconnected from the realities of teaching and learning in the schoolhouse. Real change will happen when those two realms—policy and the classroom—become better aligned.

Finally, to Chris and Ryan, my wife and son: my entire world. Thank you for your love, time, patience, humor, and willingness to let me chase my passion for teaching history.

Developing Historical Thinkers

CHAPTER 1

"But My Kids Cannot Do This . . ."

Challenging Perceptions About Historical Investigations

Leeches. For generations, doctors, or those considered to have medical expertise, used leaches to eradicate disease and coax the ill back to health. The belief, up until the mid–19th century and the emergence of germ theory, was that illness was driven by an imbalance of the four humors: blood, phlegm, and black and yellow bile. An imbalance of these four fluids would lead to illness, and thus bringing the body back to stasis would promote health. The rebalancing of humors was achieved through bloodletting. Cutting veins, lancing thumbs, and using cupping to draw blood from small cuts were all methods employed to return the humors to a healthy balance. The most famous of these techniques was the employment of leeches. Medical professionals placed leeches, bloodsuckers by evolution, on the ill to draw out blood and return people to health. Unfortunately, many of the ill either bled to death or died from shock. Thankfully, outside of some believers in "alternative therapies," the use of venesection and arteriotomy is no longer used.

What does this have to do with changes in educational practice? I have heard several educational leaders, when asked why teachers cannot continue to do things "the way they were taught" or "how things have always been done," respond by asking those teachers if they would go to a doctor who believed that the cause of illness was an imbalance of humors, and that health could be restored using leeches. The response is invariably no, of course not. So, goes the line of argument, why would we continue to use educational strategies that we know no longer, or never did, work, or could be built upon to be even more effective for more students?

For some teachers, this analogy makes sense. No one would submit themselves to a medical procedure so outdated. They value that our understanding of students, the brain, and instruction have evolved just like medical practice. For other teachers, this analogy is a false equivalency. They argue that education is different, simpler, and that change is less important than "reformers" deem it to be. These educational practitioners argue that educational research is done by people who have no understanding of what happened in the classroom or their reality. "The ivory tower," the "guys (or gals) in the suits," or "people who don't know my kids" are often the collective others pushing changes that teachers resist. But we know so much more about how students learn, what students are not being served by our current educational practices, and the needs of the current economy that continuing to apply educational leeches is willful educational malpractice.

In this chapter, I lay out my fundamental beliefs about teaching and learning in history and how these beliefs manifest themselves in the History Lab approach. In addition, this chapter will show how, for some teachers, professional learning around my approach can lead to the statement "My kids cannot do this," and thus, I will examine how taking those concerns head-on can win converts to investigating history.

MY WHY, PART I

The central theme to my professional learning is that we cannot continue to approach history teaching and learning in the same way we have for the past 120 years. It simply isn't working, and there is a rich repository of research, materials, and resources to support a transition to a more effective delivery of history instruction. Much of history instruction prior to the 1960s was predicated on a misunderstanding of Piaget's stages of cognitive development. Essentially, the belief was that students could not really understand history until they emerged into the formal operational stage because the study of the past was too abstract (Coltham, 1971; Hallam, 1970, 1971). The result was instruction that fell to memorization of discrete facts and the sharing of moralistic stories. Keep them entertained, build up their background knowledge, and eventually, the argument went, when students pass into the formal operational stage, then we can teach students real history. Research and practice indicate, though, that when students cross the threshold of the classroom, they are not entering as blank slates. In fact, they come in with many preconceived notions about the discipline and about specific events, people, and ideas from the past, in addition to factual misconceptions and oversimplifications as well as a wealth of personal insights gained through family, travel, personal experiences, and popular culture (Barton, 2008; Donovan & Bransford, 2005; Wineburg et al., 2007). Ignoring these presumptions can lead students to disregard or disconnect from school history, especially for students from groups underrepresented in the broader historical narrative (Almarza, 2001; Barton & McCully, 2005; Brown & Brown, 2010; Epstein, 2000, 2009; Good, 2009; Traille, 2007). In terms of the discipline of history, research indicates that students have a number of preconceptions about history before they enter the classroom (Barton, 2008; Epstein, 2012; Holt, 1990; Husbands et al., 2011; Lee, 2005; Lee et al., 1997; Lee & Shemilt, 2003, 2004; Shemilt, 1987). These preconceptions include believing that:

1. History is the same as the past.
2. History is a true account of the past.
3. The past is fixed, and we just need to figure out what happened.
4. Textbooks provide an unimpeachable telling of history.
5. Primary sources should be privileged over secondary.
6. There are biased and unbiased historical sources.
7. There are valid reasons why accounts of the past differ.
8. Historians develop interpretations based on "adding up evidence."
9. People in the past were not as intelligent as we are now.
10. Change equals progress.
11. Change occurs because of events causing them rather than a confluence of underlying social, political, and economic forces.
12. Singular factors explain historical change, with a bias toward individual action as the sole driver.

Unfortunately, classroom practice has followed a persistent form of instruction misaligned with best practices for student learning, generally avoidant of recognizing students' pre-existing misconceptions, and aligned to an underestimation of student interest and ability to engage in the study of history.

History education has witnessed a consistency in instructional approach focused on the dissemination of a story, told through a single source, usually via textbook or teacher lecture (Beck & Eno, 2012; Bolinger & Warren, 2007; Cuban, 1982, 1993; Leming et al., 2009; Wanzek et al., 2015; Woodward & Elliott, 1990). The "I talk, you listen" form of history instruction continues to predominate even in the 21st century (Burkholder & Schaffer, 2021; Grant, 2003, 2006; Luff, 2001; Sylvester, 1994). Social studies teachers are less likely than teachers in the other core academic areas to use alternatives to whole-class instruction. At least once a week, 78% of social studies teachers lecture students, 88% conduct a teacher-led discussion, 91% have students answer recall questions, and 94% have students read the textbook in both the classroom and at home (Leming et al., 2009). Students, though, universally dislike history when it is taught as a series of lists that must be memorized and regurgitated (Harris & Hayden, 2006; Rosenzweig & Thelen, 1998). This instructional consistency continues despite changes in technology. Film strips, reel-to-reel films, overhead projectors, VCRs, the video disk, DVDs, student electronic voting tools, document cameras, electronic whiteboards, computer labs, one-to-one computers, and a myriad of other tools have not substantively altered the traditional patterns of instruction in the history classroom. The habitual utilization of these techniques would seem to indicate that they promote student learning. Over 100 years of results throw cold water on that idea.

Information, facts, knowledge, content—whatever we name it, it matters. You cannot make a legitimate argument that the study of history should be centered only on skills. To do so would strip the power of the discipline to frame student understanding, provide much-needed background knowledge for reading comprehension, and provide a basis on which to interpret current events (Counsell, 2000; Hirsch, 1987; Neumann, 2021; Rogers, 1987; Wexler, 2019; Willingham, 2010, 2017). The reality, though, is that a history education focused only on the transmission and retention of a large volume of facts results in historical ignorance rather than knowledge (Bell & McCollum, 1917; Finn & Ravitch, 1987; McKeown & Beck, 1990; Niemi et al., 2005; Paxton, 2003; Romano, 2011; Whittington, 1991; Wineburg, 2001). As depicted in Figure 1.1, National Assessment of Educational Progress results dating from 1994 report the same dismal story: Students are not retaining much of what they are taught.

Reflecting on almost 100 years of testing data beginning in 1917, Wineburg (2001) reminds us that the NAEP data is simply a more modern example of a long-term trend. "We learn," argues Wineburg, "that there has been little appreciable change in students' historical knowledge over time . . . the consistency of these results casts doubts on a presumed golden age of fact retention. Appeals to such an age are more the stuff of national lore and a wistful nostalgia for a time that never was than a reference to a national history whose reality can be found in the documentary record" (p. 33). Let's be honest, even the much-vaunted Advanced Placement United States History program awards a score of 3 for students who have shown about 50% understanding of the material tested. A 3 is a passing score, so passing an AP exam with a score below a 4 is still not a great measure of student knowledge of history and may instead be a better measure of student preparation prior to the course, the teacher's facility with the content, or student and teacher access to resources to make the course a successful

Figure 1.1. Trend in 8th-Grade NAEP U.S. History Achievement Level Results

YEAR	below NAEP Basic	NAEP Basic	NAEP Proficient	NAEP Advanced
2018	34	50	14	1
2014	29*	53*	17*	1
2010	31*	52	16	1
2006	35	49	15	1
2001	38*	46*	14	1
2001[1]	36	48*	15	2
1994[1]	39*	48*	13	1

100 90 80 70 60 50 40 30 20 10 0 10 20 30 40 50 60 70 80 90 100
PERCENT

* Significantly different ($p < .05$) from 2018.

1 Accommodations not permitted.

NOTE: NAEP achievement levels are to be used on a trial basis and should be interpreted and used with caution.

Source: National Assessment of Educational Progress (https://www.nationsreportcard.gov/ushistory/results/achievement/)

experience. Poor student performance in history has been a hallmark of educational data for over 100 years. So, also, has been a very persistent form of instruction.

Teacher's pedagogical choices are also identified by students as a significant reason for their disengagement, as the lowest levels of intrinsic motivation and the highest levels of boredom are reported when students are engaged in listening to lectures, taking notes, or watching videos (Shernoff & Csikszentmihalyi, 2014; Yazzie-Mintz, 2010). The consistency of the results and the persistence of the instructional methodology do not paint a picture of success. Instead, they remind me of the definition of insanity: continuing to do the same thing and hoping for different results.

We know that students who are taught history as a set of facts in isolation from a meaningful historical context learn little as data since 1917 have been telling this story (Barton & Levstik, 1998; VanSledright & Frankes, 2000). Even if students retain the volume of information teachers dispense, which is unlikely if it is learned in a rote manner, if the information is not used frequently, the ability to recall that information declines over time (Bransford et al., 2000; Davis et al., 2000). This phenomenon is not isolated to American classrooms, but plagues most democratic nations (Lee & Howson, 2009; van der Leeuw-Roord, 2009). Although it is hard to prove causality, over 100 years of data clearly indicate that there is a correlation between the instruction that has persisted in history classrooms and the consistently dismal results in student learning.

Facts, absent a question to answer, are quickly forgotten (Bransford et al., 2000; Davis et al., 2000). Provided an opportunity to investigate meaty questions and develop evidence-based responses, research shows that students are more engaged, achieve better understanding of historical content, demonstrate improved historical writing, and develop historical reasoning skills (Ashby et al., 2005; Bain, 2000, 2006; Booth, 1978; Brush & Saye, 2014; Burkholder & Schaffer, 2021; Caron, 2005; Gorman, 1998; Grant & Gradwell, 2010; Monte-Sano et al., 2014; Lattimer, 2008; Lesh, 2011; Lévesque, 2009; Monte-Sano et al., 2014; Nokes, 2013; Nokes et al., 2007; Obenchain et al., 2011; Reisman, 2011; Riley, 2000; Shemilt, 1980, 1987; Smith & Niemi, 2001; Swann et al., 2018a; van Boxtel & van Drie, 2018; VanSledright, 2002, 2014; Viator, 2012; Wineburg et al., 2011). Yup, that is a tremendous amount of research that demonstrates there is an alternative path forward for history instruction. Hmmm, so there is a way to engage students AND have them learn . . . sign me up!

Central to the study of history in a disciplinary manner is the use of historical sources (Nokes, 2013; Shemilt, 1980, 1987, 2009; VanSledright, 2002). Without explicit instruction, students treat historical sources the same as they do a textbook: find the main idea (Wineburg, 1991). Teachers usually use historical sources to illustrate or reinforce "points made during the lecture" and rarely employ multiple sources or conflicting ones (Nokes, 2010).

The purpose of examining historical sources is to generate evidence to "reach a conclusion about the past," and this is only accomplished by "placing the source within a context of an inquiry" so that students can utilize sources to draw information to "reach conclusions about the past" (Barton, 2018). The application of key literacy skills that historians utilize while examining historical sources is essential to classroom instruction that encourages inquiry into the past (Nokes, 2013; VanSledright, 2002; Wineburg, 2001). Use of multiple texts results in better student understanding, writing, and learning (Hynd, 1999; Nokes et al., 2007; Voss & Wiley, 1997; Wiley & Voss, 1999). Through sourcing, contextualizing, close reading, and corroborating multiple sources, students have the tools to attack these meaty historical questions and develop responsible evidence-based responses.

When held in contrast to the persistent instruction that defines the teaching of history—a steady diet of textbook readings, recall questions, and teacher-directed instruction—historical inquiry improves student engagement and achievement (Gradwell, 2006; Grant & Gradwell, 2010; Hattie, 2009; Hillis, 2005; Newmann et al., 2001; Reisman, 2011; Smith & Niemi, 2001). Even students younger than 14 can deal with contesting historical claims, wrestle with evidence, and apply historical perspective-taking (Barton, 1997a, 1997b, 1997c; Berti et al., 2009; Dulberg, 2005; Hartman & Hasselhorn, 2008; Lee et al., 1997; VanSledright, 2002). For me, the research is clear. There is a better way to approach the teaching of history than we have done for generations. Thankfully, we had the Stanford History Education Group (SHEG) to show a better way.

THE STANFORD HISTORY EDUCATION GROUP (SHEG)

It is not often that academic research into a topic like expert readers and educational psychology can cross over into the K–12 education setting and actually influence instructional change. The work of Sam Wineburg and a growing legion of graduate students turned professors at the Stanford History Education Group (https://sheg.stanford.edu/) serves as an exception to that rule. Wineburg's research on the confluence of literacy and history has generated usable instructional materials that empower teachers to approach history differently. Teachers, departments, schools, and districts across the country have been trained on and utilize SHEG's Reading Like a Historian, Beyond the Bubble, and Civic Online Reasoning materials.

The tools found at SHEG's website empower teachers to apply and assess the disciplinary literacy skills of sourcing, contextualizing, close reading, and corroboration as well as other historical thinking skills such as causality and periodization. At the heart of the SHEG materials are two key components that alleviate teacher concerns about inquiry and facilitate use in the classroom. First, developing questions worth investigating is a key barrier to teachers adopting an inquiry-based instructional approach. Whether the lesson is World or United States History, visitors to the SHEG site will find materials organized around thoughtful questions. The second component of the SHEG methodology that smooths the obstacles in the way of inquiry-based instruction is the availability of materials that have been edited in length to no more than 250 words. Collectively, the presence of thoughtful organizing questions and approachable sources alleviates a teacher's number-one complaint: time. Teachers who do not have the time to develop lessons that incorporate elements of this approach can poach resources from the site and move students in the direction of improved literacy, historical thinking, and understanding of the past.

Kudos aside, an important caveat about the SHEG materials: The instructional materials found in the Reading Like a Historian section are labeled "lesson plans." Each contains an overarching historical question to be investigated, 2–3 sources that inform student research, and occasionally a PowerPoint to help establish background. Although labeled "lesson plans," I find that they really function more like lesson seeds. A teacher can plant them, and something will grow in the classroom, but to nurture a full-size lesson, teachers will need to supplement the SHEG-provided resources with other elements to ensure a full lesson. This could mean the addition of a few more sources, instructional materials to better flesh out students' background knowledge, and a variety of tools to scaffold the lesson and to differentiate it for various student needs. This caveat established, the SHEG methodology actualizes much of the research described above and has significantly impacted the teaching and learning of history as well as my own approach in the classroom.

So, the first part of my why is simple: The research on teaching and learning in history is clear. The way in which we have traditionally approached history instruction does not work, and there is a clear alterative with a strong research base to support this new approach. The second part of my why is the re-emergence of inquiry-based instruction, an approach that resonated with my ADHD brain and learning.

MY WHY, PART II

The notion of inquiry is not new to social studies. In fact, in the 1960s and early 1970s, the approach dominated the research, publishing materials, and instructional tools within the field. Through such endeavors as the Harvard Social Studies Project, the Amherst History Project, and the Carnegie Mellon University Social Studies Curriculum Project under the leadership of Edwin Fenton, inquiry became the heart of the "New Social Studies" (Dow, 2019; Fenton, 1990; Grant, 2018). Unfortunately, the methodology did not penetrate deeply into instruction.

By the time I hit the classroom in 1993, inquiry had literally moved to the dusty top shelf of school book rooms. It was on these shelves where I found some of the best resources to facilitate my own instructional transition, books like *Basic Concepts in History and Social Sciences*, *New Dimensions in American History*, and Edwin Fenton's *A New History of the United States: An Inquiry Approach*, *32 Problems in World History*, and *The Shaping of Western Society: An Inquiry Approach*. Finding these resources opened a window on inquiry for me. I loved how they modeled student investigation into history rather than simply facilitating student acceptance of the catechism delivered by the teacher. Unfortunately, by the early 1990s inquiry was at best on life support and at worst 6 feet under other instructional practices. Some classrooms continued to approach the teaching of social studies through the lens of inquiry, but most continued the didactic telling of stories. Lack of rich resources, the diminution of history and social studies within the broader school curriculum, and the persistence of instructional methods that have defined social studies instruction for decades brought inquiry to a close in American schools (Haas, 1977), but rest assured, as it is with most things in education, inquiry in social studies was just hibernating before reemerging in the mid/late-1990s (Foster & Padgett, 1999; Saye & SSIRC, 2013). Its re-emergence coincided with the accumulation of decades of research that points to a more effective way to teach and learn history.

THE INQUIRY ARC

The development and publication of the College, Career, and Civic Life (C3) Framework, published by the National Council for the Social Studies (NCSS), brought together the research on inquiry in social studies and gave it a clear form: the Inquiry Arc. As described below in Figure 1.2, the Inquiry Arc begins with the development of a compelling question and terminates with students communicating their response to the question. In between, students evaluate evidence within the context of the content of economics, civics, geography, and/or history. The Inquiry Arc posits an approach to instruction that places inquiry at the center and in close relationship to both content understanding and skill development (NCSS, 2015).

The work of the developers of the C3 Teachers group and some of the principal authors of the C3 Framework, Kathy Swan, John Lee, and S. G. Grant, have pushed inquiry back to the forefront of social studies education. Articulated through a series of books, articles, and, most impactfully, a series of free online inquiries, their work revitalized inquiry in social studies. This revitalization found form and function in the C3 Inquiries developed by the New York State Department of Education. Found at the C3 website, the inquiries

Figure 1.2. The Inquiry Arc

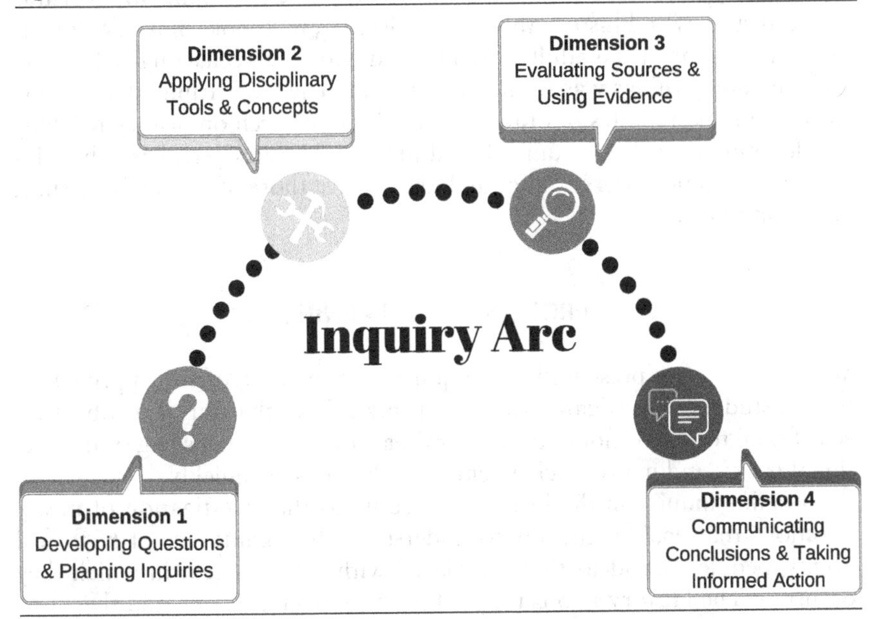

provide teachers with soup-to-nuts instructional plans that could facilitate high-quality inquiry in elementary, middle, and high school classrooms.

A significant strength of the C3 teacher inquiries is that they make a legitimate attempt to expand beyond the realm of history. Teachers can download full inquiries around such topics as:

- Does money matter in political campaigns?
- How can humans address their negative impact on the environment?
- Is free trade worth the price?
- Do any political parties represent me?
- What is the real cost of bananas?

Although there is little research on economic thinking, geographic thinking, or civic thinking commensurate with that in history, the inquiries do an excellent job of opening inquiry to these other disciplines. Visitors to the C3 site will find not only questions and numerous historical inquiries, but also inquiries focused on economics, geography, and civics.

The confluence of the research on history teaching and learning and the inquiry arc embedded in the C3 framework leads me to the final part of my why. Simply put, there are better ways to approach teaching and learning in social studies and history than simply lecture, textbook, movie, color the map, and repeat. As an adult who has lived with ADHD as long as I can remember, doing things was so much more conducive to learning than simply sitting and taking notes. As I incorporated the research on history teaching and learning as well as inquiry-based methods, I quickly realized that this kind of instruction was good for all kids, not just those of us who have short attention spans!

PROFESSIONAL LEARNING

When conducting presentations, inquiry is at the core of my approach to having students investigate history. I firmly believe that this is a robust instructional tool and should be a central part of any teacher's bag of instructional tricks, and many teachers embrace the message quickly.

I define inquiry in the history classroom as the investigation of meaty questions that enable students to understand the significance of historical events, people, and ideas that are placed within the context in which they occurred. The History Lab is the tool to move from research and theory to pragmatic instruction with teenagers.

THE HISTORY LAB 2.0

The History Lab, as outlined in Figure 1.3, is my effort to distill down all of the research into a tool that can be utilized by teachers. As outlined previously, the lab is focused on a central question to guide student investigation. Students then engage in source work where they employ historical literacy skills to evaluate the source, context, and corroborative value of a variety of historical sources, and the information gained from the sources is applied to the development of an answer to the lab's central question. Finally, the Lab requires students to develop, refine, and defend an evidence-based answer to the guiding historical question (Lesh, 2011). As outlined in Figure 1.3, the lab framework aligns with both the research on history education and the revitalization of inquiry:

The ultimate goal of a history lab is to promote thinking about a historical person, event, or idea. The relationship between the sources—contradictory and complementary—matters as much, if not morethan, simply the information they provide. In addition, during the execution of a lab, students must deal with how purpose, authorship, and time period impact the information being provided by the source and evaluate how some documents have greater weight and more corroboration than others when it comes to addressing the central investigative question. This tool, and the

Figure 1.3. The History Lab

I. Establish a focus question to guide students' investigation

- Question should be provocative and encourage investigation and discussion.
- Question should be central to the curriculum structuring the course.
- Question should deepen students' understanding of history as an interpretive discipline.
- Question should emphasize one or more of the following disciplinary concepts:
  - » Cause and consequence
  - » Chronology
  - » Multiple perspectives
  - » Historical significance

II. Initiate the Investigation

- Hook students' attention and set the context for the event, person, or idea being investigated.

III. Conduct the Investigation

- Teacher: Collect sources relevant to the central question that allow students to investigate all aspects of the event, person, or idea being investigated. Be sure to identify relevant vocabulary and edit for readability.
- Students: Analyze one document individually. Students should source the document, place it in context, and then read it closely for how the source's author(s) provides information to assist the student in developing a response to the question being investigated.
- Group students so that all documents are represented in a group, and have them generate a claim that responds to the central question being investigated.

IV. Report interpretations and class discussion

- Share group and/or individual interpretations and discuss the sources that most and least influenced their decisions and why.
- Discuss the various interpretations presented, looking for commonalities and differences.
- Reinforce that student claims should be tied to evidence drawn from the historical sources examined.
- Multiple and contrasting interpretations may emerge.

V. Debrief student investigation

- Utilize a variety of methods to allow students to discuss, challenge, and revise claims that respond to the question being investigated.
- Have students identify and rank-order the sources that most influenced their arguments and why.
- Compare and contrast student claims and how they use the evidence to support their claims.

VI. Assess student comprehension of the content and the historical thinking

- Employ a variety of formative and summative tools to assess students' understanding of the core content as well as their ability to support their claims with evidence and utilize a variety of historical literacy skills.

way in which it represents the research on history teaching and learning and operationalizes inquiry, is central to the work I have conducted with preservice and practicing teachers. Unfortunately, the History Lab is often mistaken as a document-based question (DBQ).

What Is a DBQ and Where Did It Come From?

Google "DBQ" along with almost any historical topic and you will quickly find hundreds of examples. United States History, World History, European History, and even English/language arts examples will populate your search results. As an instructional tool, the DBQ has been at the forefront of both the inquiry and disciplinary literacy movements. The DBQ originated in the College Board's Advanced Placement (AP) program in the late 1960s and early 1970s. The College Board was being pushed to consider items that more deeply measured students' ability to think like a historian (Henry, 1986). In 1973, the DBQ debuted on the AP United States History Assessment as students were asked "to analyze the factors that probably influenced Congress to pass the Immigration Act of 1924." The hope of the College Board was that by including this type of question "teachers around the country would turn to primary sources in their classrooms" (Rothschild, 2000). The item was structured so that it included an overarching question to guide student investigation, a short background reading to set the stage, and then a series of documents for students to gather information to inform their answer to the question. Initially the DBQ contained over 20 documents, but has evolved to now contain no more than 10 sources (Klein, 1983). Looking back, the DBQ has certainly provided great impetus for the inclusion of primary sources in the classroom as well as an opportunity to promote evidence-based historical writing, but does it really promote inquiry?

The DBQ is intended to facilitate students' abilities to "assess written, quantitative, or visual materials as historical evidence," and to develop an argument supported by an analysis of historical evidence." Although the specifications have been adjusted over the years, currently the College Board requires students to develop a coherent thesis, contextualize the topic within a broader historical time frame, effectively utilize evidence, and provide analysis and reasoning to support the argument being made. Of special note is that students need to analyze the documents and include outside content information in their essays. Within the scoring rubric employed by the College Board, one point is awarded for doing further analysis on four of the documents. The analysis could address:

- author's point of view
- author's purpose
- historical context
- audience

It is within the analysis portion of the DBQ rubric that there is an effort to measure student facility with historical thinking. The mnemonic APPARTS, as illustrated in Figure 1.4, is promoted by the College Board to support the analysis of the documents in a DBQ and push students to address these things in the subsequent essay (Greer, 2006).

This tool has become a staple in AP history classes. A parallel tool is found in the acronym HIPPO:

- Historical Context
- Intended Audience
- Point of View
- Purpose
- Organization/Use

Regardless of the tool that students and teachers use, they support analysis of sources and set up students with an opportunity to express their thinking in subsequent essays.

DBQs Are Great, But . . .

Two issues arise with the DBQ. The first has to do with its authenticity to the work of historians, and the second has to do with how most DBQs are implemented in the non–Advanced Placement classroom.

The DBQ's widescale embedding into instruction and assessment has brought the critical eye of educational researchers. The core criticism is that

Figure 1.4. The APPARTS Model

Author	Who created the source? What do you know about the author? What is the author's point of view?
Place and time	Where and when was the source produced? How might this affect the meaning of the source?
Prior knowledge	Beyond information about the author and the context of its creation, what do you know that would help you further understand the primary source? For example, do you recognize any symbols and recall what they represent?
Audience	For whom was the source created, and how might this affect the reliability of the source?
Reason	Why was this source produced, and how might this affect the reliability of the source?
The main idea	What point is the source trying to convey?
Significance	Why is this source important? Ask yourself "So what?" in relation to the question asked.

the DBQ is not a parallel representation of the work of historians. The authenticity argument falls flat with me and others (Grant et al., 2004). It is impossible to create a fully "authentic" experience for students. Students are in a classroom, and that classroom is defined by a schedule that teachers do not control, with resources that are limited—although certainly expanded due to the growth of internet resources. To assess the DBQ as inauthentic is simply academic myopia. The other option is generally unfeasible. Yes, teachers can move students toward developing authentic questions to guide investigations, and then head to a library or the Internet to select sources in order to develop an evidence-based argument or response to the overarching question, but the reality is that the time it would take to foster such an experience would so adversely impact the ability of a teacher to cover the required content that it is tantamount to educational malpractice to engage in such an exercise.

What researchers have found, authenticity issues aside, is that most DBQs are utilized similarly to textbook-based instruction. Despite the fact that with a rich investigative question, conflicting evidence trail, and numerous opportunities for students to engage in historical thinking, most DBQs become a read-and-write assignment, generally completed individually rather than as a real inquiry experience (Monte-Sano, 2008; Reisman & McGrew, 2018).

On a narrower level of analysis, DBQ instruction is more focused on the end product than on the steps in the process. When confronted with the overarching DBQ question, students "raid the documents for facts and quotes so that they mine the provided sources for information" so that they can "then fill the lines of an essay" (Young & Leinhardt, 1998). Having observed numerous DBQs in classroom settings, I find that the origin of the information does not matter to students. When students enter the document analysis phase of the DBQ process, they become uncritical consumers of information. To be critical consumers of information, they need to interrogate the sources to consider the value of that information. Students assiduously mine each source for facts and then place all the facts together, but never once do they source a document and consider how authorship could impact the use of that information that source provides. Rarely if ever do students contextualize a document to determine the impact the publication date of a source may have on the information they are using as support for their claim. Students do corroborate sources, but only at a surface level. They look for information that supports and contradicts information from other sources, so they can build an evidence trail to support their claim. The difference is subtle, but it comes down to the difference between information-gathering and source evaluation. "Reading historical texts," Bain reminds us, "particularly snippets of primary sources, has become a proxy for historical thinking," and this uncritical examination of where the information comes from is a key limitation of the DBQ approach (Bain, 2015). History is the process of developing evidence-based interpretations about the past, but it is clear that classroom implementation strays to a less inquiry-based direction.

Please do not get me wrong; DBQs can be rich tools to help students inquire about the past. They model meaty investigative questions, provide challenging sources, and position students to make evidence-based arguments. Implementing a DBQ well is a great stepping-off point in a teacher's evolution from history as storytelling to history as investigation, but I argue that the History Lab approach is richer, more cognitively challenging, and better aligned with inquiry than the DBQ. It also empowers higher fidelity to the work of historians.

Apostles of Disunion

When I put down Charles Dew's *Apostles of Disunion* (2002), I was reminded that history is alive. Raised in the border state of Maryland and having read my grandfather's copies of Bruce Catton and Shelby Foote, my understanding of the causes of the American Civil War downplayed the central role of slavery. The first curriculum guide I received to teach United States History placed slavery on a parallel footing with states' rights, tariffs, the failure of political parties, and other factors as the equal causes of the war. I ignored the curriculum guide, Catton, and others to teach my students that it was slavery at the heart of the war, but what I lacked was a strong set of documents that could support this interpretation. I could approach the topic through the lens of historiography, but that is a tough concept for students to wrestle with, and the sources can be long. Kenneth Stampp's *The Causes of the Civil War* (1992) became a useful tool, but again, slavery was relegated to equal footing with the specious issues of states' rights and tariffs. What Charles Dew did in *Apostles of Disunion* was to elevate the place of the Southern secession documents within the pantheon of resources considered when determining the causes of the Civil War. These documents have always been available, but previous generations of scholars did not give them as much weight as do current ones. This book immediately shifted how I approach examining the causes of the war and reminds me of the limitations of the DBQ model.

Once particular historical documents are determined to be relevant to the investigative question at hand, historians still have to determine how useful the sources are to the development of an evidence-based answer (Barton, 2018; Marino, 2022). Rarely, unless the sources have no relevance to the question being investigated, do historians simply ignore a source. The value that historians give to various sources is an integral part of the development of historical interpretations. Treating all sources equally is not akin to the way historians conduct business, as historians do not treat all sources equally, making judgments about the relative value of sources.

"Students," we are reminded, need to see "shades of usefulness depending on the purpose of the source" (P. Smith, 2001). To achieve this end, students must consider authorship, context, and the degree of corroboration between sources. As they move toward an answer to the overarching question, students should rank the sources. Some sources corroborate one another and move toward the top of the list of utility, while others—often directly related to issues with authorship, context, or lack of corroborative evidence—are ranked lower. These judgments are inherent to the work of historians and should be a part of the DBQ process. Unfortunately, the DBQ treats all sources equally and simply as repositories of information (Marino, 2022). The DBQ structure does not allow students to ask questions of the utility of the source to answer the question at hand and then to downgrade a source based on those criteria.

The strength of DBQs writ large are the way they facilitate the writing of an essay. Researchers have also questioned the utility of the essay as an effective tool for measuring historical thinking. For claim, evidence, and reasoning, DBQ essays are tremendous, but when it comes to measuring skills like sourcing, contextualizing, and corroboration, the essays fall short. "Broad essays," argue Mark Smith, Joel Breakstone, and Sam Wineburg, "like the DBQ require the orchestration of so many skills that it is difficult to draw inferences about proficiency in any particular aspect of the domain. . . . It can be difficult to untangle these factors [evaluating documents, compositional fluency, background knowledge, etc.] when so many cognitive processes are implicated at once" (M. Smith et al., 2018).

Students who are successful on the AP DBQs are well-versed in history, are tremendous writers, and can apply some historical thinking skills. Unfortunately, performance statistics clearly indicate that the lion's share of students do not demonstrate this trifecta of abilities. As demonstrated below in Figure 1.5, data from 2015–2018 as well as 2021 show that the mean performance on the DBQ is below half the available points. In addition, reviewing the comments of the Chief Readers clearly illustrates that the DBQs are not successful in assessing historical thinking.

Within the strength of the DBQ also lies its weakness. DBQs are so focused on writing and communicating content knowledge that they make it extremely difficult for students to apply historical thinking skills with any fidelity.

Ultimately, the DBQ is a limited tool when it comes to actually mirroring the work of historians. Yes, historians work with documents and the DBQ has documents; yes, historians wrestle with questions about the past and the DBQs are focused on questions; yes, historians make arguments and substantiate them with information from historical sources, but as Barton reminds us, "no historian is ever presented with sources the way students are presented with them . . . that is historians do not stumble across a set of documents and then start asking who wrote them, why they wrote" them

Figure 1.5. AP Chief Reader Comments

Year	Mean/Total Points	Chief Readers' Comments
2021	3.31/7	*The historical reasoning process of continuity and change was required in this question. Often the chronology in the responses was lacking; sometimes responses attempted contextualization or identifying the historical situation of documents with significant errors, incorrectly employing evidence from within and outside of the time period . . . Many students struggled with earning the point for sourcing. Many of the responses attempted sourcing but were not able to fully connect the sourcing to an argument or thesis.*
2018	2.42/7	*However, many students struggled with how to integrate point of view into their essays. This sourcing point was a challenge for many, especially in relation to the cartoons . . . Simply identifying one of the sourcing elements—point of view, audience, purpose, or historical situation—also does not allow them to get over the threshold for sourcing.*
2017	2.22/7	*Many responses simply stated the content of the document and did not try to explain the author's purpose in writing it.*
2016	2.29/7	No positive or negative comments provided in Chief Readers' comments.
2015	2.59/7	*Many students failed to receive extended analysis points because they failed to analyze either point of view, audience, historical context, or the purpose of the document.*

(2018). In a nutshell, DBQs are a great tool for formalizing the use of historical sources in the classroom, promoting writing and argumentation, and question-focused instruction, but if the DBQ is where teachers stop, they are missing an opportunity to deepen students' use of historical thinking skills and fully mirror the work of historians.

Please do not misinterpret this argument. I am not asking folks to throw out the DBQ baby with historical thinking bathwater. DBQs are wonderful tools and have a place within the instructional tool kit for all teachers. My argument, illustrated in Figure 1.6, is that there is a more intellectually challenging, and authentic historical inquiry process than the DBQ: the History Lab.

History Lab Versus DBQ

The intended outcome is the most significant difference between the DBQ versus the History Lab. Ultimately, the goal of the DBQ is to prepare students

Figure 1.6. The DBQ Versus a History Lab

DBQ	Historians	History Lab
✓	Driven by questions demanding answers.	✓
✓	Explore narrow historical questions.	✓
✓	Work with a variety of historical sources.	✓
	Sources provided have detailed information on the creator and the time period they were created.	✓
	Students make value judgments about the value of information provided by historical sources, ranking sources and discarding others.	✓
	Treats sources as three-dimensional repositories of information influenced by the motives of the creator and influenced by the time period the source was created.	✓
✓	Make arguments, substantiated with information from historical sources.	✓

to write an essay. Be it on the AP exam or the DBQ product materials, the intended goal of Advanced Placement is having students write. The true goal of historical investigations is to open up the debate, discussion, and thinking and not just the writing. In an investigation, source background information would increase, source credibility would be evaluated based on the impact of the sourcing and contextual information, sources would be ranked in terms of how they support the argument, some sources would have less utility than others, and some sources would not corroborate one another. Part of this difference is borne out by how the investigations are assessed, but part of it has to do with how the sources in the DBQ are questioned and utilized.

One problem with the DBQ is that in corroborating, students are still moving from the built-in assumption that all the available sources are fully credible and useful to the question at hand. This speaks to the artificiality of the task and the limitations. DBQs have an important place in the spectrum of tools that help students to think historically, but they also have limitations.

THE ONLY CONSTANT IS CHANGE!

Since the publication of *"Why Won't You Just tell Us the Answer?,"* I have made several changes to my approach to teaching history: some subtle, some dramatic. What has not changed has been my affinity for the investigative approach embedded into the History Lab. Using it with students for the better part of 20 years and seeing others use it successfully leaves me a strong advocate for the approach, but, as with any instructional approach, things improve, new research comes to the forefront, and the interaction with peers leads to new ideas. Ultimately, though, most of the changes I have made are born from the daily interactions with students and teachers. The classroom is always a laboratory that demands changes.

The most significant shift in my teaching occurred within my approach to historical thinking: I have become more precise with my language around it. There is a tendency to conflate the literacy practices promoted by SHEG with the broader kinds of thinking employed by historians. To identify what historical thinking skills to teach and assesses, I have tried to blend the thoughts of several scholars and standards bodies into one matrix. Current projects that identify and assess historical thinking skills include the Big Six historical thinking concepts out of Canada, the skills outlined in the voluntary National History Standards, the new College Board Historical Thinking Skills framework, Sam Wineburg's Beyond the Bubble, and the ARCH project. There is much overlap among these various iterations of historical thinking skills, so for my own classroom purposes, I tried to consolidate the best from each into my own model. In addition, these tools sit within a network of content that provides students with things to investigate, write about, and learn. The chart in Figure 1.7 below represents how I have parsed my thinking into three distinct, though overlapping, buckets.

This list is not exhaustive. There are some historical thinking skills that the authors identify as important that I intentionally exclude. My goal with the list is to represent skills that I can imbed into an 11th-grade United

Figure 1.7. A Broader View of Historical Thinking

CONTENT

Historical Literacy Skills
- Sourcing
- Contextualizing
- Close Reading
- Corroboration

Historical Thinking Concepts
- Historical Perspectives
- Cause and Consequence
- Continuity and Change
- Historical Significance

Argumentation about History
- Claims
- Counterclaims
- Use of Evidence

CONTENT

CONTENT

CONTENT

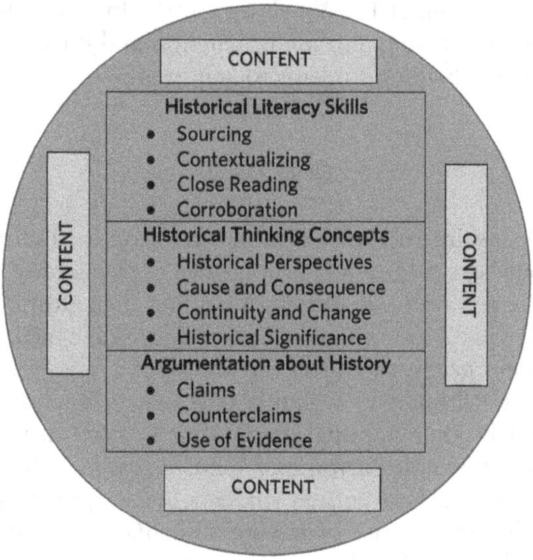

States history course. Only having students for 10 months leads me to be more pragmatic than inclusive. If a district were to adopt a set of historical thinking skills and spiral it throughout its curricula, the addition of categories such as periodization, interpretation, chronological thinking, synthesis, narrative, and the ethical dimensions of history should be added so that the skills are scaffolded throughout a student's K–12 social studies experience. A comprehensive, system-wide approach, though, is different from what I am proposing, which is teaching and assessing a specific set of historical thinking skills within one course (Phillips, 2006; Seixas & Morton, 2013).

My most significant change has been shifting to the Stanford History Education Group's sourcing, contextualizing, and corroborating—as illustrated in Figure 1.8 below—and away from text, context, and subtext. This decision was made because the terms *sourcing, contextualizing,* and *corroborating* have penetrated deeply into the instructional practices of many history teachers, and when I am developing presentations, it is easier to dovetail my approach with teacher practice than it is to try and superimpose a different structure onto them.

The movement toward a common language around historical literacy is essential, and SHEG's work provides just such a mutual vernacular. As you read the lesson examples in this book, you will find that I have dropped *text* and *subtext* and replaced them with *sourcing*, but *context* remains the same, and I have added *corroboration*. Although the language has changed, the literacy practices they embody remain constant.

This organization allows me to distinguish between reading specific-literacy skills, disciplinary-specific thinking, and oral and written argumentative-based skills (Mandell & Malone, 2008; Nash & Crabtree 1996; Seixas & Morton, 2013; Wineburg, 2001). In turn, it has enabled me to focus what I am infusing into my instruction and thus results in making me more effective in helping students to acquire these skills.

CONCLUSION

The efficacy of any instructional reform hinges on its ability to be implemented without stressing a classroom teacher's already overburdened professional life. A variety of factors, including the culture of a particular school, district-wide expectations, accountability demands, teacher confidence, and student needs, can affect the ability of a new instructional practice to take root. Ultimately, a simple cost-benefit analysis determines if the practice will become habitual or die on the vine. In many ways, this chapter responds to Keith Barton and Linda Levstik's (2003) query: Why don't more history teachers engage students in interpretation? Barton and Levstik argue that in the case of having students investigate the past, the convergence of demands for classroom control and the coverage of content

Figure 1.8. Stanford History Education Group Historical Thinking Chart

Historical Reading Skills	Questions	Students should be able to . . .	Prompts
Sourcing	• Who wrote this? • What is the author's perspective? • When was it written? • Where was it written? • Why was it written? • Is it reliable? Why? Why not?	• Identify the author's position on the historical event • Identify and evaluate the author's purpose in producing the document • Hypothesize what the author will say before reading the document • Evaluate the source's trustworthiness by considering genre, audience, and purpose	• The author probably believes . . . • I think the audience is . . . • Based on the source information, I think the author might . . . • I do/don't trust this document because . . .
Contextualization	• When and where was the document created? • What was different then? What was the same? • How might the circumstances in which the document was created affect its content?	• Understand how context/ background information influences the content of the document • Recognize that documents are products of particular points in time	• Based on the background information, I understand this document differently because . . . • The author might have been influenced by ______ (historical context) . . . • This document might not give me the whole picture because . . .
Corroboration	• What do other documents say? • Do the documents agree? If not, why? • What are other possible documents? • What documents are most reliable?	• Establish what is probable by comparing documents to each other • Recognize disparities between accounts	• The author agrees/disagrees with . . . • These documents all agree/ disagree about . . . • Another document to consider might be . . .
Close Reading	• What claims does the author make? • What evidence does the author use? • What language (words, phrases, images, symbols) does the author use to persuade the document's audience? • How does the document's language indicate the author's perspective?	• Identify the author's claims about an event • Evaluate the evidence and reasoning the author uses to support claims • Evaluate author's word choice; understand that language is used deliberately	• I think the author chose these words in order to . . . • The author is trying to convince me . . . • The author claims . . . • The evidence used to support the author's claims is . . .

conspire to poison the nascent roots of classroom investigation. As the confluence of inch-deep-and-miles-long state standards, College Board curricular expectations, or district-wide curricula merge with the need to manage the behavior of 30 to 40 adolescents, teachers abandon what they know are best practices for those that cover and control. But what happens when teachers have achieved classroom control while simultaneously rejecting the sole aim of history as simply a short-term accumulation of chronologically ordered facts? Can deep investigation of the past occur if coverage demands are made realistic and control of student behavior is established and maintained? It is my contention that an instructional approach that emphasizes the interrogation of historical sources to develop evidence-based interpretations in response to provocative historical questions can be achieved, and for all students. But as with any attempt at instructional change, some teachers register the statement that drives this book: "My kids cannot do this." This statement is usually driven by concerns about how inquiry and investigating history will impact two factors: coverage and control. Although the repository of investigations, the presence of a strong instructional framework, rich exemplars, and deep research exist, it does not mean that inquiry is now the default instructional practice in social studies classrooms. Nor does it mean that all participants in professional learning receive the information with open arms. "My kids cannot do this" has its origin as teachers consider the History Lab and inquiry through their own lenses. This book is an effort to flip that response, and have teachers consider the approach from an asset-based approach: "Yes, your kids can do this!"

CHAPTER 2

"Yes, Your Students Can Do This"

Historical Investigation for *All* Students

> I am intimidated by having to teach the [state] standards in only one semester to the non-gifted population . . .
>
> —teacher participant from a 3-day workshop

Through the doors of my classroom await this year's charges. If there are less than 30 students I count myself lucky, because the reality will more than likely be 30, 35, 40, or more students waiting for me to teach them. As the year progresses, I stop thinking of them as "my third-period class" but instead as 35 individual students who come to my room during third period to learn United States History. They each have their own personality, their individual strengths and weaknesses, and each learns in a way slightly different from the others. In addition, they are in many ways totally different from the 30-plus students in my fourth-period United States History class and from the classes I have taught in years past. Although it would be easier if I could design instruction that is deliverable to all students in the same way, when it comes to instruction, one size truly does not fit all. Welcome to teaching!

Every student I taught benefited from some adjustment to my instruction to assist them with learning the material. For some students, these adjustments are proscribed by law. Through Individualized Educational Plans (IEPs) or 504s, modifications are outlined that must be provided to assist students to be successful in the classroom. English Language Learners (ELL) also require modifications to ensure that they can meet with success. For some students, the assistance required is simple: identification of vocabulary, numbering the lines of a reading, chunking a project into smaller portions, extended time, preferential seating, or an active reminder about staying on task assisted students in their learning. But for other students the adjustments were more individualized, substantive, or both. I have taught students whose needs required me to wear an amplifying microphone, to photocopy any materials on a certain shade of green paper, to selecting readings that are five or six grade levels below that of their peers, to have a human reader or human scribe, or to print in a significantly larger font than their peers. The structure for accommodating students with special needs varies from workplace to workplace. In some school years, I taught in an inclusion model where a special educator and I worked together to ensure that instruction was adapted to meet the needs of students. The most common situation was having students with IEPs or 504s in my classroom, but the accommodations fell to me. On the other end of the spectrum, I have taught students placed in self-contained gifted and talented courses, and in other instances learners were present in a more homogenous setting. This is the truth of instruction: Teachers cannot simply dust off last year's materials, teach, assess, grade, and go home. Instead, we have to understand our students as individuals and adapt to meet them where they are so we can help them get to where they need to be.

The heart of this chapter beats with frustration about the statement that I heard so frequently while providing professional development: "My students can't do this." When sharing lessons to illustrate the approach of doing history, preservice and practicing teachers often made statements like, "But I don't teach AP," or "You don't understand my kids." These statements are proxies for insinuating that investigating the past is a strategy only implementable for advanced students or that students that do not requiring learning supports. Intertwined in these teachers' concerns are two types of students. One are those students who have identified educational needs and/or a legal remedy that teachers must accommodate so that the students can be successful. The other are students who do not have identifiable learning deficits, but instead suffer from the scourge of the classroom: apathy. These students are disaffected from school, disdainful of an academic curriculum, other-directed by interests outside of school, or just plain do not like history. Unfortunately, some teachers lump the apathetic and the needy into one group, but all of these students are capable of investigating the past if we set them up to successfully do so. Any other student who might need modifications, implies these questioners, cannot engage in the process of investigating the past. This is false.

History instruction taught through inquiry methods like the History Lab process is beneficial for all students, including those with learning differences. Often teachers perceive their students' learning differences as barriers to this type of instruction when, in reality, with sufficient scaffolding, all students can think historically (Bulgren et al., 2013). Students with learning differences are able to learn academic vocabulary related to historical literacy, actively interrogate historical sources, and corroborate information from different sources (Claravall & Irey 2022). The intentional effort to teach students with learning disabilities using inquiry methods helps them become better readers and writers, to engage in more evidence-based discussions, and to become more adept with their content understanding. Research indicates that having students that present learning differences "do history" brings about associated gains in students' knowledge about the content, a better understanding of the tools associated with historical inquiry, and improvements in their self-efficacy as learners (De La Paz, 2013, 2012; Ferretti et al., 2001; Smith, 2016).

By intentionally differentiating the process and the product, all students can actively investigate the past. Perhaps it will look different and take a little more planning and patience, but all students can engage in historical investigations through the application of modifications, accommodations, scaffolding, chunking, and differentiation. Thus, this chapter will highlight how historical investigations can be accomplished with all students, and chip away at the concern that this instructional delivery model is only the purview of the motivated, academically gifted, or students who do not possess the need for modified instruction. All students can and should have the opportunity to explore history in this manner, and all can, if teachers make an intentional effort to identify in advance the predictable barriers that may impede student success and plan for this variability, so these barriers are removed and the path to success is clear and obtainable for every student. This fact I strongly believe, but I offer the statement with a clear caveat.

The preservice and practicing teachers who offer worries akin to those from my anonymous workshop participant that frames the chapter are reflecting more than just concerns about their students. They are also giving insight into one of the significant challenges in public education. Teachers are asked to differentiate instruction to meet the needs of multiple types of students. English Language Learners and students with IEPs and 504s all require some adaptation to instruction. These adaptations are important, necessary, and beneficial, but instructional materials rarely if ever come predifferentiated. To meet the multiple needs of multiple students, teachers must adapt everything they use instructionally. As this chapter unfolds, I share useful methods to open up inquiry-based history instruction to all students, but I do so knowing that these processes are not supported with the time, professional learning, or access to high-quality instructional materials that provide this sort of differentiation.

A ROAD MAP

The reality for teachers, and the one that keeps us up at night, or at school well past 6:00 P.M., is that meeting the needs of every student is difficult to achieve. As we build years of experience, meeting these needs becomes more achievable, but when we teach three different preps, or have our schedule bounce back and forth between, say, United States History and World History, we are often pushed several steps back on the path to meeting the diverse needs of all of our students. Although some students need very specific accommodations, all students benefit from consideration of providing multiple means to "access, respond, and engage" with the content being investigated (Pawling, 2011). Universal Design for Learning (UDL) has assisted me greatly in understanding how to try and address the needs of all of the 35 individual learners in my hypothetical third-period class.

The easiest way to think about UDL is to consider a map. The destination on this map is the same for everyone: we want to arrive at the park. In a non-UDL classroom, all students migrate from the starting point to the end point using the same road, traveling at the same pace, and using the same mode of transportation. In a UDL classroom, students are provided the flexibility to travel different roads or combination of roads: They can walk, run, or skip, or they can swim, fly, hitchhike, or traverse in numerous ways, but all arriving at the same end point. Successful implementation of UDL requires the teacher (or teachers, if it is within an inclusion model) to identify the "predictable barriers" that may impact students' ability to access the content and to demonstrate their learning. The identification and generation of solutions to address these barriers must be done in the planning phase of instruction, as well as on the fly as instruction unfolds. This is the ideal, and one that research clearly shows aids in increased student achievement for all students (Novak, 2016; Pawling, 2011; Robinson & Meyer, 2012).

The trade-off is time. On average I taught between 130–150 students per year. Given the dearth of resources, finality of time, and continuous demands inherent in teaching, it is not possible to tailor instruction to the needs of every individual student. Remember, there is no such thing as a typical student. One hundred and thirty-five paths to the end destination on the map is ideal, but the closer I moved to that ideal, the costs in time eventually won out. This does not mean that teachers are empowered to ignore student needs. To do so would be instructionally tone-deaf, morally wrong, and in some instances criminal if it ignores legally binding instructional expectations outlined in a 504 or IEP. Instead, teachers must triage initially, grow over the years, and continually listen to students to ensure continual progress to a differentiated classroom.

The challenge is to be honest to the needs of students, but also respect reality. The notion that I will develop 35 ways for my third-period class to reach each daily learning objective(s) is false. But UDL prompts me as an instructor to anticipate barriers that have occurred in the past, accommodate for them in my planning, and continually look for ways to reduce those barriers to student success. The argument I will make going forward is predicated on five core beliefs:

1. Teach up, not down.
2. Accommodations are legally required and educationally necessary.
3. Modifications benefit all students, but some need more modifications than others.
4. Chunking, scaffolding, and modeling are powerful modifications.
5. The type, degree, and persistence of any modification depends on the needs of the student.

TEACHING UP

Unlike most first-year teachers, I was assigned to teach in what was designed as a gifted and talented (GT) program, in addition to students enrolled in the non-GT course. Students in both my regular and GT courses were learning American Government. There were three branches of government, checks and balances, a Bill of Rights, and federalism in both courses, albeit with slightly different district curricula. The curriculum that structured the GT course was rigorous and proscriptive, aligned to the content required for a statewide summative assessment that they needed to pass in order to earn a high school diploma, and contained an extra project that was not part of the regular American Government curriculum. The GT curricula moved at a faster pace and dove more deeply into certain concepts and topics.

The students enrolled in my GT American Government course were generally motivated, organized, and well-positioned for success. By and large, they all read on or above grade level. That said, they still had needs to be addressed to ensure they could successfully learn the material. My other students represented a wider spectrum of needs, motivations, and interests than my GT students. All these students lived in the same neighborhoods, took the same buses, to school, and ate in the same cafeteria. They were also studying the same content: American Government.

Looking back on the experience, it was the dichotomy between teaching the everyday student who populated most of my schedule and the students in my GT class that helped me understand how best to ensure that all students had the same access to a rigorous instructional experience. As I designed and implemented instruction for my regular students, they struggled more often than my GT students. Readings were too hard or too long, the sequence of activities required more chunking, and instructions necessitated greater clarity. As I made modifications to reading length, assignment length, directions, and lesson structure, what I also tended to do was reduce my overall expectations regarding the learning. Less complex topics were eliminated or pared down, and I was reducing the expectations for complexity. When my GT students were faced with concomitant challenges, I provided the modifications they needed but never reduced my expectations for them to deal with the complexity and/or depth of the topics being investigated. All my students were studying the same three branches of government, the same presidential powers, the same Supreme Court decisions, and the same landmark federal laws.

What I was doing before I had heard of the term was "teaching up" (Tomlinson, 2017). Immediately what I began to do for my other courses was to determine not what to cut, but instead how to build in the scaffolding and chunking needed to ensure that students could reach that goal. Scaffolding and chunking are complicated education terms that mean cut your food before you eat it! Instead of providing students an entire assignment and saying eat it all at once, the teacher intentionally breaks the assignment into segments to help build student confidence and skills, and ensure a greater likelihood of successful completion. The purpose of scaffolding is to assist students who struggle by providing tools that help them to move high levels of assistance toward greater independence (Jadallah et al., 2010; Smit et al., 2013). This is a process that starts with the scaffold and then, as students progress, transfers more responsibility to them until the need for the scaffold fades away (Van de Pol et al., 2010). When designing lessons for my courses, I learned to plan the same objectives regardless of whom I was teaching. Then I selected the materials of instruction that would best align with students in my GT course. For students enrolled in my on-grade level American Government course, learning the same topic, I would provide the alterations/scaffolding, modifications, and chunking to those materials of instruction to ensure that those students could reach the same learning goals, but I would not reduce the learning expectations. Scaffolding is a powerful educational tool and is the key to ensuring that all students can access a historical investigation.

BUILD SCAFFOLDS

Scaffolding, according to Bruner, "refers to the steps taken to reduce the degrees of freedom in carrying out some task so that the child can concentrate on the difficult skill she is in the process of acquiring" (1978). A scaffold on a building is a temporary structure. It exists to provide support while a building is being constructed, renovated, or repaired. These tools are temporary, adjustable, and flexible. Scaffolds in the classroom serve the same function. They exist for students to ensure they can move from the shallow end of the pool to the deep end. In the context of instruction, teachers can scaffold the task, the materials, the pacing, and the product with an eye toward building student confidence and capacity. Figure 2.1 below illustrates some of the significant scaffolds that can be employed for all students.

All scaffolds are intended to be temporary, as we aim to move students toward the confidence and capacity to engage independently. This gradual release of responsibility model varies from class to class, year to year, and investigation to investigation, but it is essential to help all students engage in this work (Fisher & Frey, 2021). With the tools to scaffold and the goal of moving toward greater student confidence and capacity for historical investigations, will model several specific touchpoints within the History Lab model where scaffolding can pay significant dividends for all students. The most essential scaffold, though, is mindset around inquiry.

Figure 2.1. Scaffolding Strategies

Technique	Purpose	Benefits
Bridging	By identifying what students already know about a topic, teachers can help link them to the new learning about to occur. Within a History Lab, this means ensuring that the necessary background knowledge is provided before diving deeply into the question being investigated.	Allows teachers to build on what students already know and use that knowledge as a stepping-off point for new learning.
Modeling	Achieved by a teacher proving clear examples of what is required of them to complete a task, utilize a skill, or express understanding. A teacher verbalizing how they sourced a document or corroborated across multiple sources would be immensely helpful modeling strategies for a History Lab.	Allows students to see and or hear how a skill is to be utilized, a process is to be implemented, or a product is to be developed.
Chunking	Breaking a set of directions, the steps in a lesson, or the elements of a longer-term project into smaller segments. Within a History Lab, teachers can separate the sourcing of a document from the close reading or allow students to consider each historical source completely before they examine a second or third.	This allows students to focus on discrete parts of the skills being employed or the steps in a full lesson arc and not get lost in the longer term.
Visual representation	Directions, steps in a process, key things to consider, and other elements of a lesson can be depicted visually.	Visual representations provide students with something to which they can refer back to when they need a reminder.
Acronyms	Directions, steps in a process, key things to consider, and other elements of a lesson can be depicted with an acronym. The tools TACOS, APPARTS, and SOAPS discussed below are examples that could be employed during a History Lab.	Acronyms provide students with something to which they can refer back to when they need a reminder.

(*continued*)

Figure 2.1. (*continued*)

Technique	Purpose	Benefits
Graphic organizers	Provide students with graphic organizers (Venn diagrams, spiderwebs, concept maps, sequence chart, etc.) during a history lab. They can be employed during the analysis of sources, during the corroboration of sources, and/or when students are linking evidence to claims.	These tools help organize thinking, make comparisons, and ensure that students can move back and forth between analyzing evidence and using the evidence to support a claim.
Exemplars	Provide students with examples of what each step of a lesson looks like. Previous students' work, videos of class discussions, or the sharing of information from sources are all places within a History Lab that exemplars can be utilized.	Sharing with students examples of a completed chart or assessment provides them with a target for their efforts. Knowing what their end product should look like can reduce student anxiety, build confidence, and increase the overall quality of their work.
Pacing	Adjusting how quickly steps in a lesson progress from one step to another can ensure that students are understanding rather than complying. Going slow early, so you can go fast later, is always helpful as students become familiar with the demands of a History Lab.	By adjusting the pace or an element of a lesson, teachers can develop student confidence and capacity with a particular skill or task.

IN THE CENTER RING, INQUIRY VERSUS COVERAGE AND CONTROL

In the teachers' lounge, there is a variation of George Carlin's seven dirty words that are guaranteed to raise a teacher's blood pressure. One of those words is *inquiry*. For many teachers, the mere mention of the word directly challenges the two factors that are perceived to be at the heart of teacher success: control and coverage (Barton & Levstik, 2003). When teachers hear "inquiry," they tend to think of an unstructured, Montessori-esque classroom where children follow their own path. The practice of student inquiry conjures up images of poor Arnold Schwarzenegger as the kindergarten teacher in *Kindergarten Cop* (Reitman, 1990). Schwarzenegger is unable to stop the children from running around, throwing toys, painting one another, and other types of off-task behaviors. Frustrated with his lack of control, he runs out of the school screaming. Inquiry is often interpreted by many teachers as diametrically opposite of control, and Schwarzenegger's primal scream is one that all teachers want to avoid emitting, as it signifies a loss of control.

In addition to being contrasted with control, inquiry is also interpreted by many teachers as a direct threat to their ability to cover all the material they are required to teach. If students are taking the time to inquire about things the teacher already knows and can simply tell students, this line of argument goes, then it limits the number of things that the teacher can share with students. Those opposed to or intimidated by inquiry argue that we already know answers can be efficiently communicated to students by teacher-controlled dialogue, thus ensuring that all the required information is covered; therefore, inquiry is a solution chasing a problem. Inquiry is perceived to be on a collision course with the ability to control student behavior and cover core content, but this is often due more to how it is presented than a realistic appraisal of the pedagogy.

How inquiry is packaged makes a huge difference in teacher receptivity. Inevitably, when professional development presentations are made regarding moving from lecture to inquiry approaches, they are presented as an either-or scenario: Either you are student-centered and students are investigating on their own, or you are teacher-centered and telling students everything you know about a topic. This either-or mentality is then accentuated with arguments about the organization of a classroom.

There has been a significant push to have teachers abandon the industrialized factory model of a classroom in rows to a more modern "Information Age" classroom of clusters, or other nontraditional room arrangements. This false syllogism sets up a purity test for inquiry that hinders its implementation: rows = no inquiry, clusters = inquiry! As a teacher who arranged desks in rows for 22 years, I can tell you that my room organization did nothing to impede my students' ability to investigate the past, work in groups, jigsaw, conduct historical trials, and hold congressional investigations. Instead of explaining that various room arrangements best facilitate certain types of instruction and that teachers need to adjust room arrangements as instruction merits, this illogical thinking of rows = no inquiry, clusters = inquiry often deters teachers from even trying inquiry.

Another false diametric is the nostrum that is always part of training on inquiry: that the only way that inquiry can work is for "teachers to be a guide on the side, rather than being a sage on the stage." Straight lecture and inquiry do not work together, but, as I will demonstrate below, inquiry is a process that students must scaffold into, and without a teacher's guidance they will drown, and the inquiry will fail.

When presented to teachers in this manner, inquiry is seeming to say that everything you are doing is wrong; give up control, give up coverage, run screaming like Schwarzenegger in *Kindergarten Cop*! As this type of messaging converges with inch-deep and miles-long state standards and district-wide curricula merge with the need to manage the behavior of 30 to 40 adolescents, teachers often abandon inquiry-based practices for those that protect their ability to cover content and control student behavior. Though these teacher decisions are based in pragmatic realities, inquiry is not diametrically opposed to either control or coverage, and if done well, it can enhance both—if it is scaffolded for both students and teachers.

SCAFFOLDING TO SUCCESS

Good inquiry is neither unstructured nor rarely completely student-driven, but is instead a scaffolded, evolutionary approach that varies depending upon several factors (Alfieri et al., 2011). Levstik and Barton (2023) speak to this in *Doing History*:

> As every teacher knows, few students have the skills necessary to conduct inquiry on their own. Although inquiry is essential to education, simply assigning such tasks won't guarantee meaningful results. Most students need direct help to make the most of their experiences, and teachers' most important responsibilities is to provide them with the structure they need to learn—a process known as scaffolding.

The best representation of the reality of scaffolded inquiry in the classroom is encapsulated in the infographic in Figure 2.2.

The analogy of learning to swim and not starting in the deep end beautifully and powerfully captures what the challenges around inquiry are. If a teacher starts their students in the deep end, the pupils will panic and flail, and teachers will have to spend all their time saving students from doing something that they were not prepared to do. "Free inquiry" demands that students form the overarching question that guides their inquiry, find the resources and apply those resources to the guiding question, and construct an evidence-based response to the overarching question while the teacher serves as a resource rather than the leader. Starting inquiry here, in the deep end, is what many teachers think of when they hear student-centered inquiry, but for inquiry to have a chance, teachers must see that they can both maintain control and ensure curriculum coverage. In short, teachers and students need to start in the shallow end of the inquiry pool (Gorman, 1998; Grant et al., 2017, 2018; MacKenzie, 2019).

Instead of the toss into the deep end, students and teachers benefit from starting inquiry from a structured approach in the shallow end of the pool. "Teachers," as a mentor once told me, "cannot assume anything and must teach students exactly what they should do to be successful in

Figure 2.2. Trevor Mackenzie's Types of Inquiry

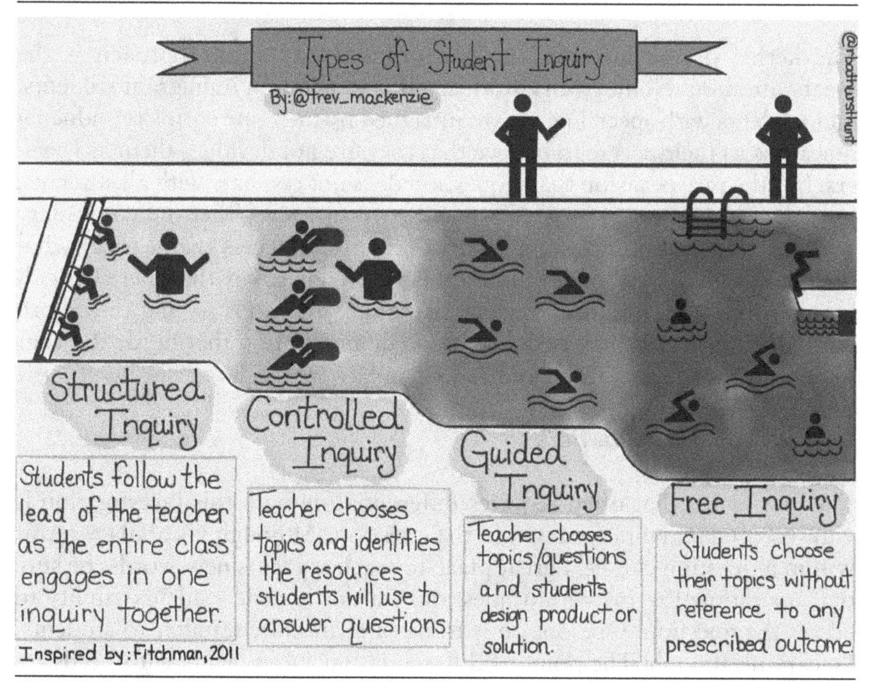

Reprinted with permission from Trevor Mackenzie Sketch notes (https://www.trevormackenzie.com/sketchnotes).

the classroom." This means that how to take notes, how to behave during the announcements, how to format an essay, how to study, or how to conduct oneself in an inquiry, student success stems from teacher instruction. When initiating an inquiry, teachers are best served by providing explicit instructions regarding procedures, modeling strategies, and chunking and scaffolding the inquiry (De La Paz, 2005; Downey & Long, 2016; Fisher & Frey, 2010; MacKenzie, 2019; Nokes, 2011). As students and teachers become more comfortable with inquiry, they can pull back some of the scaffolding and empower students to take on more of the responsibility for guiding the inquires. In these controlled and guided phases, the students have more independence.

Assuaging these concerns about inquiry-based instruction and history teaching and learning that is not centered on the textbook and lecture are at the core of the "My kids cannot do this" comment. Helping teachers to realize that they are still using instructional leeches instead of more research-based methods to teach the subject is the first step toward reorienting them away from a deficit-minded—*cannot*—and into an asset-based—*can*—mindset.

MAKING THE INQUIRY QUESTION ACCESSIBLE FOR ALL

The kernel of the historical investigations/History Lab approach is the meaty question. Nonmajority students, first-generation immigrant students, and students with special needs are intrigued by the same curiosity-inducing questions as their peers. To believe that they are not devalues them as learners. It is the rare occasion that a question does not resonate with all students, but when it does not it is usually one of two factors: Either the vocabulary within the question impedes a student's ability to access the heart of what the question is asking, or the question is worded in a way that there is a colloquialism or other cultural barrier. Tweaking questions so that they work with all students is much easier than the differentiation that needs to occur with both historical sources and assessments.

Address Vocabulary Barriers

The first factor that often requires differentiation with this investigation is with vocabulary employed within the question. Although vocabulary terms within a question can be a great place to teach students new words, be sure that operational terms within questions do not impede students' ability to access the question. One option is to use a term more familiar to students. Be careful, though: The point of differentiation for students with needs related to reading is not to make everything easier. Teach up, not down. Just dropping in a word better aligned with students' reading level may not always be the best choice

Scaffolding and Framing Operational Terms

Another barrier for students' ability to access an investigatory question can be the operational terms that guide student focus, phrases such as *to what extent, the degree to which, significance,* or any term that provides parameters to the student's investigation. Other disciplinary terms like *despot, lord,* and *revolutionary* may also require scaffolding and framing. Teachers can anticipate problematic terms and either provide synonyms or definitions, or prepare explanations that can assist students with understanding the terms. The key is to avoid dumbing down the terms so that they alter the nature of the investigative question.

A final and extremely useful tool is for students to annotate the question they are wrestling with. Underling the key focus of the question and circling any key terms can help students focus on the key points of an investigative question. This can indicate to the teacher the terms that students are struggling with. This active marking of text, as illustrated in Figure 2.3, also ensures that students are considering what they are wrestling with. To extend the annotations, students can also web the question or restate the question in their own words. The end destination is that all students understand exactly what they are being asked to investigate. Some students will not need any of these strategies; some students will need them initially and then progress away from them as confidence grows and responsibility is released; but having them in your toolbox ensures that no student is denied access to this instructional approach.

Setting the Stage

One of the biggest realizations for me after presenting historical investigations to teachers across the country is that most of my investigations occur from the middle to the end of a unit. Noodling over that insight, it became apparent that the reason why had to do with background knowledge. In order for students to engage effectively in any deep-dive investigation, they need some level of knowledge. I was using the first few lessons in every unit to build students' understanding of the time period, personalities, vocabulary, and concepts that were essential knowledge for a deep dive into a topic. Common sense and the research indicate that this is good practice (Foster & Yeager, 2001). Setting context involves helping students to understand the interplay between chronological, spatial, political, economic, and social factors during the time period being studied (Dawson, 2009; Havekes et al., 2012; Huijgen & Holthuis, 2018; Neumann, 2021; Shemilt, 2009; van Boxtel & van Drie, 2012; Wilschut, 2012). Setting the context can be achieved in a number of ways, but regardless of how it is done, students must have a solid grounding in the time period before they can confidently attack a meaty historical question through the lens of historical sources.

With a full understanding of the investigative question under their belt, students are now ready to wade into the sources compiled to support the investigation. Providing a diversity of sources for students when investigating a meaty historical question is an important consideration. Text sources usually dominate, and so teachers are always looking for visual sources to include to diversify the source trail. Having scaffolded the question, students are now ready for a dive into the sources. It is here that teachers can have the biggest impact on opening up historical investigations for all students.

No, Just Because It Is in a Box Does Not Mean It Is Directions and You Can Skip Reading Them!

Before any historical source is scaffolded, there should be a uniform formatting and annotation strategy utilized. By having uniformity in formatting, I can help students become more effective in accessing key sourcing and contextualizing information. The source information is essential so that students can mimic the process that historians use when examining sources (Wineburg, 2001). Since historical sources are "drawn from a world different from that of the students in time or place, or both, teachers should provide historical context for their students by giving them information about the time, location, and purpose for the creation of the source" (Neumann et al., 2014). We know that most students jump right into the source and usually do not take the time to first understand who wrote the source, why they wrote it, and what was going on when the source was created. Simply providing what I refer to as background information is not enough to ensure that students pay heed to it (Popp & Hoard, 2018). Instead, consistent formatting can help students habitually access this essential sourcing and contextualization information.

Associated with the consistent formatting is including an annotation strategy. Annotation while reading is a powerful strategy (Aulls, 2008). The power of the annotation is that it gets away from source evaluation as a series of questions and answers. Turning source evaluation into a worksheet activity can often dull the flow of the lesson and limit the student's interest in investigating. Annotating, on the other hand, empowers students to look for key information that addresses the literacy concepts they are applying. As I show in Figure 2.3, the formatting of the sources facilitates annotation and places emphasis on sourcing and contextualizing all historical sources.

This change has formalized the process and provided a device to remind all students that attacking sources is not something we do every once in a while, but is as imbedded into our instruction as following the order of operations is to teaching and learning mathematics. With a uniform formatting approach and annotation strategy in place, greater focus can be placed on how to scaffold visual and text-based historical sources.

ADAPTING HISTORICAL SOURCES: POLITICAL CARTOONS AND IMAGES

I love visual sources, and so do students. Compelling photographs, thought-provoking art, statues, and other visual sources all supply change to the normal text-heavy diet that dominates the history classroom. I especially love political cartoons! Outside of music, they are my favorite historical source to use in the classroom.

For students though, political cartoons are more of a love–hate relationship. The visual nature, often heavily sarcastic messages, and powerful artistic representations of significant people and events—and the fact that it is not another paragraph to read—attract students to these sources and constitute the "love" end of the relationship. On the flip side, political cartoons present people or events that students are unfamiliar with and assume readers have significant background knowledge that most students do not. In addition, they require the ability to infer and extrapolate meaning from images that utilize exaggeration, symbolism, irony, analogy, captions, stereotypes, references to popular culture, humor, and caricatures. The "hate" side of the

Figure 2.3. A Model for Formatting Sources

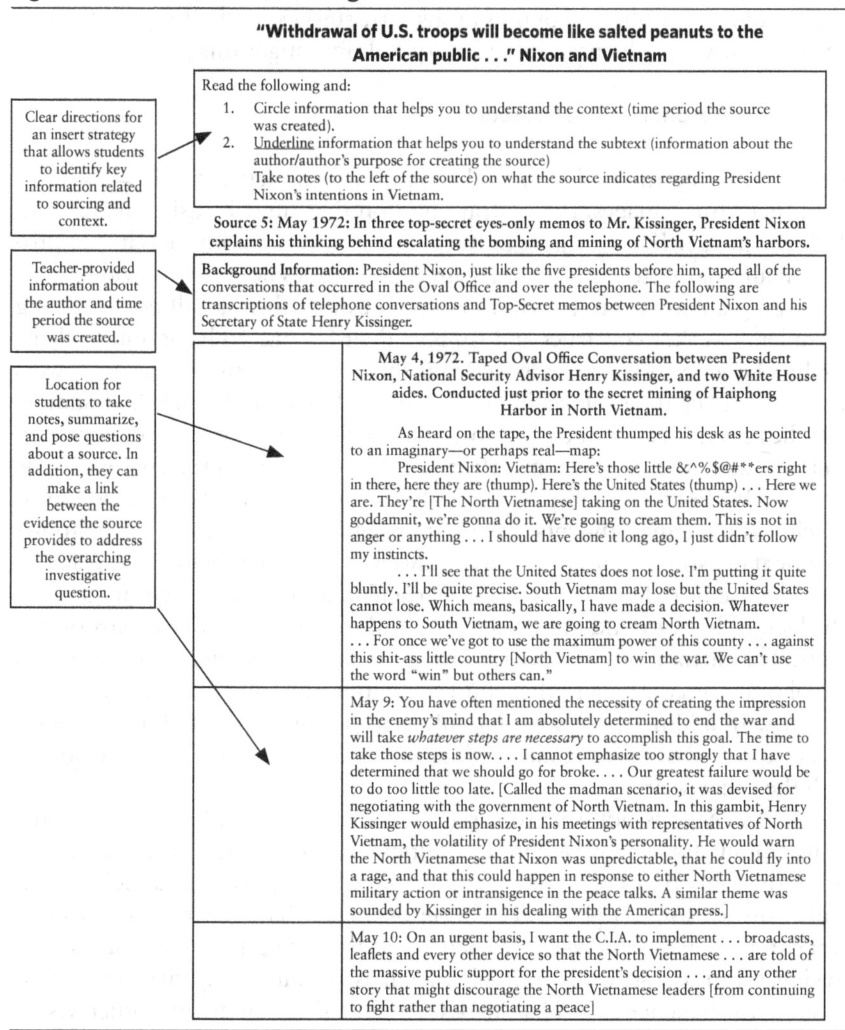

"Withdrawal of U.S. troops will become like salted peanuts to the American public . . ." Nixon and Vietnam

Read the following and:

1. Circle information that helps you to understand the context (time period the source was created).
2. Underline information that helps you to understand the subtext (information about the author/author's purpose for creating the source)

Take notes (to the left of the source) on what the source indicates regarding President Nixon's intentions in Vietnam.

Source 5: May 1972: In three top-secret eyes-only memos to Mr. Kissinger, President Nixon explains his thinking behind escalating the bombing and mining of North Vietnam's harbors.

Background Information: President Nixon, just like the five presidents before him, taped all of the conversations that occurred in the Oval Office and over the telephone. The following are transcriptions of telephone conversations and Top-Secret memos between President Nixon and his Secretary of State Henry Kissinger.

	May 4, 1972. Taped Oval Office Conversation between President Nixon, National Security Advisor Henry Kissinger, and two White House aides. Conducted just prior to the secret mining of Haiphong Harbor in North Vietnam. As heard on the tape, the President thumped his desk as he pointed to an imaginary—or perhaps real—map: President Nixon: Vietnam: Here's those little &^%$@#**ers right in there, here they are (thump). Here's the United States (thump) . . . Here we are. They're [The North Vietnamese] taking on the United States. Now goddamnit, we're gonna do it. We're going to cream them. This is not in anger or anything . . . I should have done it long ago, I just didn't follow my instincts. . . . I'll see that the United States does not lose. I'm putting it quite bluntly. I'll be quite precise. South Vietnam may lose but the United States cannot lose. Which means, basically, I have made a decision. Whatever happens to South Vietnam, we are going to cream North Vietnam. . . . For once we've got to use the maximum power of this county . . . against this shit-ass little country [North Vietnam] to win the war. We can't use the word "win" but others can."
	May 9: You have often mentioned the necessity of creating the impression in the enemy's mind that I am absolutely determined to end the war and will take *whatever steps are necessary* to accomplish this goal. The time to take those steps is now. . . . I cannot emphasize too strongly that I have determined that we should go for broke. . . . Our greatest failure would be to do too little too late. [Called the madman scenario, it was devised for negotiating with the government of North Vietnam. In this gambit, Henry Kissinger would emphasize, in his meetings with representatives of North Vietnam, the volatility of President Nixon's personality. He would warn the North Vietnamese that Nixon was unpredictable, that he could fly into a rage, and that this could happen in response to either North Vietnamese military action or intransigence in the peace talks. A similar theme was sounded by Kissinger in his dealing with the American press.]
	May 10: On an urgent basis, I want the C.I.A. to implement . . . broadcasts, leaflets and every other device so that the North Vietnamese . . . are told of the massive public support for the president's decision . . . and any other story that might discourage the North Vietnamese leaders [from continuing to fight rather than negotiating a peace]

equation is that students think images are easier to use but soon realize that they require more thinking than reading a paragraph.

Visual images aid with the transfer of learning, comprehension, and retention (Mayer, 2008; Sousa, 2017). Sadly, research indicates that students often struggle to understand the message of political cartoons, as do adults, and that many teachers restrict their use to older and more advanced students (Bickford, 2010a, 2010b, 2011; Heitzman, 1998). Fortunately, with a set of taught skills, all students can effectively use political cartoons and other images in historical investigations (Burack, 2010; Wilson, 1928).

Although the guidance I discuss below is specific to political cartoons, it is, and should, be applied to photographs, art, statues, and all types of visual sources that would be used in a History Lab investigation.

What's the Purpose of the Cartoon?

Before exploring the tools required to empower students to utilize cartoons and other visual images, the central question that must be asked is, why include the image? If the purpose of the political cartoon or image is just to provide an alternative to a text-based source, and it does not provide evidence for developing an answer to the overarching question, then it will be distracting to students as they construct and support their claims. To be useful, students need to be able to draw evidence from the political cartons that empowers them to answer the overarching question (Callahan et al., 2019). Assuming that the visual image is included to provide evidence, then the most essential skill that assists students' comprehension is to understand the context of the cartoon. Without an ability to place the cartoon within the time period to which it is referring, students cannot appreciate the value of the image to the historical question being investigated. This is often at the root of why teachers limit the use of political cartoons in particular, and visual images in general. The lack of background knowledge can lead to frustration of the part of students. The cartoon or visual image incorporated into the investigation should corroborate or contradict other source(s) within the source trail provided for students. In addition, the sourcing information and context should provide fodder for discussion as students align the political cartoon or visual source with the other sources.

If the image is not able to serve as evidence, it could still serve as the launch point for an investigation. Political cartoons and other images are powerful tools that can evoke questions and emotions and launch significant investigations. A political cartoon or image that initiates an investigation can thus also serve as a great bookend to closing the investigation and serving as an assessment tool. Whether it is to launch an investigation or to serve as evidence in a History Lab, political cartoons and other visual sources cannot simply be given to students. They must come with scaffolding and tools to ensure that students can use them effectively.

Scaffolding Political Cartoons for All Students

A political cartoon, especially one from before the 20th century, can be overwhelming. The unfamiliar figures, the allusions to events or people unknown, the dual meaning of words or images, and the substantive dialogue can be sensory overload for students. As a result of the stylistic differences, the scaffolding of political cartoons is differentiated by the century of their production. Modern cartoons require less adaptation than those from the 17th,

18th, and 19th centuries. Modern cartoons are streamlined in comparison to their earlier kin. Cartoons from before the dawn of the 20th century require a few more modifications. I will use the cartoon "Bonaparte Establishing French Quarters in Italy" as the foil for my discussion of how to scaffold political cartoons. The Napoleon image is utilized as part of a World History investigation that focuses on the question, How Should We Remember the Reign of Napoleon Bonaparte? Ensuring that students have the sourcing and contextual information as well as using tools to bring to the surface elements of the image that might not be within their scope of knowledge empowers students to use the source. The North Star for the use of political cartoons and all types of visual sources is to make students proficient enough that they employ these strategies naturally whenever they meet a political cartoon or visual image in a History Lab. Figure 2.4 provides this cartoon in the form in which it is found online, while Figure 2.5 presents the same image in an adapted form.

Provide the Sourcing and Context for Political Cartoons

Too often political cartoons are not presented as you would a text source. Instead of considering them as a multidimensional representation of an artist's view of the events of a particular time period, they are presented as

Figure 2.4. Bonaparte Establishing French Quarters in Italy

Source: Copyright © The Trustees of the British Museum. Used with permission.

Figure 2.5. Annotated "Bonaparte Establishing French Quarters in Italy"

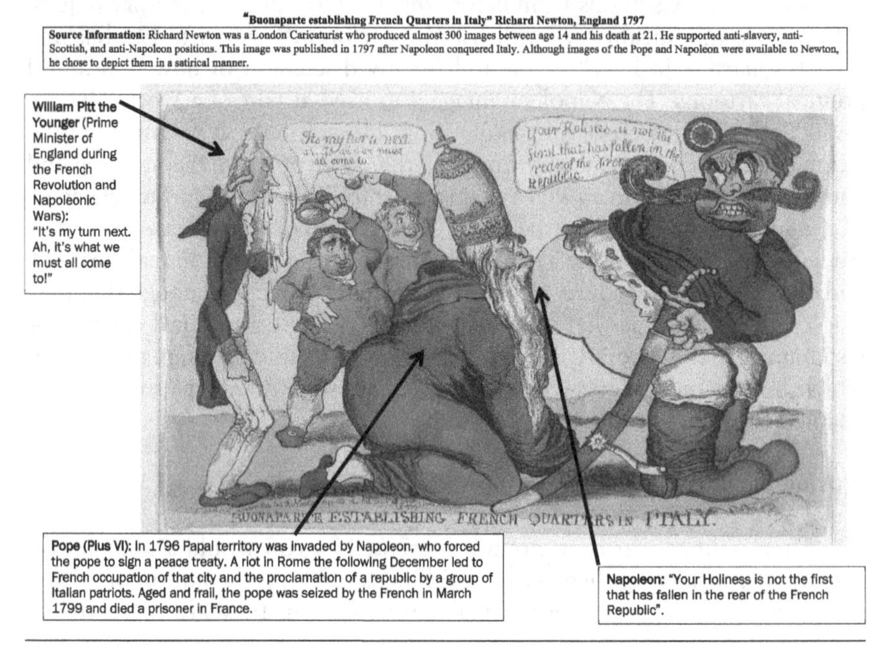

Source: Copyright © The Trustees of the British Museum. Used with permission.

one-dimensional. Students do not know who the artist was, what motivated their creation of the image, or what their connection was to the events or beliefs of the time period. To fully draw evidence from the source, students must know these things. As you can see in Figure 2.4, no information or scaffolding is provided for students about the image. In Figure 2.5, students now have information about the artist and the time period. In particular, it is an essential scaffold that all visuals include information about the artist and the context in which it was created (Harris et al., 2021). The presence of this information deepens students' ability to use the image as evidence and not just as a repository of information.

Equally essential is the scaffolding that allows students to understand the image. Political cartoons, particularly those from the 18th and 19th centuries, are remarkably busy and dialogue-heavy, and presume that the student knows the people depicted. Each of these elements is a barrier to the use of these rich sources as evidence in historical investigations.

Scaffolding to Make Language Accessible

Eighteenth- and 19th-century versions of political cartoons are often text-heavy. Massive text bubbles emerge from the mouths of the multiple characters populating the image. Unlike modern cartoons that either function with few to no words or employ a greater economy of words to communicate the cartoon's message, pre-20th-century cartoons have a greater reliance on text. To neutralize the potential for the saturation of text to interfere with a student's ability to interpret a cartoon, it is best to make that text accessible. As you can see in Figure 2.4, the text is only available in the bubbles provided in the cartoon. It is difficult to read and could cause students to shut down. In Figure 2.5 I have adapted the cartoon by pulling out the text. This process also allows you to define terms needing definition and, as discussed below, aid students with the identification of individuals they may not have a connection to.

Do Not Assume That Students Will Recognize the People in the Images

The students in your classroom are anywhere from 10 to 40 years younger than you. Their sense of what is "the past" is much narrower than yours. Your lived experience is not theirs. So while you may recognize the large nose of a depiction of President Bill Clinton or the long, saggy face of President Ronald Reagan, students do not know them from Julius Caesar. Do not assume that students know who the people are depicted in an image. Even if an image is used as an assessment at the end of a lesson where that person or people have been taught, students may not recognize the image unless that person's visage is part of the instruction. When in doubt, label the people in the image.

Provide Magnifying Glasses

A magnifying glass is an essential tool for accessing the nuances of these images. The magnifying glass allows students the autonomy to explore the image and to draw out aspects that are hard to discern with unaided eyes. Their inclusion in the tool kit reinforces the idea that students are literally investigating the past. Of course, magnifying glasses are only useful if students have a physical copy of the cartoon they are examining. If the images that students are examining can only be accessed online, many online sites have magnifying tools that serve the same function. The online tools often benefit from a higher-quality image as well, which increases the power of the magnification tool. Regardless, if a student is forced to confront an image and they cannot access all of the elements employed by the artist, it can cause them to either shut down their examination or to use the inaccessibility of the image to support an argument that the image is not helpful.

From Big to Small, or Small to Big?

Armed with their history magnifying glasses and with a political cartoon or visual image that is contextualized, sourced, and annotated, the question for teachers is how to attack the image. A quick Google search of "political cartoon analysis techniques" leads to examples from the National Archives, Library of Congress, Colonial Williamsburg, the College Board, and numerous other less reputable sources. Essentially, these tools can be grouped into two categories: big-to-small analysis tools and small-to-big ones. It comes down to examining the image in small parts and then building to the full image or starting with the full image and moving to the smaller elements. Which approach to utilize depends on the time of the year, the complicated nature of the image, and the relative strengths of the students. Generally my rule of thumb is to start students with tools to examine elements of an image and then gradually move them to being able to examine an entire image. Because most political cartoons have layers of meaning, it helps to systematically unpack those layers rather than assuming students can digest all these elements at once (Thomas, 2004). That gradual release of responsibility allows teachers to align the analysis of these sources with the growing levels of students' confidence.

Small-to-Big Tools

The small-to-big tools are simply variations on the same idea that students will become more effective in their analysis of political cartoons and other visual images if they isolate elements of the image, explore that element in depth, and then move to another element. There is no research base behind these techniques, but there are thousands of teachers who employ them with remarkable success. The most often employed is the Crop It method. When students are supplied a political cartoon or visual image, they, or the teacher if the image is being projected, use L-shaped paper to block out parts of an image and to focus on other elements (Bondie, 2010; Weibe, 2016). A similar tool is to quarter the political cartoon or visual image. The political cartoon or image is divided into quadrants, A, B, C, and D, and students, or the teacher if the image is being projected, cover all but, say, the right-hand quadrant, have students examine the image, then unveil the top left quadrant, and continue until the entire image is revealed. This approach can calm student anxiety about images that can be challenging and teach them the skills that they will slowly be able to employ on their own.

Big-to-Small Tools

The alternative to segmenting the analysis of political cartoons and other visual images is to have students analyze the entire image. Especially at the start of the school year, I try to avoid these types of tools. They tend to become either very formulaic or increase the cognitive load for students to the point that they shut down. There are many commercially available tools that are organized as acronyms that fit this mold. Depicted in Figure 2.6 are two of the more frequently employed, from the College Board.

Figure 2.6. SOAPS and TACOS Models for Visual Source Evaluation

SOAPS	
S	What is the Subject? The general topic or event dealt with in the cartoon?
O	What are Objects? Describe the objects and even the people you can identify in the cartoon.
A	Who is the Audience? Who do you suppose the artist wants to see his cartoon and leave with a message?
P	What is the Perspective? What is the artist trying to say in the cartoon? Describe his viewpoint or perspective.
S	Identify the Symbols. What symbols does the artist use to represent an idea or group of people, etc.? Is this an appropriate symbol? Why or why not?
TACOS	
T	Time: When was this created? Occasion?
A	Action: What's happening?
C	Caption: What textual clues are included?
O	Objects: List everything item you can identify.
S	Summary: What is the message of this cartoon?

A parallel tool is the use of Evidence Analysis Window Frames. The window frames are thick plastic sheets that have preprinted questions on the margins that guide student analysis of a political cartoon or an image. Students use overhead markers to engage the image and annotate or respond to the questions directly on the sheet (Weibe, 2017).

One of my favorite approaches that moves from big to small is to pose four questions for students to address as they analyze the political cartoon: What do you see, think, feel, and wonder? These questions allow students to enter the image without getting lost in trying to "figure out" what the political cartoon means. Cognitively unburdened by having to come to an immediate analysis of the political cartoon or visual image, these questions put students in the driver's seat, which allows their impressions to drive the initial exploration of the image. This is empowering and will lead to the generation of questions that can launch an investigation, draw out information that can align with an investigative question (See, Think, Wonder, 2019). A similar model is Visual Thinking Skills, which has students pose the same three questions to any visual they encounter: What's going on here? What makes you say that? What more can we find? (Kerr & Adams, 2017).

Scaffolding the use of political cartoons and other visual images is essential so that these types of historical resources can be a part of any History Lab investigation. Political cartoons and other visual images are powerful tools that break up the daily diet of text, stimulate students' thought, and broaden the literacy skills that the History Lab approach promotes.

MODIFYING A TEXT SOURCE

Text-based historical sources are the most frequently used sources in the history classroom. The rise of the Internet has made text sources easier to access. Poems, song lyrics, speeches, letters, newspaper articles, you name it—there are tons of options for text-based sources. Nevertheless, text sources, if not handled correctly, can be as deadly boring as a history textbook, and more confusing (Howells, 2007; Sipress, 2004). There is no reason that a student needs to read the entirety of Henry Clay's speech on the American System. Two days long, forty pages of text, and paragraph after paragraph, the speech, as riveting as it may have been on its delivery, should never be used in its entirety with students, and yet, I have seen this speech and others like it assigned as homework or incorporated as part of a classroom lesson.

Unfortunately, in the few instances where historical investigations have been done with students reading significantly below grade level or needing accommodations to align with educational needs, these students are offered a reduced number of sources (De La Paz, 2005). Although limiting the number of sources is a good scaffolding strategy as we allow for students to gain confidence in the cognitive moves necessary to be successful in a History Lab, "limiting exposure to sources does not give students with a learning disability an equal chance to participate in rich elementary and secondary classroom experiences" (National Center for Technology Innovation & Center for Implementing Technology in Education, n.d.). The key is to recognize that all students need and benefit from instructional scaffolds. Determining what scaffolds, how long to utilize them, and when to remove them is where teachers can make inquiring about history accessible for all students.

All Those Ellipses Worry Me!

Once, when presenting to a group of teachers alongside a university historian, the discussion of source adaptation came up. I took the position that if a student cannot access the source, then they will shut down and no learning will occur. Therefore, within reason, we must make the adaptations necessary to ensure that all students can access historical sources. I shared my sources for a lesson on the Mexican-American War, and my historian partner interjected that the presence "of all those ellipses worry me." For the historian, shortening the source, using ellipses to eliminate redundancies, and providing definitions or synonyms for challenging vocabulary all ran the risk of turning a historical source into something it was not intended to be.

Yes, adapting sources without care can lead to distortions, misrepresentations, or outright altering the intent of the author, artist, or source creator. Too many ellipses can make the source seem like a string of disconnected statements rather than a coherent narrative. Substituting too many synonyms can reduce the student's ability to understand the past from the lens of those who lived at that time. Thus, the adaptation of historical sourcesis a fine line between "tampering with history" and leaving your students unable to access the historical materials that their peers with different reading abilities are able to utilize (Wineburg & Martin, 2009). Because "every adaptation is a trade-off," teachers should determine if the "adaptation is necessary for students to access, understand, and analyze the" historical source ("Adapting Documents for the Classroom," n.d.). Once a historical text is selected to be part of the source trail in an investigation, teachers must make some preliminary choices about how much of the source students need. My suggestion, in keeping with the idea of "teaching up," is to make the initial selection of sources based on students who would not need any modifications. This allows you to start with a strong sense of what is the most that students can handle before applying select modifications. Then apply the adaptations below to meet the needs of the students in your classes.

The One-Page Rule!?

The adaptations for text-based historical sources below are divided into things that should always be done, versus tools that should be employed predicated on the needs of the students and time of year (earlier rather than later), and are designed to be removed as the year progresses. In addition, I will illustrate the application of these adaptations using one source from a historical investigation on the Disability Rights Movement of the Late 20th Century.

Adaptations that should always be employed:

1. **Provide sourcing and contextualization information.** Providing source information helps students to understand the author of the source and when the source was created. Do not assume that students will have the background knowledge about the author or the time period. Instead, provide this information and encourage students to source and contextualize the document first, before diving into the text. This ensures that students will treat the source as three-dimensional and not simply as a snippet of text. Providing this information empowers students to question authorship and intent as they use the source as evidence in the investigation.
2. **Excerpt the source.** Provide text-based historical sources that are focused enough to serve as evidence, but not so short that they are divorced from the context of the source. Excerpting eliminates student frustration with information extraneous to the question

being investigated and allows the teacher to ensure that students are able to draw meaning from the source. The length of the excerpt should increase as students gain confidence, increase their reading comprehension, and advance in grade.

3. **Follow the one-page rule.** This rule is hardly scientific or research-based, but I promise you, it is rooted in student behavior and teacher practice! I discovered this rule from years of watching students when they are handed a text-based historical source. Invariably, the first thing they do is turn the paper over to see if the source runs onto the back. If it does, they think it is too long and disengage. If the source does not run onto the back, then they are more likely to persevere through it. Even the size of the font is less demoralizing than a source that runs to the back of a page!
4. **Present the source in a uniform manner.** As outlined in Chapter 1, I structure all sources in a uniform manner so that students can take notes, annotate, and interact with all historical sources in the same way.

The source found in Figure 2.7 models the four adaptations above. This source, including the source information, is 407 words and is excerpted from a book of 240 pages.

Next come the kinds of adaptations that enable students who require scaffolds to be able to utilize the same historic text as their peers, adaptations that should be employed depending upon the students' needs, the time of the school year, and the grade level. In addition, unless these adaptations are required by an IEP or 504, they should be viewed through the lens of a scaffold that can and should be removed as students grow more confident or their reading comprehension increases.

1. **Simplify sentence structure, syntax, spelling, grammar, vocabulary, etc. This is tricky work.** I do not endorse the idea that teachers should "rearrange sentence sequences" or make use of tools like Text Compactor or Rewordify. It is not difficult to unintentionally alter the intent of a source by making such changes. Wineburg and Martin (2009) make a compelling argument that the "crisis in adolescent literacy" demands that we adapt historical sources so that students can access the information, but there is a fine line between adaptation and simply turning a historical source into just text. Although I do not suggest "rearranging sentence sequences," I do suggest the judicious use of ellipses, providing definitions, and aligning spelling with modern conventions. The source that remains after adaptation should more resemble its creator's intent than not. Yes, in many instances we teach students who are reading significantly below grade level, and in these cases teachers must

Figure 2.7. Original Source: No Modifications Other Than Excerpting From the Original

"We Won't Go Away": The Fight for Equal Treatment for People with a Disability

Source A: *Being Heumann: An Unrepentant Memoir of A Disability Rights Activist*, by Judith Heumann, 2020, Beacon Press.

Read the following and:

1. Circle information that helps you to understand the context (time period the source was created).
2. Underline information that helps you to understand the information about the author/author's purpose for creating the source.
3. Take notes (to the left of the source) on what the source indicates regarding if the 504 sit-ins were more historically significant than the passage of the ADA in 1990.

Source Information: Judith Heumann contracted polio in 1949 and became a quadriplegic. She was a pioneer in the disability rights movement. Heumann successfully sued the New York Department of Education to receive her tearing license, founded the Center for Independent Living, planned, and led the sit-ins that occurred in 1977, and was a central figure in getting the Americans With Disabilities Act (ADA) passed in 1990. This excerpt is taken from her autobiography.

When I look back now, I see that one of the greatest aspects of the 504 sit-ins was the way it united us. We weren't focused on how we were different—we were focused on our common goal, our collective purpose. We looked beyond how we each spoke and moved, how we thought and how we looked. We respected the humanity in each other. We stood for inclusiveness and community, for our love of equity and justice—and we won.

We have come a long way from my youth. The legislation we worked so hard to get passed still stands: The Americans with Disabilities Act, Section 504, IDEA, and numerous other federal and state laws validate and protect the civil rights of people with disabilities. Disabled children are no longer allowed to be denied the right to an education. Calling a child a fire hazard is illegal . . . If you're of an age where you have grown up with all these benefits—curb cuts, disabled kids in class, captioning and audio description on television, and the myriad other ways disabled people are integrated into our communities—you would be forgiven for thinking that this is how it is, how it's always been and how it will always be.

(continued)

Figure 2.7. (*continued*)

	The Section 504 sit-in was an exceedingly complex operation. First, it took years to develop the enabling regulations and create the American Coalition of Citizens with Disabilities . . . then it took many months and a multitude of meetings to organize the protest outside the San Francisco Federal Building. Our work was grounded in an enormous amount of networking among civil rights groups, involving more people than you can imagine. Behind each name I've mentioned in this book were thousands of others, radiating outward. We had committee after committee. Everyone had a role, and everyone had ownership . . . we believed that every single person had a role in producing change. We knew our success would hinge on collaboration. Our power would only come from the people who identified with and felt ownership of a movement.

make more significant alterations than normal. But these scaffolds should be walked back as students gain more confidence and increased reading comprehension. As illustrated in Figure 2.8, the source is reduced from 407 words to 306 and the complexity of the vocabulary is reduced as well.

2. **Chunk text.** Dividing the text into sections allows students to focus on smaller parts of the text, draw conclusions, and then move to the next section. Chunking of text also enables the teacher to check for understanding more frequently. This can be accomplished by simply breaking the text into sections or utilizing questions to focus students on each section. Figure 2.9 models chunking. Note that the source information as well as the text of the source is chunked and scaffolded with questions.
3. **Word bank or parenthetical vocabulary.** Students often shut down when historical sources employ unfamiliar vocabulary. Students can benefit from having definitions and key vocabulary terms provided in either a word bank or defined parenthetically within the source. The choice of word bank or parenthetical is preferential, and often depends on the number of words needing definitions and the impact that may have on the length of the source. Figure 2.9 below utilizes a word bank.
4. **Number lines.** Numbering lines provides both the teacher and the reader benchmarks to allow students to read efficiently and to reference where they find information when discussing.

All of the adaptations described above help all students access the historical investigation process. By removing barriers to the sources of

Figure 2.8. Modified Source 1: Reduced Complexity and Length

"We Won't Go Away": The Fight for Equal Treatment for People With a Disability

Source A: *Being Heumann: An Unrepentant Memoir of A Disability Rights Activist*, by Judith Heumann, 2020, Beacon Press.

Read the following and:

1. Circle information that helps you to understand the context (time period the source was created).
2. Underline information that helps you to understand the information about the author/author's purpose for creating the source.
3. Take notes (to the left of the source) on what the source indicates regarding if the 504 sit-ins were more historically significant than the passage of the ADA in 1990.

Source Information: Judith Heumann was a pioneer in the disability rights movement. She successfully sued the New York Department of Education to receive her teaching license, founded the Center for Independent Living, planned, led the sit-ins that occurred in 1977, and was a central figure in getting the Americans with Disabilities Act (ADA) passed in 1990. This excerpt is taken from her autobiography.

	When I look back now, I see that one of the greatest aspects of the 504 [**Part of a federal law that requires schools to provide students with disabilities an equal opportunity to participate in school services, programs, and activities**] sit-ins was the way it united us. We weren't focused on how we were different—we were focused on our common goal, our collective purpose. We looked beyond how we each spoke and moved, how we thought and how we looked. We respected the humanity in each other. We stood for inclusiveness [**including everyone**] and community, for our love of equity and justice—and we won. We have come a long way from my youth. The legislation we worked so hard to get passed still stands: The Americans with Disabilities Act, Section 504, IDEA [**Individuals with Disabilities Education Act; a federal law ensuring all students have access to an education**], and . . . other federal and state laws validate and protect the civil rights of people with disabilities. Disabled children are no longer allowed to be denied the right to an education. . . . If you're of an age where you have grown up with all these benefits—curb cuts, disabled kids in class, captioning, and audio description on television . . . you would be forgiven for thinking that this is how it is, how it's always been and how it will always be.

(continued)

Figure 2.8. *(continued)*

	The Section 504 sit-in was a . . . complex operation . . . Our work was grounded in an enormous amount of networking among civil rights groups, involving more people than you can imagine . . . We knew our success would hinge on collaboration. Our power would only come from the people who identified with and felt ownership of a movement.

information, all students can stand on the scaffolding they need to engage in the investigation of meaningful questions about the past. Teachers exert their expertise when they utilize these scaffolds and later remove them. As student confidence and skills increase, the scaffolds employed can be removed. The need for and the level of which the scaffolding is provided depends on the needs of the students in the room, just as the pace at which they are removed depends on each group of students.

SCAFFOLDING THE PROCESS

The final consideration for making History Labs accessible for all students is how to modify the process while not cheapening it for students who may require modifications or who read below grade level. Significant research indicates that all students from upper elementary through high school and from those enrolled in advanced classes to those needing educational accommodations are able to learn historical literacies in a scaffolded environment (Nokes et al., 2007).

1. **Model the process.** Although starting the year with a full-on jigsaw would be wonderful, the reality of that choice depends on a multitude of factors. Jumping into the deep end of the pool depends on the maturity of students, their confidence with what they are being asked to do, and their understanding of the cognitive moves involved in sourcing, corroborating, and contextualizing. If that is the choice you make, then be sure to model what an effective jigsaw looks and sounds like. The most powerful tool is for students to see other students engaged in an effective jigsaw. Film students from the previous year and show this as a model for students. Ask them to critique their predecessors. Within this modeling, be sure to model how to source, contextualize, and, especially, corroborate. At the start of the school year, analyze a document for students and verbalize how you source and contextualize a historical source. Students are more adept with analyzing one source, but as Weinburg (2001) has

Figure 2.9. Modified Source 2: Reduced Complexity, Word Bank, and Scaffolding Questions to Chunk Reading

"We Won't Go Away": The Fight for Equal Treatment for People With a Disability

Source A: *Being Heumann: An Unrepentant Memoir of A Disability Rights Activist*, by Judith Heumann, 2020, Beacon Press.

Read the following and:

1. Circle information that helps you to understand the context (time period the source was created).
2. Underline information that helps you to understand the information about the author/author's purpose for creating the source.
3. Take notes (to the left of the source) on what the source indicates regarding if the 504 sit-ins were more historically significant than the passage of the ADA in 1990.

What about the author might impact the information provided about the significance of the sit-ins and the passage of the ADA?	**Source Information:** Judith Heumann was a pioneer in the disability rights movement. She successfully sued the New York Department of Education to receive her teaching license, founded the Center for Independent Living, planned, led the sit-ins that occurred in 1977, and was a central figure in getting the Americans with Disabilities Act (ADA) passed in 1990. This excerpt is taken from her autobiography.

Word Bank

Inclusiveness: Including everyone in something.

IDEA: Individuals with Disabilities Education Act, a federal law ensuring all students have access to an education.

Section 504: Part of a federal law that requires schools to provide students with disabilities an equal opportunity to participate in school services, programs, and activities.

Why does the author feel the sit-ins were important?	When I look back now, I see that one of the greatest aspects of the 504 sit-ins was the way it united us. We weren't focused on how we were different—we were focused on our common goal, our collective purpose. We looked beyond how we each spoke and moved, how we thought and how we looked. We respected the humanity in each other. We stood for **inclusiveness** and community, for our love of equity and justice—and we won.

(*continued*)

Figure 2.9. *(continued)*

What evidence does the author use to support her argument that the disability rights movement was successful?	We have come a long way from my youth. The legislation we worked so hard to get passed still stands: The Americans with Disabilities Act, **Section 504, IDEA**, and . . . other federal and state laws validate and protect the civil rights of people with disabilities. Disabled children are no longer allowed to be denied the right to an education. . . . If you're of an age where you have grown up with all these benefits—curb cuts, disabled kids in class, captioning, and audio description on television . . . you would be forgiven for thinking that this is how it is, how it's always been and how it will always be.
What point is the author making here?	The **Section 504** sit-in was a . . . complex operation . . . Our work was grounded in an enormous amount of networking among civil rights groups, involving more people than you can imagine . . . We knew our success would hinge on collaboration. Our power would only come from the people who identified with and felt ownership of a movement.

demonstrated, when they have to corroborate across multiple sources, especially ones that provide conflicting and contradictory information, students need more scaffolding and support.

2. **Stairstep the process.** If a full-blown jump into the inquiry deep end is not the optimum pedagogical choice for your students, then chunk the process. Conduct a Lab with three sources, then four, then five, and build students up to six sources. Find the "Goldilocks" point where students feel comfortable enough to succeed, but not so comfortable that they are bored or so uncomfortable that they shut down (Willingham, 2010). Once you find that point, slowly move students out of the shallow end of the pool and into deeper territory. This "gradual release of responsibility" will recognize student growth and enable all students to move toward ever more complex History Lab experiences (Ferretti et al., 2001; Fisher & Frey, 2021).
3. **Provide variation in the format.** Although the optimal format is a jigsaw, there is nothing written in pedagogical stone to say that this is always the format that should be utilized. As discussed in forthcoming chapters, the investigations can take the form of a history trial, a mock Supreme Court hearing, a meeting of a presidential cabinet, or

another context for sharing. Some students liked to read all of the sources themselves (more power to them!); in other instances, students benefit from working through the sources together

4. **Utilize strategic graphic organizers.** Provide students with organizers that aid with the sourcing and contextualizing of documents as well as with corroborating. "Embedded scaffolds can help students look across sources to synthesize the multiple perspectives they encounter. An interactive graphic organizer can also help students look at key points in each source and then compare across sources" (National Center for Technology Innovation & Center for Implementing Technology in Education, n.d.). My preference is to utilize a fairly simple tool that prompts students to consider the impact of the source and context and then to draw information that helps to support a claim about the overarching question. This structure allows students to have all of their information in one place. In addition, you will notice that in the example provided in Figure 2.10, the students have also used numbers to indicate how they are ranking their source and lines/arrows to show sources that corroborate or challenge others. These tools are the by-product of an emphasis on annotating any source that students encounter.

In most of my writing, practice, and professional learning, the ideal structure for a History Lab is for students to engage in a jigsaw. This instructional approach is "one of the most powerful strategies" to use "across surface, deep, and transfer levels of learning" (Hattie et al., 2020). In this format, students are provided one of six sources that are being used to develop an evidence-based claim in response to the investigation's overarching question. The students source, contextualize, and closely read their source to determine how it can be used as evidence to support the claim they are making in response to the investigation's overarching question. Then students are grouped so that each group has one student with each of the sources. The students then share their sources, explain how the source and context impacted their understanding of the source, and then explain what evidence it brings to bear regarding the question. Next, student groups debate various claims and how the evidence supports those claims. This is a cognitively challenging series of student moves that takes time for students to practice, gain confidence, and perfect. Needless to say, few students or classes are ready for this on their first trip through a History Lab. Thus, scaffolding the process can be as, if not more, essential to success than the scaffolding of the question or the sources.

The scaffolding can be provided at several points in the process. Each tool can be used individually, all together, or piecemeal, based on the needs of the students. As students progress in their confidence and facility with the cognitive moves required of a History Lab, these scaffolds can be removed

Figure 2.10. Student Annotations and Source Ranking

Source	How does the subtext/context of the source influence the portrayal of American impact on the Philippines?	Information
(2) **Source A:** *The Boston Sunday Globe*, "Expansion, Before and After." March 5, 1899.	- Newspaper—American's point of view - Made in Boston not in Phillipines	-It purtrays the transformation of Filipinos before and after the expansion
(3) **Source B:** Smith, Warren D. "The Philippine Question." *Economic Geography*, Vol. 9, No. 3 (Jul., 1933), pp. 303–320.	- He wanted U.S to take control over the Philippines >Believed that it was for the Philippines benefits	- Shows the economic trends in Phillipines.
(4) **Source C:** Chris Andrews, "American Imperialism in the Philippines" From *Fourth International*, February 1946, Vol.7 No.2, pp.41–44.	-Taken from a social magazine written at the end of WWII -Communist international organization consisted of followers that supported socialism	- talks about economic changes in Phillipine throughout the war and how U.S can improve the economy.
(5) **Source D:** *This is America's Story*, 1950.	-Taken from a text book, used in American schools during the 1950s. -U.S was fighting Soviet union and communism	-Some people in Phillippines wanted the U.S to grant their independence.
(5) **Source E:** *Stanley Karnow, In Our Image: America's Empire in the Philippines*, 1990.	-Covered Asia from 1959 to 1974. - Present in Vietnam in July 1959 during the war. -Impacted deeply by the American loss in the war.	-U.S tried to helped the Fillpinos but the Phillippines turned against them.
(5) **Source F:** David J. Silbey, *A War of Frontier and Empire: The Philippine American War, 1899–1902*, 2007.	- Written and published during American invasion of Afghanistan and Iraq, after 9/11. - A military historian.	-After the war, both sides lived peacefully and Phillipines became America's "favored race"
(1) **Source G:** Clouie. "How the Americans Hampered Philippine Progress in the 20th Century...". Definitely Filipino: The Blog for Online Filipinos, 2011.	- A block for online Fillipinos - "Clouie", he is Filippino - Blamed U.S for all the problems in the Philippines.	talks about how imperialism affected the Fillipinos.

or scaled back. There is no exact recipe for what tools to use, how many to use, and when to use them; that is the alchemy that makes teaching challenging and rewarding. It is what teachers do best: creating environments in which all students can be successful.

CONCLUSION

Yes, all students can and should have the opportunity to do inquiry about rich historical questions, interrogate a range of historical sources, and develop claims. The key is that teachers cannot simply roll out the materials and put the students to work. This is akin to dropping a non-swimmer into the deep end of the pool and letting them figure out how to swim on their own. When teachers at professional development sessions respond that historical investigations are "not for the kid that they teach," my response is always the same. Yes, your kids can do this, but not without supports. All students need supports to be successful with History Labs. Some need more supports for longer periods of time; others need fewer and for shorter periods. Some students need accommodations to align with their 504s or IEPs. Other students need scaffolding due to reading comprehension issues. UDL reminds us to anticipate barriers that students might encounter along the way and provide the scaffolds they need to eliminate these barriers. When we do that, we provide opportunities for all students to investigate the past rather than simply just digest stories.

CHAPTER 3

"Is Every Day a Lab?"

What Happens Between History Labs?

Is every day a lab?

—Kristen Rentschler, teacher in Indiana

I still remember the first unit plan I ever developed. It was for my undergraduate social studies methods course, and even though it was written in the 1990s, I still have it! Typed on an electric typewriter—and in retrospect, not deserving of the grade I received—my Vietnam War unit was twenty days long! It included a crossword puzzle, a film strip, and a full day of map coloring (make sure the water is blue!). To my current satisfaction, it did include historical sources and a decent historical question for one of the lessons, but looking back at this now-30-year-old document, I realize quickly that there is absolutely nothing from it that I use in my current Vietnam unit. Despite the limitations of the instructional approaches embedded in this unit plan, I realize that planning, both short- and long-term, is the most essential ingredient—and second most time-consuming after grading—to effective teaching and learning. Looking back on this unit plan also helped me to contextualize a question raised at professional development sessions: "So what do you do between labs?" I recognize it as a question about how to plan so that students can be successful in learning and applying historical thinking in the classroom.

Unlike current efforts to "teacher-proof" education through prepackaged instructional materials and programs, true planning requires a teacher to consider how each lesson fits into the entirety of a unit and a course (Cuban, 2009, 2012; Curwin, 2012). Because of the heavy lifts required to move away from history as a good story told and to have students engage in studying the past, teachers need to be active planners (Levstik & Barton, 2023; Lesh, 2011; Nokes, 2013, 2019; Swann et al., 2018a; Waring & Hartshorne, 2020). It is also essential for transitioning to teaching history as an investigative approach. Owning the development of lessons, units, and the scope of a course allows a teacher to think about how each aspect aids in students' understanding of the content and the skills being utilized. When teachers simply pick up a curriculum guide or a prepackaged lesson and "teach it," they lack the ownership that empowers reflective instruction. We know that access to high-quality lessons can increase the effectiveness of both novice and struggling teachers because these lessons serve as exemplars to follow (Chenowith, 2009; Goodwin, 2016). And yes, there are times when "borrowing" a lesson from a curriculum guide, a colleague, or a commercial product is necessary and, at times, better than what an individual teacher can create. Nevertheless, even the best prepackaged high-quality instructional materials must be adapted to meet the needs of the learners in front of you, or they will not successfully promote student learning. For me, teacher creativity and effectiveness lie at the intersection of stealing good materials from others and developing your own. Do not fear: The time spent planning pays long-term dividends.

THE TWINKIES OF LESSONS

In the context of planning, the idea of designing an effective inquiry lab can be simultaneously invigorating and daunting. Developing a History Lab or historical investigation takes time, more time than the development of a typical lesson. That said, these types of lessons that have the sweat equity of a teacher within their DNA always have a longer shelf life than a lesson developed 20 minutes before it is taught. There are always lessons that you develop or borrow that you know are not very good, and even before you implement them you know in your teacher heart that they will have to be replaced before you teach that topic again next semester or next year. It is rare, though, that a well-developed History Lab is replaced that quickly. By the end of my time in the classroom, there were History Labs that I had been using, generally unchanged, for over a decade. Yes, sometimes I would find a better resource or would tweak the question, but the bones of the investigations remained sturdy. Just like a Twinkie, History Labs last longer, stay fresher, and are always delicious whenever you use them!

"IS EVERY DAY A LAB?"

Recently, I had an extended email conversation with a teacher from Indiana. She was interested in determining what a unit would look like "if every day is a lab." Over the course of several emails, she helped me to see that in many ways it is what happens before, after, and between History Labs that makes the endeavor successful. Without having sources, questions, literacy skills, and historical thinking skills at the forefront of every lesson, the History Labs would be perfunctory at best and failures at worst. Suffice it to say, what I do not do between History Labs is simply revert to the pedagogy that has dominated history instruction for hundreds of years. It is not lecture, movie, coloring maps, History Lab, and then book work. Variety is the spice of the classroom, so every unit should have a variety of instructional approaches. I also look for instructional strategies leading up to and after labs that enable me to support the skills needed to effectively conduct deep dives into "meaty" historical questions, but also ensure that kids do not see class as "we do the same thing every day." It is not just listing the topics to be covered that day, but thoughtful, intentional unit and lesson planning that enables teachers to bring clarity to their instruction and to see how the time between historical investigations are essential to the successful execution of those experiences.

An important reminder, though, especially to pre-service teachers: The unit that I model below is the result of several years of development. Lessons were crafted, some failed and were jettisoned, and all needed revisions. The product you are looking at is the result of the constant cycle of planning, teaching, revision, and reflection. A rich unit of diverse lessons is the goal, but it is important to respect the journey we take to get to this point and not think that all our units should look like this when we are 1st-, 2nd-, or even 3rd-year teachers.

Having had the fortunate opportunity to work with numerous teachers in many states, the prevalence of the question posted by my Hoosier pen pal helped me to realize that one of the holes in my first book is the spaces between the deep-dive historical inquires that I described. In this chapter, I intend to shine some much-needed light into the instruction that occurs in the gaps between History Labs and help to demonstrate how teachers need to reverse-engineer the elements of a History Lab into the lessons that occur beforehand so that the skills utilized in an inquiry lab are taught, practiced, and expanded prior to the actual lab. A failure to backwards-map these skills into your instruction can lead to a lab experience that may not be as productive or enjoyable for students as it could be with advanced planning. To facilitate this exploration, I am going to discuss my unit on The Great War, break it down into its constituent parts, and use it to provide insight into how historical thinking is woven into lessons that are not historical investigations. The focus will be on the skills introduced in Chapter 1, illustrated again here in Figure 3.1.

SERIOUSLY, NO TRENCH FOOT, OR TANKS, OR MUSTARD GAS?

The Great War has become a unit that I look forward to every year. One, it is a marker for progress. If I finish World War I by the end of December, I will be able to get to the 21st century by May. But it also became a

Figure 3.1. A Broader View of Historical Thinking

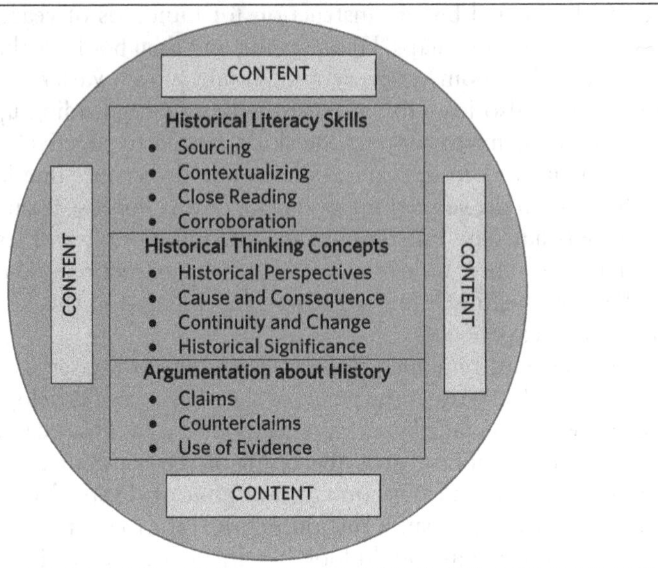

favorite because of the domestic lens I brought to its investigation. In Figure 3.2, you will notice that I examine more of the domestic aspects of the Great War than the foreign. This is intentional. Because my students take World History the year prior to my course, we organize the World History analysis of World War I to look at causes, the battlefield experience, and the outcome. Instead of repeating wonderful lessons on the "isms" (militarism, nationalism, and imperialism), trench warfare, and the mechanization of warfare, I made a conscious decision to provide a distinctly different view of the war in American History than what students get the previous year in World History. Pre-assessment of students often identifies that they remember these aspects from the previous year's World History course, and reteaching would be to no one's benefit. This is simply how we approached things within my school and district. Other schools and districts may not benefit from the same sequencing, may not function within a collaborative environment as I did, or may just like to teach about trench foot, the Second Battle of the Somme, or no man's land. The approach to teaching World War I in the context of United States History will vary from classroom to classroom and district to district, but the essence of the unit is the transformative impact the war had on political, economic, and social relations in the United States and its relationship to the rest of the world.

In terms of time, you will notice that I spend 11 days on the unit. Because I live in a state that divides United States History between two

Figure 3.2. The Great War Unit Outline

Lesson	Central/Key Question	General Instructional Approach	Historical Literacy Skills	Historical Thinking Skills	Argumentation about Historical Issues
The Road to War	Was American neutrality driven more by economic concerns or a concern about immigrants?	Decision-Making Simulation	Sourcing Contextualizing	Historical Significance Cause and Consequence	Claims Use of Evidence
Home Front Mobilization	How mobilized was the nation?	Source Evaluation Mini-presentations Argument Development	Sourcing Contextualizing		
The Great Migration	Is the artwork of Jacob Lawrence or oral histories a better representation of the experiences of African American migrants?	Comparing and Contrasting sources	Sourcing Contextualizing Corroborating	Cause and Consequence	Claims Use of Evidence
Anti-German Reactions	Did the United States people and government over or underreact to the presence of German Americans?	Decision-Making	Contextualizing	Historical Perspectives	
Civil Liberties and WW1	Do civil liberties demand more or less protection during times of war?	Decision-Making			
Suffrage	What was the best path to suffrage: Working within or outside the political system?	Simulated Debate	Sourcing Contextualizing	Historical Perspectives	Claims Counterclaims Use of Evidence
Temperance	Is Carrie Nation the best spokesperson for the Temperance Movement?	Source Evaluation Mini-presentations Argument Development	Sourcing Contextualizing Corroborating		
Versailles Treaty	Should the United States ratify the Treaty of Versailles?	Simulated Debate		Continuity and Change	Claims Use of Evidence
Palmer Raids	Were the Palmer Raids legal and justified?	History Lab	Sourcing Contextualizing Corroborating	Historical Perspectives	Claims Use of Evidence

grades, with industrialization as the overlapping bridge unit, I am afforded the time necessary to dive deeply and am not saddled by the ridiculous strictures imposed by a full survey. Students in Maryland can look deeply at events, individuals, and ideas that make up the tapestry of the American past. This is not a luxury that all teachers experience, but as you can see, the benefits far outweigh the costs of not doing a full survey every time a student studies American History. If you teach a full survey, obviously you would have to make harder choices about what topics to cover and how much time World War I gets relative to the rest of the curriculum. Nonetheless, there are still ample opportunities even in a survey structure to dive deeply into significant aspects of World War I and to have time for one historical investigation.

WOVEN INTO EVERY UNIT

The most significant conclusion to draw from the unit outline in Figure 3.2 is the intentional weaving of the skills central to literacy concepts related to evidence, disciplinary concepts specific to the study of history, and skills particular to argumentation about historical issues throughout all the lessons. By the time students get to the Palmer Raids History Lab occurring toward the end of the unit, they have practiced sourcing, contextualizing, corroborating, close reading, and argument development, and considered causality, significance, and interpretation. Weaving these essential skills into lessons that precede and follow deeper investigations builds student confidence and makes the implementation of the lab more effective for both student and teacher (Hattie et al., 2020). Without weaving historical literacy and historical thinking skills, as well as the use of a variety of historical sources, students will find the laboratory experience so daunting that they may shut down rather than dive in.

In addition to literacy skills, I also embed at least one of several historical thinking skills. This ensures that students are thinking and moving beyond simply the memorization of names, dates, or concepts. I limit the number of these skills in both a unit and a course because keeping the number limited helps students to develop greater facility with their use. My suggestion when building lessons is to label these skills and processes so that you are aware of when students are sourcing or corroborating or ascertaining historical significance. By making these skills apparent when planning, it will ensure that you are also embedding them into your instruction.

To highlight the weaving of key skills into every nonhistorical investigation lesson in my World War I unit, this chapter will employ a series

Figure 3.3. Historical Thinking Symbols

	**Historical Literacy Skills** • Sourcing • Contextualizing • Close Reading • Corroboration
	**Historical Thinking Skills** • Historical Significance • Continuity and Change • Cause and Consequence • Historical Perspectives
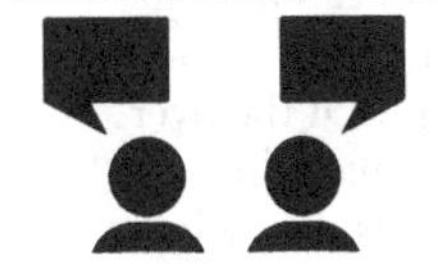	**Argumentation About Historical Issues** • Claims • Counterclaims • Use of Evidence

Source: Icons from The Noun Project (https://thenounproject.com)

of symbols as illustrated in Figure 3.3. As I unpack my World War I unit, I will demonstrate that not every lesson should be an investigation, but every lesson should employ historical literacy, historical thinking, and argumentation.

Lesson 1: "There Is Such a Thing as A Man Being Too Proud to Fight": President Woodrow Wilson, America, and the World

The first lesson in my World War I unit sets the stage for the international and domestic events that students will examine throughout the unit. The lesson is a congressional simulation based on Ted Dickson's article "The Road to United States Involvement in World War 1: A Simulation" (2002). The activity has been adapted so that students are forced to view the events within and outside the United States through the lens of the decision-makers during the time period. As with any simulation, this is not a reenactment. My students are not repeating the words of historical actors on a stage dramatizing the event. Instead, they are attempting to understand generally how people thought from 1914 to 1918 and how the events of the time period were interpreted through those lenses.

In this modified simulation, students take on the role of a senator from one of 10 key states. Students review the information regarding their state's economy, demographic makeup, and the alliance preference of its main immigrant groups. The example in Figure 3.4 comes from the state of Massachusetts, but the full lesson involves 10 states.

Figure 3.4. Sample State Information Card

The Great War in Europe: Neutrality or War?

Massachusetts

Massachusetts' economy is based on manufacturing finished products and trade with foreign nations. Factories in Massachusetts produce ammunition, steel, clothing for uniforms, and other material used in the war. Many of the materials made in New Jersey are exported through the port of Boston, one of the largest port cities in America. In addition, many citizens of Massachusetts have long-standing ties to banks and manufacturers in Great Britain. Manufacturing in Massachusetts boomed between 1914 and 1919 as the result of producing materials and food for the European nations fighting in the war.

Many immigrants, particularly from Eastern and Southern European nations such as Austria-Hungary and Italy, reside in Massachusetts. In addition, German and Irish immigrants also make up the largest immigrant groups. Of the over 3 million people living in Massachusetts, 56% are foreign born, including 1% from Germany, 3% from England, and 7% from Ireland. There is a very large Irish American community in Boston that dominates that city's politics.

Agricultural	Yes	No
Manufacturing	Yes	No
Immigrant Population	Yes	No
Immigrants linked to:	Allied Powers	Central Powers
Would prefer:	Neutrality	War with: Allied Powers/Central Powers
Issues that could push the United States to war:		
Factors that would keep us neutral:		

After completing the analysis of their particular state, groups decide if they would prefer neutrality or war. If they select war, they must decide if they will ally themselves with the Central Powers or the Allied Powers. At the end of each round, groups post their vote on the chart displayed in Figure 3.5 below.

In 1914, the majority of states vote to remain neutral. Discussion ensues as to why, and the majority of states identify the fact that they are making money via international trade and/or they have immigrant groups within their state that would not be happy with their decision to fight one side of the war or the other. After their initial decisions, students read a short description of the global events occurring in 1914, as illustrated in Figure 3.6. I provide the description of each year on separate sheets of paper, each year on a different color (easier to collect and reorganize for the next class). The

Figure 3.5. Student Voting Chart

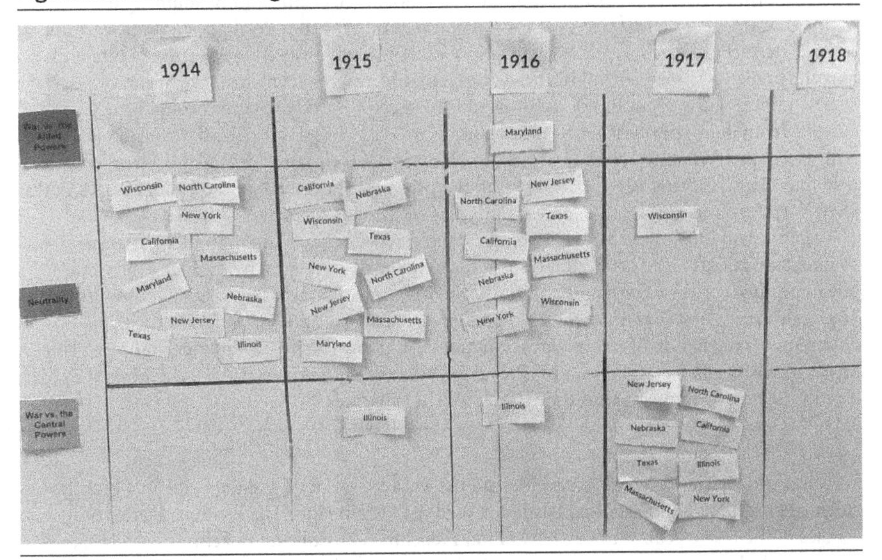

group then discusses their "vote" for 1914 and either moves their Post-it to the war column or keeps it at neutrality. Students discuss the events of the year and how or why it altered their thoughts regarding the issue of neutrality. Cognitively, students need to weigh the events occurring in that year against the needs, concerns, and goals of their state. In addition, they need to consider how significant each event that occurs is relative to the goals of the nation and the leadership of President Wilson.

By 1917 in the simulation, many states have moved away from their concerns regarding immigrant allegiances and the impact of war on the economy and more toward supporting war to protect American lives, sovereignty, and/or honor. Unrestricted German submarine warfare, trade, and British propaganda enable students to see those events through the lens of the time period. To ensure that students do not assume that by the end of 1917 they should be voting for war, there is a fake narrative describing "events" in 1918:

> In early February 1918, the Germans bombed the American naval base at Pearl Harbor. This attack was unprovoked and was followed up by a German invasion of Maryland. The Germans burned the White House and almost captured Fort McHenry. German troops also invaded New Mexico and killed several American citizens. Finally, the Germans were detected setting up nuclear missiles on the island of Cuba.

Figure 3.6. World War I Simulation: The Road to the Great War

1914

In Europe: Germany invades Belgium even though Germany and Belgium signed a treaty guaranteeing German respect for Belgian neutrality. From Belgium, Germany advances toward Paris, France. Paris almost falls into German hands—the Allies near Paris block the assault. England sets up a **total blockade** of Germany and major neutral European ports, severely limiting the types of goods allowed into neutral ports. England forbids British citizens from doing business with Americans accused of violating England's rules on trade with Germany. When America protests the blockade of Germany, Sir Edward Grey of Britain responds that the British are just following the practice established by the United States in the Civil War. England and France increase imports from the United States.

Impact on the United States: England interferes with American mail in an attempt to intercept military and economic information intended for Germany. England **cuts the telegraph link** between Germany and the United States, so all war news must come through England. British newspapers begin to report on German atrocities in Belgium such as chopping off the hands of babies, attacking nuns, and destroying universities, but most stories are "yellow journalism" at its finest. President Wilson wants Americans "to be neutral in fact as well as in name; impartial in thought as well as in action."

1915

In Europe: Trench warfare develops on the Western Front and millions die in a bloody stalemate as the war settles into a battle for yards of French land. The French advance only 3 miles in the entire year, yet over 1.5 million Frenchmen are killed. On February 4, 1915, Germany declares a war zone around the British Isles in which their submarines will operate freely thus blockading any trade with England.

Impact on the United States: Germany places advertisements in American newspapers urging Americans not to travel on British ships. Wilson insists that under international law Americans have the right to travel on any ship. He warns Germany that it will be accountable for any loss of American ships or lives:

- On March 28, the British ship *Falaba* is sunk in the Irish Sea and one American drowns.
- On May 1, the American tanker *Gulflight* is sunk off England, and two Americans die.
- On May 7, the British luxury liner ***Lusitania* is sunk** off the coast of Ireland. One thousand one hundred ninety-eight (1,198) people die, including 128 Americans.

Americans are outraged, calling the sinking "mass murder." Wilson demands an apology and reparations. The Germans point out that they warned Americans not to travel on the ship and that it was carrying arms and ammunition. In June, Wilson repeats his demands in stronger terms. On August 19, the British passenger liner Arabic is sunk, and two Americans are killed. Germany responds by paying an indemnity, and on September 1, Germany issues the Arabic Pledge promising not to sink anymore passenger ships without a warning and without providing for the rescue of the passengers.

Great Britain extends its blockade and announces that it will seize vessels carrying goods to or from Germany wherever they are found. In addition, Britain severely restricts United States trade with neutral countries in Europe. England also continues to increase its purchase of many tons of supplies from the United States. Fearing a possible depression, Wilson lifts all loan restrictions, and United States bankers arrange a $500 million loan to Britain and France.

James Bryce, former British ambassador to the United States, publishes the **Bryce Report** in the United States. The report accuses the German military of heartlessly killing civilians, burning villages, taking hostages, and wantonly destroying property. It further claims that the German military uses civilians as a shield for Germany's advancing armies.

Henry Ford, American automotive maker, pays for a private group to visit Europe to attempt to negotiate an end to the war. Political parties, such as the American Union against Militarism, the Women's Peace Party, and the Socialist Party, rouse public opinion against the war. In December 1915, despite opposition to the idea of war, Wilson asks Congress for money to build new naval ships and increase the army's size as part of his Preparedness Campaign.

Figure 3.6. (*continued*)

1916

In Europe: Trench warfare continues on the Western Front. At the Battle of the Somme, which lasts five months, more Germans are killed than all Americans killed in the Civil War (600,000). Zeppelins begin to bomb London.

Impact on the United States: Germany violates the *Arabic* pledge by sinking the French liner *Sussex* on March 24. Two Americans are injured. Germany again apologizes, and in May issues the ***Sussex* Pledge** promising that its U-boats will not sink any passenger or merchant ships. American trade dramatically increases with England. Between 1914 and 1916:

- United States munitions sales to England increase from $40 million to $1.3 billion.
- United States trade with Britain and its allies grows from $800 million to $3 billion.
- United States loans to Allied governments reaches $2.3 billion, compared to loans of $27 million to the Central Powers.

British and the United States issue the House-Grey Memorandum that says that if England and France call for a peace conference and the Central Powers refuse, the United States would probably join the Allies. Wilson wins a very close re-election campaign on a platform of neutrality and war preparedness. His most famous campaign slogan is "He kept us out of war!"

Pancho Villa leads a rebellion against President Carranza in Mexico. Villa's troops repeatedly attack across the border into the United States and burn the small town of Columbus, New Mexico, killing 17 Americans. Wilson responds by sending General John Pershing and 6,200 troops across the border to chase Villa. Villa is not caught. Pershing's invasion into Mexico angers Mexican people. Spring 1916, the Irish rebel in Dublin and the British harshly suppress this rebellion. Many Irish-Americans respond by expressing a wish for Germany to defeat Britain in the war.

1917

On January 22, President Wilson makes public his proposals for a fair peace to end World War I and to prevent future wars. President Wilson's Peace Plan calls for:

- Peace without victory—no country should win or lose the war.
- Recognition by all countries of the basic concept of the rights of neutral nations and the freedom of the seas for ships of all countries.
- A League of Nations to insure peace in the future and democracy for all nations.

In January 1917, President Wilson orders General Pershing home from Mexico. On January 31, Germany announces it is resuming unrestricted submarine warfare, effective the next day. Any ship in the war zone will be sunk. On February 3, Wilson breaks off diplomatic relations with Germany. The same day, an American ship is sunk.

On March 1, newspapers publish the **Zimmerman Telegram**. The German Foreign Secretary, Arthur Zimmerman, asks Mexico to join the Central Powers. In exchange, the Central powers would provide financial aid and assistance in helping Mexico regain territory, specifically Texas, New Mexico, and Arizona.

On March 15, a revolution overthrows the Czar of Russia. Russia seems close to surrendering to Germany. Germany is now able to fight on only one front, combining its armies for a final overwhelming assault. The Allies are now all democracies.

Germany declares unrestricted submarine warfare on the United States, attacking all ships without warning. On March 16, German submarines sink three American ships in the North Atlantic. Six Americans are killed. Two more American ships are sunk later in March. In April, Wilson addresses a special session of both houses of Congress and asks Congress for a declaration of war. Wilson also accuses Germany of having spies in the United States since before World War I started.

Once students go, huh, and realize that the events of 1918 as described are false, we revisit the actual events of 1917 and how those events led to the United States Congress declaring war on the Central Powers. Students weigh the relative impact of economic and immigration on their decision-making and the decision-making of the United States as a whole.

The lesson concludes with students completing impact thermometers for any two events that occurred from 1914 to 1917. The assessment, illustrated in Figure 3.7, requires students to work back-and-forth between the events and the concerns of the nation at that time. To complete the assessment, students consider the event and extrapolate the impact the event had on American neutrality. In the justification section, students must clearly articulate the connection between events and consequences.

Throughout this decision-making simulation, students have practiced evaluating the historical significance of particular events, understanding the relationships between cause and consequence, considered events from multiple perspectives, and using evidence to support a claim. Were students to simply take notes on the domestic and foreign events between 1914 and 1917, they would not have had an opportunity to develop facility with historical literacy skills, historical thinking skills, and argumentation. This lesson is devoid of any student analysis of primary or even secondary sources, and that is okay! Not every lesson requires the use of historical sources. In this instance, the emphasis is on historical thinking skills. Students need as much practice with these skills as they do with the literacy ones. By weaving these skills into all lessons, the stage is set for students to apply them eventually in a full-blown History Lab while maintaining the need for variety within the instructional approaches utilized.

Lesson 2: "The Yanks Are Coming"

The second lesson in my World War I unit explores the challenges of mobilizing for war. To initiate the lesson in class, students listen to excerpts from two songs: "Over There," and "Hunting the Hun," depicted in Figure 3.8. While listening and following along with the words, students are asked to list a term or sketch an image or symbol that describes the mood of the song and to identify what they believe to be the purpose of the songs. Music is an excellent historical source to use with students. Most students enjoy music, but generally do not see it as something that reflects the times in which the songs were created and made popular. A word of caution, though: Students have a predilection for their own music. Music from a historical period will often engender the same reaction that you get from your own kids while driving in the car and playing the radio: an eye roll and a request to

Figure 3.7. Road to War Assessment

On the Way to War: Raising America's Temperature

Using what you know about America's movement from neutrality to involvement in the Great War in Europe, fill in the thermometer to represent how the specific events raised/lowered/failed to change the temperature for war in the United States. Describe how or why they impacted America's movement away from neutrality. Be sure to consider: What happened in each event and how the United States reacted.

The Sinking of the Lusitania

100°=War

0°=Neutrality

The Sussex Pledge

100°=War

0°=Neutrality

Zimmerman Telegram

100°=War

0°=Neutrality

Figure 3.8. World War I Music Lyrics

Over There Words & Music by George M. Cohan http://www.firstworldwar.com/audio/overthere.htm	*Hunting The Hun* Music by Archie Gottler and words by Howard E. Rogers http://www.firstworldwar.com/audio/huntingthehun.htm
Johnnie get your gun, get your gun, get your gun, Take it on the run, on the run, on the run, Hear them calling you and me; Every son of Liberty Hurry right away, no delay, go today, Make your daddy glad to have had such a lad Tell your sweetheart not to pine, To be proud her boy's in line. **Chorus:** Over there, Over there Send the word, send the word, Over there That the Yanks are coming, The Yanks are coming, The drums rum-tumming everywhere So prepare, Say a Prayer Send the word, Send the word to beware We'll be over, we're coming over, And we won't come back till it's over Other there. Johnnie get your gun, get your gun, get your gun, Johnnie show the Hun, you're a Son-of-a-Gun, Hoist the flag and let her fly Like true heroes do or die Pack your little kit, show your grit, do your bit, Soldiers to the ranks from the towns and the tanks,	Over in France, there's a game that s played, By all the soldier boys in east-brigade. It's called hunting the Hun, this is how it is done. First you go get a gun, then you look for a Hun, Then you stalk on the run for the son of a gun. You can capture them with ease, All you need is just a little limburger cheese. Give 'em one little smell, they come out with a yell, Then your work is done. When they startle with fear, shoot 'em in the pants, At the games called hunting the Hun. First you go get a gun, then you look for a Hun, Then you stalk on the run for the son of a gun. You can capture them with ease, All you need is just a little limburger cheese. Give 'em one little smell, they come out with a yell, Then your work is done. When they startle with fear, shoot 'em in the pants, At the games called hunting the Hun I met a soldier and he told me, It's just the latest thing across the sea. It's a game that is new, They are all doing it too. First you go get a gun, then you look for a Hun,

(*continued*)

Figure 3.8. (*continued*)

Over There Words & Music by George M. Cohan http://www.firstworldwar.com/audio/overthere.htm	*Hunting The Hun* Music by Archie Gottler and words by Howard E. Rogers http://www.firstworldwar.com/audio/huntingthehun.htm
Make your Mother proud of you and to Liberty be true.	Then you stalk on the run for the son of a gun.
Chorus:	You can capture them with ease,
Over There, Over There	All you need is just a little Limburger cheese.
Send the word, send the word,	Give 'em one little smell, they come out with a yell,
Over There	Then your work is done.
That the Yanks are coming,	When they startle with fear, shoot 'em in the pants,
The Yanks are coming,	At the games called hunting the Hun.
The drums rum-tumming everywhere	First you go get a gun, then you look for a Hun,
So prepare,	Then you stalk on the run for the son of a gun.
Say a Prayer	If you want to bring them out,
Send the word,	offer them a little bit of hot sauerkraut.
Send the word to beware	They come over the top with a pip and a hop,
We'll be over, we're coming over.	Then your work is done.
And we won't come back till it's over	When they're starting to eat, cut of every creep,
Over there.	At the games called hunting the Hun.
	First you go get a gun, then you look for a Hun,
	Then you stalk on the run for the son of a gun.
	You can always make them pay,
	Let them know there's going to be a pinochle game.
	They come over the top with a pip and a hop,
	Then your work is done.
	When they first show their face, clump 'em with a mace,
	At the games called hunting the Hun.

change the channel! Push past this response, and students will quickly come to enjoy the sounds of the past and will become very adept at analyzing them as historical sources.

Students select words like *gun* and *drums*, or will draw things like flags, soldiers marching, fireworks, cheese (!), or other patriotic images. I use these images and words to debrief the songs and focus on the idea of mobilization. A brief discussion of the things a country would need to prepare for a war—especially one across the Atlantic Ocean—leads into a discussion of the challenges of mobilization and a discussion of the homework illustrated in Figure 3.9. For homework, students examine a variety of programs distributed in anticipation of or to prepare the United States to intervene in Europe.

For homework, students read the descriptions of each program and, using an insert strategy, label the efforts with the appropriate symbol(s). Some programs can, and should, have more than one symbol. Students then explain any three programs and why they selected the symbol they used. The best strategy for debriefing the homework after the music hooks students into the challenges of mobilization is to start with the programs students labeled with a question mark. It will become apparent to students that the expansion of governmental power during World War I threatened civil liberties, the free market, and the ability of Americans to meet the demands made by their government. In addition, students see that the industrial growth of the nation was being transformed into a tool of war. The discussion of the homework slides into the introduction of the lesson's focus question:

How mobilized was the nation?

At the heart of this question is a deep look at propaganda and what limitations there are on using it to evaluate American mobilization.

The lesson segues into the analysis of primary sources, in this case propaganda posters and speeches by the Four Minute Men employed by the Committee on Public Information (CPI). Students are assigned two sources and asked to identify the mobilization program(s) related to the source, identify the main message(s) communicated by the source, identify images/symbols and so forth used to convey the message, and determine the propaganda method utilized. The propaganda methods listed below in Figure 3.10 is content that students often confront when examining political advertisements in their American Government course and other nations' propaganda in their World History course.

Figure 3.9. Mobilization Reading

Winning (or Losing?) the Hearts and Minds of Americans: Mobilizing for the Great War

Read the descriptions of the programs created to help the United States mobilize for war. Label the efforts with the appropriate symbol(s). Some programs could have more than one symbol. Be sure to explain why in the why column.

- **P**=if it helped to mobilize people
- **$**=if it helped to pay for the war
- **M**=if it helped to produce the materials needed to fight the war
- **USA**=if it helped to promote the cause and generate support for the war
- **?=if you think this government program might cause problems**

War Time Program	Symbol	Why that symbol?
Revenue Act of 1917: Imposed a tax of 63% on the nation's largest incomes and taxed all business profits that were considered to be "excessive."		
Selective Service Act (SSA): Registered over 24 million men, between the ages of 18 and 45, for service in the United States military. Married men and men with dependents were exempted from military service.		
War Industries Board (WIB): Coordinated the American economy for wartime production by allocating raw materials to companies, establishing production priorities, and encouraging businesses to use mass production techniques to help reduce the waste of precious resources. Threatened companies with military takeover if they refused to comply with the quotas they set. As a result, American production rose 20% and corporate profits soared as the American economy supplied both the Allies and themselves.		
National War Labor Board (NWLB): Contained representatives from organized labor, business, and the public. Members were responsible for mediating labor disputes, protect workers' rights to fair wages and hours, and ensure collective bargaining. Was created to reduce class conflict that could lead to strikes or lockouts.		

(continued)

Figure 3.9. *(continued)*

Fuel Administration (FA): organized by the government to help ration coal, heating oil, and gasoline. Promoted such programs as "gasless Sundays," "heatless Monday's," and "lightless nights." In addition, the FA created Daylight savings time to take advantage of summer weather and help conserve fuel.		
Food Administration (FA): Managed agriculture to produce food for troops and allies overseas. The agency engaged in a massive publicity campaign asking Americans to believe in the "gospel of the clean plate." To conserve food for the troops, the FA promoted "Meatless Mondays, Sweetless Saturdays, Wheatless Wednesdays, and Porkless Tuesdays." Americans were encouraged to plant Victory Gardens to grow their own vegetables and school children planted gardens in city parks to help provide more food for the war effort.		
Committee on Public Information (CPI): Published over 100 million books, articles, slides, movies, paintings, posters, cartoons, and sculptures communicating the patriotism necessary to win the war in Europe. Theaters showed films like *The Kaiser: Beast of Berlin* and *To Hell with the Kaiser* to stir American passions and hired 75,000 "Four Minute Men" to give speeches on bonds, the draft, rationing, victory gardens, and why the war was necessary. Over 7.5 million speeches were given to over 314 million Americans. Distributed 7 million copies of *How War Came to America,* and 60 million pamphlets in English, Swedish, Polish, Dutch, Italian, Spanish, Czechoslovakian, and Portuguese, to help drum up support for the war.		
Espionage and Sedition Acts: Levied a fine of up to $10,000 and/or 20 years in prison for interfering with the draft, the sale of war bonds, or saying anything disloyal. In addition, any profane, abusive, or disloyal speech about the government, the war effort, the Constitution, the flag, or the military was made illegal. Finally, the acts allowed the Postmaster General to stop/ban any mail that was considered treasonous. Over 6,000 arrests, 1,200 convictions, numerous deportations, and the removal of the mailing privileges for 45 newspapers were direct results of these acts.		
Liberty Loans: Using slogans like "Halt the Hun," four Liberty Loan drives helped the United States Government net over $21 billion dollars to help pay for the costs of the war. The remainder of the funds came from the sale of "Liberty Stamps" to children and a dramatic increase in the Federal income tax.		

Figure 3.10. Propaganda Methods

1. Bandwagon: Urging voters to support the war effort because everyone else is.
2. Half-Truths/Card-Stacking: Giving only one side of the facts to support the war's position.
3. Transfer: Associating a patriotic symbol with the war.
4. Plain Folk: Identifying the war as fight for "the common people."
5. Testimonial: A celebrity endorses the war.
6. Glittering Generalities: Using impressive language to influence the public.
7. Labeling/Mudslinging: Name-calling, using slurs, making the enemy appear inhuman.
8. Allegory and Mythical Figures: Associating historic figures or past historic events.

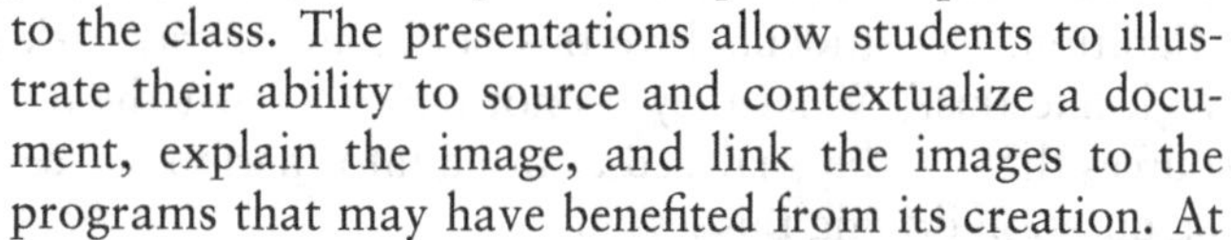

After analyzing their sources, student pairs make quick mini-presentations to the class. The presentations allow students to illustrate their ability to source and contextualize a document, explain the image, and link the images to the programs that may have benefited from its creation. At the end of each mini-presentation, students discuss how the evidence influences their thoughts regarding the lesson's overarching question, ***How mobilized was the nation?*** Discussion of the central investigative question requires students to link the programs to the propaganda and to consider how and why they might work to bring the nation together or to generate resistance.

Within this lesson, students are required to practice the historical literacy skills of sourcing, contextualizing, and close reading. It is important to recognize that the source work is not the lesson itself, but is woven into the lesson. Content does not take the day off while students apply their skills, nor do skills take the bench when students learn content: They work together. The skills help students to acquire, apply, and extend the content. Too many times teachers compartmentalize content and skills, as in, "today we are learning history, but tomorrow we are doing source work." As students are analyzing their sources, they need to consider who created it, why it was created, and the intended audience, and place it into the context of mobilizing for World War I. Because this unit occurs at the midpoint of the school year, the divide between skills and content is seamless. It is essential to recognize that within this lesson, students are not applying all of the literacy skills, or any of the disciplinary concepts specific to the study of history. This is intentional. By focusing on a few particular skills, students can balance the application of skills with the acquisition of content. This process is also an essential element of the third lesson in my unit on the Great Migration.

Lesson 3: Corroborating Sources and the Great Migration

The third lesson in my World War I unit examines the changes wrought by the domestic mobilization necessary to fight and win a global war. One of the most significant changes exacerbated by the mobilization of people, material, and support to fight in Europe was the migration of African Americans from the South to Northern cities. Seeking the high wages offered by factories ramping up production for war, and fleeing the harsh realities of disenfranchisement, debt peonage, sharecropping, and lynching in the South, over half a million African Americans migrated northward.

To initiate this investigation, I provide my students with a copy of *The Great Migration: An American Story* by Jacob Lawrence (Lawrence & Meyers, 1995). The book incorporates all 60 panels of his Migration Series paintings with captions that describe the motivations for, process of, and results of the Great Migration. My students love this book, and always ask for "more homework like this." What they do not realize is that the images are historical sources that can be analyzed to bring information to bear on the overarching question driving this lesson:

Is the artwork of Jacob Lawrence or oral histories a better representation of the experiences of African American migrants?

To explore this question, students are asked to examine the images and complete a graphic organizer illustrated in Figure 3.11 that outlines the factors that pushed African Americans out of the South and pulled them to the North.

The in-class portion of this lesson begins with a full-class discussion of Lawrence's work and a review of the push and pull factors that students identified from the paintings. Students discuss their thoughts about the artwork and how effectively it represents the mass movement of African Americans northward. The art is extremely accessible for all students. The book does a great job of illustrating Jim Crow laws, sharecropping, and violence, as well as labor recruiting, the job opportunities available in Northern factories, and other push/pull factors. Students are also able to evaluate the tools Lawrence employs to depict this mass movement.

To contrast the secondary sources created by Lawrence in the 1940s, students listen to excerpts from *Field to Factory: Voices of the Great Migration* (Crew, 2010). The collection is amazingly rich, but it is not very teacher-friendly as originally published. The full collection of oral histories and narration by

Figure 3.11. Great Migration Organizer

"One Way Ticket"-The Great Migration: African Americans head North 1910-1920 (and until 1980ish)

As you examine the book, *The Great Migration: An American Story* by Jacob Lawrence, complete the following charts. Be specific with the information that you record.

PUSH FACTORS (Things that pushed African Americans out of the South: Things occurring in the south)

PULL FACTORS (Things that pulled African Americans to the North and West: Things occurring in the north and west)

Dr. Spencer Crew is over an hour long, so I selected about 8 minutes' worth of stories for students to hear. To develop the resource of the oral histories I wanted to highlight for my students, I employed the skills developed in making mixtapes in middle school. In the age of streamed music, pulling out my old boombox to play my edited cassette tape was always a bit anachronistic and always hilarious to my students! The selections I chose begin with push factors and then conclude with pull factors and serve as nice counterpoints to the images presented by Jacob Lawrence. While listening to the oral histories, students are corroborating sources while also adding to the list of push and pull factors they developed while analyzing Lawrence's art. While Lawrence's art emphasizes certain aspects of the migration, the oral histories, through the storytelling abilities of the interviewees, cast greater depth on other aspects not as well developed by the artist's brush. The role of labor recruiters, the fears of migrants, the impact of violence, and the intrusive nature of sharecropping on the economic life of Southerners emerge from the oral histories. Once students learn to understand the deep Southern drawl that punctuates the interviewees' comments, they gain even more insight into the motivations of millions of migrants headed north.

To reinforce the building and supporting of historical arguments, the class discussion that ensues after analyzing both sources centers on students making and supporting claims regarding the lesson's central question: Is the artwork of Jacob Lawrence or oral histories a better representation of the experiences of African American migrants?

Claim construction is initiated by having students visually demonstrate their response to the overarching question. Magnetized name cards that I have for each student are placed along the continuum at the front of the room. The physical representation of student views allows for a conversation. I randomly call on students to explain why they placed their card at that point on the continuum. Discussion ensues, and students are able to connect their claim to evidence, challenge the claims of others, and construct a well-supported argument. The conversation is filled with students using specific examples of push and pull factors to substantiate their interpretation of the sources. The marriage of content both historical literacy (sourcing, contextualizing, corroboration), historical thinking (cause and consequence, historical significance), and argumentation (claims, use of evidence) makes this lesson a great example of how a teacher can have students employing all of these skills while not engaging in a full-scale investigation.

The lesson concludes with students completing the assessment depicted in Figure 3.12, which requires them to develop new stanzas for a Langston Hughes poem about the Great Migration. Their responses reflect the information they gained from contrasting Jacob Lawrence's work with that of the oral histories.

Lesson 4: Anti-German Reactions

Sometimes a historical source jumps out and demands that a lesson be developed around it. When I discovered the enemy alien registration documents, I knew it was time to use them to explore the efforts during World War I to suppress dissent. Fully digitized, the repository of these documents is available at the National Archives. They are easily accessible to students, have zoom tools that further empower student investigation, and offer enough sources that each student can examine a different one. The power of the enemy alien registration materials, as well as the various reactions that Americans had to Muslim Americans after 9/11, led me to carve out a 45-minute lesson that examined how German Americans were treated during World War I. Prior to discovering these documents, I used a series of other sources to set the stage for the Supreme Court lesson that is explained in Lesson 4.

Figure 3.12. Great Migration Assessment

Now that you are the school expert on the Great Migration, the estate of Langston Hughes has paid you to complete two more stanzas of his poem "One-Way Ticket." Consider everything we discussed regarding the factors that led to the Great Migration and develop two more stanzas of the poem. **One stanza should focus on the push factors for migration, and one should focus on the pull factors.**

Stanza	Text	Stanza	Text
1	I am fed up With Jim Crow laws People who are cruel And afraid who Lynch and run, Who are scared of me and me of them.	2	
3		4	I pick up my life and take it away On a one-way ticket Gone up North Gone out West Gone!

The lesson begins with students confronting the images in Figure 3.13 and addressing the associated questions.

Students speculate about age, gender, patriotism, and loyalty. The reality is that both Sister Mary Agnes and Albert Sockland were born in Germany and immigrated to the United States. Their status as immigrants

Figure 3.13. Enemy Alien Registration Images

Why was this Union Army Civil War Veteran not allowed to take a balloon ride?	Why was Sister Mary Agnes not allowed to aid injured American soldiers at Ft. Leavenworth, Kansas?

Source: National Archives, Enemy Alien Registration Affidavits, 1917–1921 (https://catalog.archives.gov/id/286238 and https://catalog.archives.gov/id/289064)

made them enemy aliens, and this required them to register with the U.S. government.

Students are assigned a link to one of the registration forms found at the National Archives site. You can use QR codes, direct links, a trip to the computer lab, or even paper copies so that students can research one of the immigrants who was required to register under Regulation 19 of the declaration of war that required all enemy aliens to register with the federal government. Students are asked to examine the document and to take notes on what these documents tell us about the federal government's concerns.

After 15 minutes, we come back together as a class and discuss. Students clearly and quickly understand that the U.S. government was concerned about the ability to identify, track, and locate German immigrants. The inclusion of images and the use of fingerprints—a new technology at the time—clearly communicates the desire to clamp down on the potential for domestic dissent.

The discussion of the enemy alien registration materials, segues into the focus question for the lesson:

Did the United States people and government over- or underreact to the presence of German Americans?

A think-pair-share structure is used to initiate the conversation about the overarching lesson question. After reading the information found in Figure 3.14, students use small, student-size whiteboards, students make their initial claim. Students generally realize that these actions appear to have no underlying cause other than the ethnicity of those attacked. Actions certainly, but evidence beyond ethnicity, certainly not: This phase of the discussion usually peters out as most students see the reaction as unnecessary, racist, and overblown. After reviewing the claims, I ask students what other information or sources they would need to make a stronger claim. Responses range from letters, newspaper articles, and police reports to examples of German Americans actually doing something wrong. To complicate their thinking, students need to consider not only the actions taken by the government and individual Americans, but also the contextual events that precipitated these actions.

To foster a deeper debate, I share the information depicted in 3.15.

After reading the information, students engage with a new partner for a think-pair-share discussion of the new information. They start by readjusting their initial claim on the whiteboard and then explain their decision to change or maintain their claim based on the new evidence. I prompt the discussion by posing the question: Do the efforts of some German Americans to sabotage the war effort justify the stereotyping and limiting of the rights for all? After discussion with their new partner, students make their final readjustments to their claims addressing the lesson's overarching question, Did the United States people and government over- or underreact to the presence of German Americans? The final claim serves as the assessment for the lesson.

Where Is the History Lab??

Four lessons into my World War I unit and students have not completed a full historical investigation, and that is okay! Students have wrestled with historical questions; interrogated a variety of historical sources; considered questions of significance, causality, and change; and developed and reinforced claims using a variety of evidence. All of these skills must be employed at once within a full investigation, but by separating them and practicing a few within each lesson, students become more comfortable and adept for when they have to go the full historical monty. As we move into the last five lessons, consider how some lessons emphasize one particular skill versus those that require a blend of skills. Think about how this would overlap with any unit you teach and how you could develop a similar emphasis within the lessons you have already designed.

Figure 3.14. Anti-German Reactions Organizer

"Buy What I can and blow up the Rest...": American Reactions to German Americans

Alien Enemy Registration (Federal Government)
German Americans were
- Forbidden from owning guns, traveling, moving, or going to the beach
- Arrested and interned 6300 in Georgia and Utah
- Required to register with the United States government if they were 14 years and older who were not naturalized citizens (450,000)

Alien Property Custodian Program
(Federal Government)
The Federal Government seized from German Americans:
- Companies and businesses
- Patents for inventions
- Millions in bank assets

Companies were then sold to Americans for bargain prices.

American Protective League
(Formed with support from the federal government)
- Mobilized 250,000 people across the United States
- Spied on neighbors
- Burglarized homes
- Opened mail
- Organized "slacker raids" to target anti-war protesters and draft dodgers
- Intercepted and opened the mail and telegrams of people suspected of disloyalty

American Reactions to German Americans

- Libraries removed German books from shelves and had them burned
- People with German names were barred from working for the Red Cross.
- German folksongs were removed from children's songbooks.
- Some considered pro-German were forced to quit their jobs and change their names.
- In 16 states the teaching of German language was banned.
- Sauerkraut was renamed "Liberty Cabbage," hamburgers became "Liberty Sausage," German Measles became "Liberty Measles," and Dachshunds became "Liberty Pups."
- Some Symphonies refused to perform classical music written by Bach, Brahms, and Beethoven.
- The California State Board of Education banned the teaching of German, called a "language that disseminated the ideals of autocracy, brutality and hatred."
- Rose Stokes was sentenced to 10 years in federal prison for writing a letter to the editor opposing the war.
- J.P. Doe was sentenced 18 months in federal prison for penning a chain letter questioning if Germany had pledged to end unrestricted submarine warfare.
- Reverend Clarence Waldron was sentenced to 15 years in Federal prison for distributing pamphlets stating that the war was "un-Christian."
- Robert Goldstein was sentenced to 10 years in Federal prison for making a movie called Spirit of '76 about the American Revolution where America's current allies, the British, were depicted in a negative light.
- 45 newspapers had their rights to published revoked.

Figure 3.15. Acts of Espionage During World War I

Espionage That Occurred During the War That Was Public Knowledge

In 1914 U.S. federal agents uncovered a German plot to destroy a Canadian canal that was important to the shipping of goods to the Allies.

In 1915 a German agent set off a bomb on a railroad bridge between Canada and the United States.

Franz von Rintelen developed a cigar-shaped lead tube bomb that could be placed on ships and would explode once the ships were in the middle of the Atlantic Ocean. In 1915, the cigar bombs destroyed nine American ships and were discovered on four other ships. Before the plot was uncovered, 36 ships were attacked, destroying millions of dollars of cargo.

American Secret Service agents stole a briefcase from the editor of a German-language newspaper and found documents indicating plans to disrupt war shipments from U.S. corporations to the Allies and a nationwide plot to blow up bridges and tunnels. These documents, under the direction of the White House, were leaked to the American press.

By the end of 1917 there were 43 unexplained fires or explosions at American munitions plants, causing an estimated loss of $6 million.

Rudder bombs were developed and placed on American ships. The motion of the rudders would cause the bombs to detonate.

New York City police discovered in the apartment of a German agent 25 sticks of dynamite, 450 pounds of explosive materials, 200 bomb cylinders, and a detailed chart of New York Harbor

In July 1915, Erich Muenter detonated a bomb inside the United States Capitol building and then boarded a train for New York. The next day he invaded the home of J.P. Morgan, one of the richest men in the world and a key source of loans to American allies, and attempted to kill him.

Espionage That Occurred During the War That Was Confirmed Later

In July 1916 there was a massive explosion on Black Tom Island off the coast of New Jersey that destroyed $20 million of ammunition and ships. In the 1930s, the United States government found the evidence linking this to German agents.

In an effort to destroy the horses and mules that were essential to fighting the war and were overwhelmingly exported from the United States, German agents imported anthrax and other germs to the United States. The germs were grown and then injected into the horses and mules so that they would die. Several Germans were killed by the anthrax.

Lesson 5: Civil Liberties and World War I

The Anti-German Reactions lesson sets the stage to examine the impact of the Supreme Court on the issues of civil liberties during times of war. This lesson also serves as proof that sometimes the lesson you think is mundane works well not because of the structure, the historical sources, the overarching question, or a song and a dance by the teacher, but instead works because the content is compelling and applicable well beyond the confines of the unit.

The lesson starts with students taking the oath of office to serve as a Supreme Court Justice:

> I, ________, do solemnly swear (or affirm) that I will administer justice without respect to persons, and do equal right to the poor and to the rich, and that I will faithfully and impartially discharge and perform all the duties incumbent upon me as ________ under the Constitution and laws of the United States; and that I will support and defend the Constitution of the United States against all enemies, foreign and domestic; that I will bear true faith and allegiance to the same; that I take this obligation freely, without any mental reservation or purpose of evasion; and that I will well and faithfully discharge the duties of the office on which I am about to enter. So help me God. (https://www.supremecourt.gov/about/oath/oathsofoffice.aspx)

Students are asked to decide what they believe should be the relationship between civil liberties and war. Armed with a sticky note labeled with their name, students adhere the note to one of the three signs below:

Civil liberties should only be suspended in times of national crisis.	Civil Liberties are nonnegotiable and should be vigorously defended no matter the circumstances.	Certain civil liberties should be negotiable and altered to reflect the time period and conditions.

Discussion of student responses is associated with a debrief of a homework that explores First Amendment case law in times of war prior to World War I, or it can be buttressed with a quick overview of the decisions made by President Lincoln and the Supreme Court during the American Civil War. Students ALWAYS use more modern touchpoints to support their arguments, and that is fine. After students explain their beliefs regarding civil liberties, I introduce the overarching question structuring the lesson:

Do civil liberties demand more or less protection during times of war?

I assign students to mini-mock Supreme Courts (usually 9 or fewer students) and assign them the first case: *Schenck v. United States* (1919). Students silently read a teacher-generated summary of the case and then discuss and vote on whether Schenck is guilty of violating the Espionage and Sedition Act of 1917 or whether the Sedition and Espionage Acts violate the First Amendment of the Constitution. Each court reports their decision and the explanation for the decision, and then I pull back the curtain and reveal how the court decided. The same process continues with *Debs v. United States* (1919) and *Abrams v. United States* (1919). Ultimately, students return to the overarching question and stake a claim as to whether civil liberties demand more or less protection during times of war. The content of this lesson is very engaging for students because the topic cuts across many events in the post-911 world, although the immediacy of 9/11 declines with distance. The conversations are rich and cut across time, often bouncing back and forth between World War I and current events.

Please note that this lesson did not earn any of the three symbols that have been affixed to the other lessons. Its inclusion in this chapter seems to undermine my main argument that between History Labs students should be practicing historical literacy skills, historical thinking concepts, and argumentation about historical issues. Students are developing a claim in the lesson, but they are not doing so to the degree that it merits a symbol. I could make the argument that students are considering continuity and change, but that is more a by-product of the lesson-generated conversations than an intentionally emphasized element of the lesson. Students are engaging the past through the lens of a question and are studying an important issue that impacted the United States both during World War I and after. The lesson is good, students are engaged, and they learn, but sometimes you just need a good lesson and to set aside the overarching emphasis on skills. Absence makes the heart grow fonder, and those skills will again take center stage in lesson 6.

Lesson 6: But the Other Class Is Watching a Movie!

In 2004, the HBO film *Iron Jawed Angels* was released to the acclaim of both critics and history teachers (von Garnier, 2004). The film, staring Hilary Swank as Alice Paul, Anjelica Huston as Carrie Chapman Catt, and Frances O'Connor as Lucy Burns, is excellent. Students are mesmerized by the scenes of Alice Paul's hunger strike and subsequent forced feeding. Many teachers incorporated either clips or the film in its entirety into their units on either Progressivism or World War I. I did not, and paid the price with student complaints!

Films in the classroom are great tools, and if used correctly can be interrogated as a historical source. Unfortunately, in too many instances, films have come to be a substitute for good instruction (Paxton & Marcus, 2018). Films are shown for days, and students answer questions or take notes to show that they are watching the film. The most significant deleterious impact of this instructional choice is felt at the end of the year. Individual lessons that take more than two instructional periods accumulate quickly, and this aggregation of time makes it difficult to give coverage to the full scope of a course. "I never have enough time" is often the by-product of instructional decisions made during the year rather than having too much to cover. The best choice is to incorporate film clips into instruction rather than showing one, two, or three entire films or documentaries over the course of a school year/semester. Rather than spending the better part of a week showing a Hollywood film, the lesson I implemented was on suffrage and focused on the comparative roles played by Alice Paul and Lucy Stone, but it did so through a paired debate. Much to the chagrin of my students, *Iron Jawed Angels* became a supplement to my lesson but not the centerpiece.

The lesson begins with students analyzing the image in Figure 3.16. Students are asked to determine the message the artist is trying to convey. This image helps students to understand how entrenched the bigotry, sexism, xenophobia, and scientific racism was in the United States in the late 19th and early 20th centuries. As a result, it is important for students to understand the image in the context of the time it was created. Students initially interpret the image as showing "that women should be treated the same way as others that are considered not human." On the surface this appears to be the artist's intent. Women's peers are natives who are not citizens and are not considered human; they are prisoners who have transgressed social norms and are receiving punishment. They are seen as mentally challenged individuals who are separated from society to ensure they do not infect others. They are the insane divining for water. The true message is much more complicated than this surface evaluation.

To fully evaluate the image, students must source and contextualize it. Once this is done, students see the dissonance created between the image and the sourcing information and challenge the face value reading of the image.

Source Background: Henrietta Briggs-Wall, a member of the Kansas Equal Suffrage Association, had the postcard created to celebrate the work of Frances Willard. The image was displayed at the World's Columbian Exposition of 1893 in Chicago, and photographic postcards of the picture were available for purchase during and after the fair and were sold throughout the United States.

Figure 3.16. American Women and Her Political Peers

Source: Kansas State Historical Society (https://www.kansasmemory.org/)

Henrietta Briggs-Wall's connection to suffrage leads some students to posit such ideas as: "I think it is saying that it is bad that women are seen as equals to these people and that they should not be." The discussion is rich as students toggle between their reading of the image, the context of its creation, and their knowledge of the author. If students struggle, I will share the language that accompanies some of the postcards sold with the image.

American Woman and Her Political Peers

In many states women are classed politically with idiots, convicts, the insane and Indians—not allowed to vote . . . Women do not, however, escape taxation.
"Taxation without representation is tyranny."
"Resistance to tyranny is obedience to God."

This information helps students to understand the power of the image and its intended use to promote women's suffrage. Important, though, is to remind students that although the image was a tool to promote suffrage, it also clearly represents the bigotries of the time period. The image provides an opportunity to connect back to scientific racism and eugenics.

Discussion of the image leads to a debrief of a homework reading that outlines the legal, political, social, and economic status of white women at the turn of the 20th century. Highlighted in the reading and subsequent debrief are concepts like coverture, the cult of domesticity, the debate over the 14th and 15th Amendments, *Minor v. Happersett*, 88 U.S. 162 (1874), and social housekeeping. Finally, the division of the suffrage movement into two competing organizations, the American Women's Suffrage Association (AWSA) and the National Women's Suffrage Association (NWSA), is explained. With the AWSA focused on a state-by-state approach and the NWSA focused on a constitutional amendment, the stage is set for the paired debate.

To prepare for the paired debate, my students are assigned the role of either Alice Paul or Carrie Chapman Catt. A teacher-prepared guided reading helps students prepare to represent the individual in a mock debate. The readings are designed in a parallel structure to help promote conversation and to highlight areas of agreement and disagreement.

In paired debates, students are required to represent the individual and to argue from that person's point of view. A flip of the coin determines who gets to respond first to the question. The first person gets 1 minute to respond to the question prompt. The opposite person can only listen. After the minute is up, the second person can respond to the prompt and to the argument made by the first speaker. Each question ends with a 30-second open discussion where either participant can participate. The discussion then proceeds until all the questions depicted in Figure 3.17 below have been debated. Essential to the success of the debate is that students are not simply filling in a graphic organizer or taking notes. I want them to be actively listening, reacting to what they hear, and engaged, not seeing the discussion as just sharing information to complete a chart.

My students love these mini-debates because instead of a performance in front of their peers and the anxiety that can generate for many students, they are only required to work with one other person. This reduces their stress and makes them more willing to play the role and participate. The debate leads to a discussion of the central investigative question for the lesson:

What was the best path to suffrage: working within or outside the political system?

Figure 3.17. Debate Prompts

- What is the best method for women to achieve suffrage?
- Suffrage for woman has been granted by numerous Western states already. Shouldn't women stop pushing and allow things to happen naturally?
- Isn't President Wilson an ally in the fight for women's suffrage?
- Isn't it better to move slowly, working from state to state, than trying to push the President and the federal government to grant suffrage all at once?
- The United States has entered into war against Germany. Shouldn't women put their push for suffrage aside and support the country?
- Mrs. Paul, why should you get more of the credit—and not Mrs. Catt—for the passage and ratification of the 19th Amendment providing women with the right to suffrage?
- Mrs. Catt, why should you get more of the credit—and not Mrs. Paul—for the passage and ratification of the 19th Amendment providing women with the right to suffrage?

Students, having participated in a debate representing the efforts of two women representing both sides of this question, must draw on their understanding of the context of the time period and the significance of the efforts made by both Paul and Catt to engage in an informed discussion. This discussion is accomplished using the Four Corners strategy and then debating individual decisions. To facilitate the discussion, students vote with their feet and stand in the corner that best represents their claim. A teacher-guided discussion ensues in which students justify their choice and challenge the choice of other students. Key to this phase is that students apply the information gleaned from the paired debate about the efforts, tools, and impacts of Alice Paul and Carrie Chapman Catt. The discussion allows students to develop and defend a claim and support it with historical evidence.

The suffrage lesson is not a historical investigation, but is driven by an overarching investigative question, populated with a variety of historical sources, and emphasizes historical literacy skills, historical thinking skills, and skills around argumentation about historical issues. Again, although not a History Lab, the lesson embeds the kinds of skills that students will need facility with when they encounter a fully fleshed-out investigation. My suffrage lesson also provides variety—in this case a paired debate and then a full-class continuum discussion. I still get flack while my peers show *Iron Jawed Angels*, but the debates are spirited, the content is rich, and I just saved 4 days for other topics later in the year!

Lesson 7: "Total Abstinence From the Things That Are Foul": Temperance

Just as the push for suffrage received a huge boost from World War I, so too did the call for temperance. While suffrage advocates utilized the war to demonstrate their patriotism and the contrast between fighting authoritarianism abroad with the limiting of women's rights at home, temperance promoters accomplished their goals within the same context. By the start of World War I, the road to prohibition was well-paved. Three states had passed temperance laws; moral arguments about the impact of alcohol consumption on women, the family, and children had penetrated the American consciousness, and organizations such as the Anti-Saloon League had worked to elect two-thirds majorities in both the House of Representatives and the Senate that fully supported prohibition of alcohol. The advent of global war brought tensions over immigration and temperance to a head. Much of the temperance movement found its adherents in rural, native-born, and fundamentalist communities that connected alcohol consumption to saloon-going, urban populations of German, Irish, Catholic, and Jewish immigrants. As the war evolved, alcohol consumption, anti-German sentiment, patriotism, and much of the propaganda produced by the Anti-Saloon League connected in the public mind beer and brewers with German treason, which congealed into a stew that pushed Prohibition across the finish line. Politicians, many elected with support of pro-temperance organizations, and emboldened by a national income tax, which eliminated the need to tax alcohol to fund the federal government, passed the 18th Amendment (McGirr, 2016; Okrent, 2010; Pegram, 1998; Rorabaugh, 1979; Sismondo, 2011). Although I know many curricula and textbooks teach the temperance movement as part of the Progressive Era, I center it in World War I to demonstrate the connections between Progressive reform and the war.

My temperance lesson focuses on one of my favorite historical figures: Carry A. Nation. Nation is a fascinating personality whose passions fall in line with historic figures like John Brown, Mother Jones, Stokely Carmichael, and Nat Turner. The unique combination of zeal, drive, religion, anger, mission, and perhaps a touch of insanity makes Nation's efforts to draw attention to the issue of temperance well worth a lesson, but Nation is not synonymous with the movement, and exclusively focusing on her hides the arguments, methods, and motivations of the numerous people and organizations involved. As a result, students wrestle with a question that uses Nation as the foil for the entire movement. By examining the overarching question below, students must contextualize Nation's actions, methods, and motivations against a broader examination of the movement for temperance:

Is Carry A. Nation the best spokesperson for the Temperance movement?

I initiate the lesson by reading aloud to the class the description found in Figure 3.18 of Nation and her actions and beliefs provided in her own words and then asking students to sketch either an image or generate a description of the person portrayed in the reading. Invariably, students sketch or describe a large man with rocks. After a quick discussion of what they believe to be the individual's motivations, goals, and methods, I share with them an image of Nation (Figure 3.19).

Students are dumbstruck by the difference between their vision and the actual historical figure. I use this description above as the basis for their sketches because there is no reference to gender, and it always fascinates me that kids think the person should be male. The image leads to a short

Figure 3.18. Carry A. Nation Reading

I got a box that would fit under my buggy seat, and every time I thought no one would see me, I went out in the yard and picked up some brickbats, for rocks are scarce around Medicine Lodge, and I wrapped them up in newspapers to pack in the box under my buggy seat . . . I hitched my horse to the buggy, put the box of "smashers" in . . .

I put the smashers on my right arm and went in. He and another man were standing behind the bar. I said: "Mr. Dobson, I told you last spring . . . to close this place, and you didn't do it. Now I have come with another remonstrance. Get out of the way. I don't want to strike you, but I am going to break up this den of vice." I began to throw at the mirror and the bottles below the mirror. Mr. Dobson and his companion jumped into a corner, seeming very much terrified. From that I went to another saloon, until I had destroyed three, breaking some of the windows in the front of the building. In the last place, kept by Lewis, there was quite a young man behind the bar. I said to him: "Young man, come from behind that bar. Your mother did not raise you for such a place." I threw a brick at the mirror, which was a very heavy one, and it did not break, but the brick fell and broke everything in its way. I began to look around for something that would break it. I was standing by a billiard table on which there was one ball. I said: "Thank God," and picked it up, and threw it and it made a hole in the mirror. The other dive keepers closed up, stood in front of their places, and would not let me come in. By this time, the streets were crowded with people; most of them seemed to look puzzled. . . . I stood in the middle of the street and spoke in this way: "I have destroyed three of your places of business . . ."

Source: The Use and Need of Carry A. Nation, by Carry A. Nation (Topeka: F. M. Steves & Sons, 1904), p. 60–62 (https://web.archive.org/web/20080516223351/http://etext.lib.virginia.edu/toc/modeng/public/NatUsea.html)

Figure 3.19. Carry A. Nation

Source: Kansas State Historical Society (https://www.kansasmemory.org/)

introduction of Nation, the growth of beer consumption in the United States, and the long push for temperance, and it sets students up for investigating whether Carry A. Nation is the best spokesperson for the temperance movement.

The core of this lesson is source work. Students are assigned one of seven sources. Because this is not a traditional investigation, I use more than my recommended four to six sources. The sources in Figure 3.20 provide a cross-section of the people, methods, motivations, and arguments that defined the push for temperance that resulted in the 18th Amendment.

Students work individually to analyze their source and determine the method and message employed by the individual or group working toward temperance. Next, students group with others who have the same source to share, compare notes recorded in the organizer found in Figure 3.21, and come to consensus on

Figure 3.20. Sources Used in Temperance Lesson

Source A: Mother Stewart and the Women's Crusade
Source B: Mary Hanchett Hunt and Scientific Temperance
Source C: Reverend Billy Sunday
Source D: Women's Christian Temperance Union (WCTU)
Source E: Women's Christian Temperance Union (WCTU)
Source F: The Anti-Saloon League
Source G: The Prohibition Party

the two continuums built into the organizer. Student groups next prepare for mini-presentations that explain information about their group or person (who were they, what did they do, why did they do it, and how did they do it?) to their peers.

The graphic organizer in Figure 3.21 is utilized by students both to track the information gleaned from their source as well as to take notes from the mini-presentations. When groups finish their presentations, they place an X along both continuums that are displayed in the front of the classroom. The first continuum indicates how like or unlike the source's methods were compared to those employed by Carrie A. Nation, and the second continuum specifies how like or unlike the source's arguments were to those proffered by Nation. As the mini-presentations stack up, students quickly see that although the central messages made by all supporters of temperance were religious and family-focused, the methodology employed was significantly different from that employed by Nation.

At the close of the mini-presentations, students employ a 0–5 finger ranking to demonstrate the degree to which Carrie A. Nation's methods were like (5 fingers) or unlike (0 fingers) the overall temperance movement, and do the same for her arguments. This quick, informal formative assessment can be followed with students making a claim supported with evidence as to whether Nation is the best spokesperson for the movement. The discussion at this phase is rich, steeped in historical examples, and allows for multiple opportunities to link temperance to the passage of the 18th Amendment.

The lesson concludes with a quick assessment asking students to consider who Carrie A. Nation would "friend" or "not friend" on her anachronistic Facebook page. This assessment, illustrated in Figure 3.22, allows students to make a claim (to friend or not friend) and to use evidence to support their claim in a manner different than an essay. Kids enjoy it, and it is fun to grade!

Figure 3.21. Temperance Lesson Organizer

"Total Abstinence from the things that are foul.": Progressives and Temperance

Notes on Carry Nation and the movement for temperance

Group or Individual	Method	Message	Evaluation
Source A: Mother Stewart and the Women's Crusade			*Methods* *Like* *Unlike* *Arguments* *Like* *Unlike*
Source B: Mary H. Hunt and Scientific Temperance			*Methods* *Like* *Unlike* *Arguments* *Like* *Unlike*
Source C: Reverend Billy Sunday			*Methods* *Like* *Unlike* *Arguments* *Like* *Unlike*
Source D: Women's Christian Temperance Union (WCTU)			*Methods* *Like* *Unlike* *Arguments* *Like* *Unlike*
Source E: Women's Christian Temperance Union (WCTU)			*Methods* *Like* *Unlike* *Arguments* *Like* *Unlike*
Source F: The Anti-Saloon League			*Methods* *Like* *Unlike* *Arguments* *Like* *Unlike*
Source G: The Prohibition Party			*Methods* *Like* *Unlike* *Arguments* *Like* *Unlike*

Notes:

Figure 3.22. Temperance Assessment

"Total Abstinence from the things that are foul": Progressives and Temperance

Carrie Nation, has set up a page on Facebook (Yeah, I know 100 years too early but just go with it). The following people have asked Nation to be her friend and allow them access to her page. Determine if she would allow each person access and then defend your answer. When formulating your responses, be sure to consider:

- The efforts made by Carrie Nation and her relationship to the Temperance Movement
- The various arguments made by the WCTU, Anti-Saloon League, and others opposed to Prohibition
- The various methods employed by the WCTU, Anti-Saloon League, and others opposed to Prohibition

1. A member of the Woman's Christian Temperance Union (WCTU) would like to be your friend:

Yes No
Why?

2. The owner of a saloon in Pittsburgh would like to be your friend:

Yes No
Why?

3. Mary H. Hunt, the Reverend Billy Sunday, or Mother Stewart (you pick) would like to be your friend:

Yes No
Why?

WHERE ARE THE INVESTIGATIONS!?

Seven lessons into the unit and no History Lab! I am sure you are thinking, oh, so the investigation of history really isn't that central to what you do. In that assumption you are wrong. The investigative approach is the heart of my argument about effective history instruction, but you cannot conduct them for every topic, every lesson, or every day. Instead, as these seven lessons demonstrate, you must center the skills and concepts that support investigation. Focusing students on meaty questions, having them apply literacy skills and historical thinking concepts, and making and critiquing arguments must be practiced consistently so that when students dive into investigations, they have practiced these skills. So don't worry, this unit does have a full-fledged investigation. But to answer honestly the question posed by the Indiana teacher I discussed at the outset of this chapter, it is paramount that we see how to set students up to be successful before they make a deep dive into an investigation.

Lesson 8: Don't Reinvent the Wheel When You Don't Have To!

Sometimes you just run into instructional materials that are so good and dovetail so smoothly with your own instructional approaches in the classroom that you know in your teacher's heart that it is not worth your time to develop something else. In the case of the Treaty of Versailles, I found just such a resource in the materials produced by the Choices Program. From Brown University, Choices provides units that are based on a central driving question, supported with resources that provide multiple viewpoints, and allow students to develop thoughtful, evidence-based answers. It is an excellent repository for materials.

I make some adaptations to the materials, but the core of the lesson is to have students simulate a congressional debate regarding the ratification of the Treaty of Versailles. I assemble this debate as a modified Structured Academic Controversy where one student is essentially undecided and must be persuaded by the facts presented to cast a vote (Johnson & Johnson, 1988). Students represent one of three viewpoints, and a fourth student represents an undecided member of the Senate. Students representing the Reservationists, the Irreconcilables, and the Progressive Internationalists utilize the Choices materials to develop an argument they will present during the Senate debate. Because these materials are copyrighted, I cannot share them here, but they can be found at the Choices website at Brown University (https://www.choices.edu/). I modify the Choices materials to help students prepare for their mock congressional debate.

Preparation time is essential to the success of this activity. I usually assign these roles and the materials a week ahead of time, and provide students with 10 minutes a few days prior to the actual lesson to meet with other students who were assigned the same role to talk about their side of the argument. Because the Choices materials are concise and precise, students rarely have difficultly developing their positions and preparing for the debate. Student research focuses on

- Three main points
- Benefits of choosing your options for the United States
- Specific facts, data, examples, or quotes that support your position
- 5–7-sentence opening statement
- The 5–7-sentence concluding statement or summary you want to end with

The undecided members of the Senate preview a summary of each of the three arguments that will be presented and develop questions to ask each group. Students are allowed to bring the organizer, an example of which can be found in Figure 3.23, to their session of Congress, but they are reminded not to read directly from it.

The debate is a structured discussion with the prompts outlined in Figure 3.24 used to configure the conversation. I set a timer and usually provide 2 minutes each for opening and closing statements and 4 minutes for the broad questions.

At the conclusion of the debate, the undecided member of the foursome must explain their vote, the reasons that most persuaded them, and the issues they had with the opposing sides. At this point, students are allowed to abandon their pre-assigned positions and cast a vote based on what they feel was the most persuasive argument. We then tally the votes of the entire class and determine how our Senate voted. The subsequent discussion enables me to unpack the actual vote and the final fate of the treaty.

The lesson concludes with students assessing a political cartoon for how it assigns blame for the failure of the Treaty of Versailles to be approved by the United States Senate. Students are provided one of 20 political cartoons depicting the outcome of the debate over the treaty. Having knowledge of the people and ideas that populated the debate, students are able to place the cartoons into context and analyze them. Student analysis focuses on the Senate as a whole; the Irreconcilables specifically; President Wilson's health; the foreign entanglements embodied in the treaty; Wilson's failure to include any Republican senators in the United States peace delegation to Paris; the "reservationists" in the Senate, led by Senator Henry Cabot Lodge, who disliked Article X, regarding the League of Nations; and/or Henry Cabot Lodge, the Republican leader of the Senate, who disliked President Wilson. Depending on time, students can complete the assessment as a written assignment, or they can make short presentations of their image to the class and explain the artist's interpretation.

Figure 3.23. Versailles Treaty Organizer

"The World Must Be Made Safe for Democracy": President Woodrow Wilson and the Treaty of Versailles

You are a member of the United States Congress who has made your decision regarding the recently negotiated Treaty of Versailles. The Treaty was negotiated and signed by President Woodrow Wilson, but the United States Constitution stipulates that all treaties must be ratified by a 2/3rds vote of the Senate. Your job will be to participate in a debate about the treaty and persuade an undecided member of Congress to vote your way.

Much of the debate over the treaty has been over Article X, which discusses the creation of a League of Nations that would be responsible for arbitrating all problems that occur between nations and to end war forever. The League would require the United States to participate in any military actions that involved other members of the League. In addition, the League could overrule American actions in other parts of the world.

Your task is to argue your position regarding the ratification of the Treaty of Versailles with three other Senators. Your arguments should convince the other Senators that your option is the best choice. You **MAY NOT** read directly from the sheet. Your job is to summarize the argument, provide facts, figures, and quotes to support your option, and then answer questions from the other Senators. Complete the following questions as you prepare for your debate.

The three main points you wish to make are:

The benefits of choosing your options for the United States are:

Specific facts, data, examples, or quotes that support your position are:

The 5–7 sentence opening statement you will make:

The 5–7 sentence concluding statement or summary you want to end with is:

Figure 3.24. Debate Starters

- Should the United States ratify the Treaty of Versailles?
  Option 1—Go
  Option 2—Go
  Option 3—Go
- America avoided European problems for over 100 years. When we finally assisted these nations, it cost 48,000 American lives. Shouldn't we return to isolation from Europe's problems?
- If the United States does not join the League of Nations, doesn't that send the message to the rest of the world that we believe we are more important than other nations?
- Doesn't membership in the League of Nations endanger America's ability to make its own decisions about war by taking the power away from Congress and giving it to the League?
- Closing Statement:
  Option 1—Go
  Option 2—Go
  Option 3—Go

The Palmer Raids

And now, finally, we arrive at this unit's investigation! The full History Lab that I use in my World War I unit is on the Palmer Raids. It occurs at the end of the unit; thus, students have a strong background of information on the war, and it serves as a nice bridge into some of the social reactions to immigration that impacted the 1920s. Reflecting on the question "Do you conduct a History Lab every day?," I have realized that often the investigation occurs from the middle to the end of a unit. This is due to students' need to be grounded in the unit before they can dive deeply. Although as my proficiency with the approach grew I conducted investigations in the earlier part of a unit, for the first 6–7 years that I conducted labs, they did tend to aggregate in the middle or end of units. In addition, placing the investigations later reinforces the need for students to practice the historical literacy, historical thinking, and argumentation skills throughout the lessons prior to the investigation.

The focus of this chapter is not on any particular aspect of implementing a historical investigation. As a result, I will not spend too much time outlining the Palmer Raids lesson. The central question framing my Palmer Raids lab has students inquiring:

Were the Actions of Attorney General A. Mitchell Palmer Legal and Justified?

Because the growth of federal power was a significant strand that students explored during the unit on World War I, this question is in line with what they have been considering since the lesson on mobilization.

Through a short reading, I provide students with background on postwar domestic events. The legality of the Palmer raids raises a rich historical question for students to investigate. The sources listed in Figure 3.25 structure the lab.

"Legal When, By Whose Standards, and How Do We Determine Justifiability?"

Student discussion centers on the differences between legality and justifiability as well as "whose values" we should use to evaluate Palmer's actions. For some students, the legality of actions taken by the U.S. government is the most essential issue, while for others legality is less important that the necessity of undertaking the actions. The discussion allows teacher to have students consider presentism and whether it is appropriate to evaluate the actions of historic figures using modern values. Most students understand that the question of legality is something that must be considered through the lens of what was or was not legal at the time the event occurred. Judging a historical actor's choices using current laws as the measuring stick is not a good application of historical thinking. Understanding the circumstances that led to a decision helps both to humanize the actor and to generate a more historically accurate understanding of the events, people, and ideas being studied. The Palmer Raids put to bed, it is now time to revisit the query I have received numerous times from teachers: *"So, what do you do when you are not doing labs?"*

WHAT HAPPENS BETWEEN HISTORY LABS?

Imagine participating in the Palmer Raids investigation not having had the opportunity to practice sourcing a variety of historical sources, learn how to understand sources in the context of their creation, or know how to read those sources closely or corroborate across multiple sources in order to make a claim and support it with evidence. In the preceding lessons, students were able to focus on claim construction (Anti-German Reactions), consider cause and consequence (The Great Migration), wrestle with questions of significance (The Road to War), and corroborating (Temperance). The lack of opportunity to practice these skills in the lessons preceding the investigation would lead to a great deal of anxiety, confusion, and limited success for students.

So, no, every lesson does not need to be a lab or investigation. In fact, doing so would have a negative impact on the efficacy of the approach. Any

Figure 3.25. Palmer Raids Sources and Source Information

Source	Background Information
Source 1: *Hearings before the Committee on Rules, House of Representatives, Sixty-sixth Congress, Second session*, 1920.	The following report came after public backlash against the Palmer Raids. With the help of J. Edgar Hoover, the new Bureau of Investigation director who believed an international conspiracy against the U.S. government was under way, the Department of Justice prepared the following testimony to defend their actions in a series of hearings before the Committee on Rules Congress.
Source 2: Statement by Emma Goldman at her federal deportation hearing, New York, October 27, 1919.	A Russian immigrant known by her critics as the "most dangerous woman in America," Emma Goldman was perhaps the most famous anarchist in the United States. She agitated for workers' rights and women's rights, and in 1917 Goldman was sentenced to two years in jail for conspiring to "induce persons not to register" for the draft. When she was released in early 1919, she was again arrested in December 1919 when Palmer's agents seized 249 resident aliens. Those seized were placed on board a ship, the *Buford,* bound for the Soviet Union. She was permanently exiled from the United States.
Source 3: National Popular Government League: "To the American People: Report upon the illegal practices of the United States Department of Justice," May 28, 1920.	Louis Post, a lifelong liberal, was responsible for overseeing the federal deportation cases. Although he signed off on deporting Emma Goldman, when he reviewed the files, he found that in 3 out of 4 cases the Bureau had violated the law and that many detainees were not communists. Post and his lawyer organized the National Popular Government League, which was dedicated to protecting First Amendment civil liberties in the United States.
Source 4: A. Mitchell Palmer, "The Case Against the Reds."	After the outbreak of strikes and riots in 1919, Attorney General A. Mitchell Palmer organized a carefully coordinated series of raids against communists and anarchists on January 3, 1920. Driven by hatred of foreign radicals and a desire to gain the Democratic presidential nomination in 1920, he often acted on his own without informing or consulting President Wilson.
Source 5: "Fear, Not Freedom, Our Real Danger" by Judge Anderson, *The World Tomorrow,* February 1920.	The following journal article is a transcript of Judge Anderson's address to the Harvard Liberal Club in Boston. Judge Anderson had issued a writ of habeas corpus shortly after giving this speech to challenge the Department of Justice's legality of the arrests in Boston during the Palmer Raids.

instructional method, be it lecture, debates, movies, research projects, group work, or historical investigations, wears out its welcome quickly if it is the only thing on the instructional menu. If you try to make every lesson a full historical investigation, students will tire of it, and the efficacy of their use of these skills will atrophy. Instead, a buffet style of instructional approaches leads to more student interest, engagement, and learning. What I will say, and I hope that this chapter was able to address, is that although not every lesson is an investigation, every lesson should incorporate some elements of historical literacy, historical thinking, and historical argumentation. The infusion of these elements into every lesson, regardless of whether that lesson is a simulation, discussion, lecture, or research project, ensures that students are engaging in the subject in a disciplinary manner and setting the stage to be confident and skilled when they do dive deeply into an investigation. The next time you are planning a unit, use the symbols in Figure 3.3 (p. 63) and consider what aspect is addressed in each lesson. Focusing on these elements will make the full historical investigations richer, more successful, and more anticipated by students than doing one every day.

CHAPTER 4

"Is There an Easy Way to Develop Questions . . . ?": Sorry, No

> Teachers introduce a sense of mystery . . . by raising thought-provoking questions, ones that demand answers supported by reasons, by evidence . . .
>
> —David Gerwin and Jack Zevin,
> *Teaching United States History as a Mystery* (2010)

During my youth, trips to my grandparents' house were always punctuated with access to memorabilia: helmets, uniforms, medals, pictures, and often-rumored other "things" in the attic. My curiosity was further piqued when I discovered a Hitler Youth identification card in a pile of possessions in my grandparents' basement. The name was German, but the picture on the identification card was not of anyone I recognized. Why would my grandfather have this item? As I grew older, I came to realize that what was war memorabilia for me were the accoutrements of an earlier life lived by my grandfather. Since he was long reluctant to tell much about his experiences in World War II, I was left to figure out as much as I could about this phase of my grandfather's life. I talked with my mom and grandmother, read books, asked questions of my grandfather when I could muster the courage, and, whenever possible, went searching in the attic, which I had been forbidden access. My interest has continued over the years. I have accessed government documents, discovered pictures that captured snapshots of his service, and, upon his death, accessed the multitude of items squirreled away in the attic. What I discovered was military service at the heart of the Allied invasion of Europe and a fascinating personal story that gave me insight into a transformative global event. This is the power of a question: It can motivate all sorts of actions on the part of the person posing the question and lead to greater knowledge and, of course, more questions!

The challenge for pre-service and practicing teachers addressed in this chapter is how to construct questions that can motivate a teenager to want to explore something about the past. All students have questions about the world around them, but often those questions are driven more by pop culture, peer relationships, or more temporally contiguous issues. The right question can promote anything from a lesson, to a unit, to a research project, but finding those questions is the most difficult aspect of this approach to investigating history rather than simply telling historical stories.

ONE-STOP SHOPPING

When working with teachers, I am invariably asked if there is a "database" or "website" to find the questions I use for my investigations. Unfortunately, no, there is not. It would be awesome if a teacher could go to a webpage and enter the content needed to be covered, the grade level, and something about the students and then an algorithm would generate the perfect question. Alas, and I think in everyone's best interest, there is no such tool. Although there has been an increase in materials that support question-focused instruction, there is not one go-to location for inquiry questions. The Stanford History Education Group (SHEG) has some intriguing questions, and C3 Teachers have some as well. Other tools include the University of Maryland, Baltimore County, Center for History Education's History Labs (https://www2.umbc.edu/che/historylabs/)) the National Archives' DOCs Teach (https://www.docsteach.org/), and Historical Scene Investigations from William and Mary (https://hsi.wm.edu/), but the best questions come not from an algorithm or preexisting materials but instead from a confluence of the curricular demands of the teacher's district, the strength and weaknesses of the students in a teacher's classroom, and the teacher's knowledge of history.

In professional development settings, the formulation of questions concerns teachers, not because their kids cannot investigate questions: I never get the statement that "my kids can't" investigate questions. Instead, the question I hear revolves around how teachers can find or develop their own questions. Central to teachers' concerns is the time it takes to develop a good one. There is no doubt that question development is the most time-consuming aspect of the planning around this type of instruction, and so in this chapter, I will address a significant underexplored area in *Why Won't You Just Tell Us the Answer?:* the development of meaningful and engaging questions. After setting the stage, I will use a lesson on Marcus Garvey to model the development and evolution of a question.

THE ENGAGEMENT CLIFF

Every classroom teacher has witnessed disengagement firsthand. It might be when trying to teach in a room where it is over 90 degrees, and it is simply too hot to concentrate. For some it is the last class on a Friday, while for others it was that lesson that just bombed, and you are trying to salvage it with a song and dance. Regardless of the situation, we have all witnessed the lifeless stares, the not-so-surreptitious glances at phones sequestered in crotches, or the myriad number of off-task behaviors that emerge when student engagement drops. Disengaged students are one of the clearest signs that learning is not happening.

We also know what engagement, not compliance, but legitimate cognitive engagement, looks like. Hands are in the air, student-to-student conversation fills the classroom, teachable moments occur as students generate questions, and content-rich work fills the time from bell to bell. This kind of engagement is not the temporary type generated by offers of candy, a nonacademic movie, or a "Fun Friday." Instead, students need to be involved because schoolwork is cognitively engaging (Geraci et al., 2017; Willingham, 2010). Getting an education requires students to invest hours of time investigating meaty topics, reading, taking notes, engaging in discussions, studying, writing, and revising, and these actions are often not immediately rewarding. For students to reap the benefits of school and "to enhance achievement," teachers "must first learn how to engage students" (Newmann, 1992). Unfortunately, as Figure 4.1 shows, student engagement drops significantly over the course of their education, and thus the challenge to the teacher to learn how to generate true engagement is both difficult and important.

Part of this drop is simply the fact that as students get older, they begin to see disconnects between the education they are receiving and what they perceive as their life path, but that caveat aside, it is hard to look at this graph and not ask: "What could be done to reverse the stark disengagement trend?" Students spend 8 hours a day, 180 days a year in school for 13 years from

Figure 4.1. The Engagement Cliff

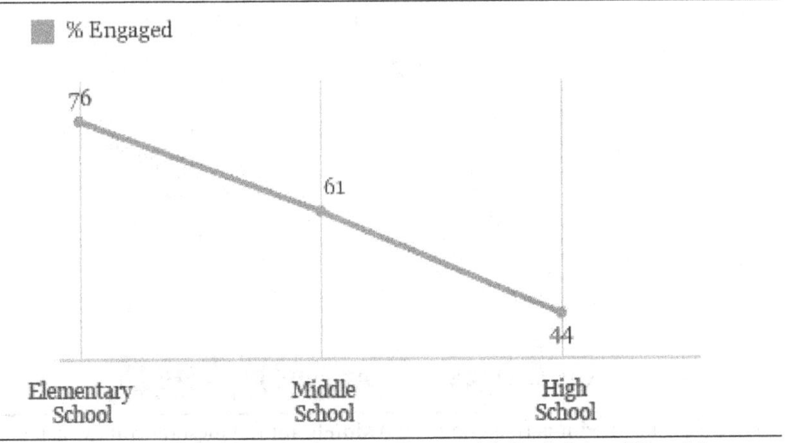

Source: "The School Cliff: Student Engagement Drops with Each School Year," by B. Busteed, January 7, 2013, Gallup (http://www.gallup.com/opinion/gallup/170525/school-cliff-student-engagement-drops-school-year.aspx).

kindergarten through high school. This means that much of this time they feel disengaged from the experience of learning (Berger, 2014). That is scary.

A key indicator of engagement is a student who asks content-pertinent questions. The inverse is a one-way dialogue where only the teacher has questions, which is not a recipe for deep learning. As demonstrated in Figure 4.2, student-generated questions peak at age 4 and begin to drop as children enter school.

By about age 10, students asking questions is eclipsed by reading and writing. As I outline in Chapter 5, teacher-provided questions come to dominate the discourse in most classrooms. Thus, "As kids stop questioning, they simultaneously become less engaged in school" (Berger, 2014), and we see student engagement dropping as teacher talk, reading, and writing overwhelm student inquisitiveness. No, this is not causal, but it is four separate actions that at least appear to be connected. Even if ultimately they are not statistically connected, having taught and observed others teaching, they have some relationship. A metanalysis of studies about the relationship between student engagement and student achievement indicates a strong correlation between the two. The more time students are engaged, the higher

Figure 4.2. Trends in Students Asking Questions

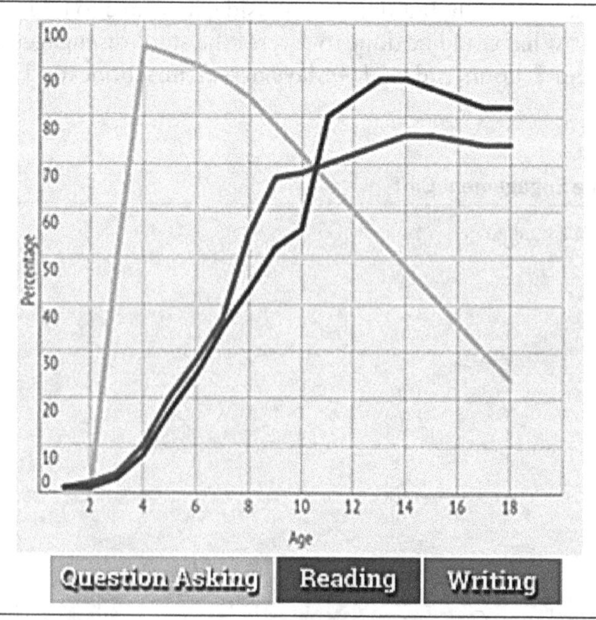

Source: Reprinted with permission from AMoreBeautifulQuestion.com, which created this chart based on a similar version originally created by the Right Question Institute (rightquestion.org).

their achievement (Lei et al., 2018). My belief is that questions, even if they are designed by the teacher, have a unique power to reinvigorate student engagement—even if it is just for 45 minutes at a time.

THE BRAIN AND QUESTIONS

Getting a student's attention is essential for ensuring engagement, and much of the instructional potential possessed by questions lies in their ability to spark curiosity. A good question's power to motivate and increase student engagement is directly linked to the human brain, which is wired to respond to curiosity, or what neuroscientists refer to as novelty. When the brain confronts something novel—an idea, an image, a provocative quote, a conundrum, or a compelling question that creates dissonance—the brain releases dopamine, which activates several parts of the brain associated with attention and focus. Research indicates that learning is facilitated when the brain is confronted with things that generate curiosity. When people are highly curious to find out the answer to a question, they are shockingly better at learning that information. When in a curious state, people are also better able to retain the information learned. When curiosity is stimulated, there is increased activity in the brain circuitry related to reward, and when curiosity motivates learning, there is increased activity in the hippocampus, a brain region that is important for forming new memories, as well as increased interactions between the hippocampus and the reward circuit (Gruber et al., 2014; Kidd & Hayden, 2015). That is a lot of science to simply reaffirm what we witness as teachers—when students are engaged, they are talking about content, solving problems, and learning at much greater rates than when they are not engaged. But what do questions that stimulate curiosity have to do with social studies, a discipline that has always been approached as the teaching of answers?

WHY QUESTIONS IN SOCIAL STUDIES?

Knowledge of social studies is usually measured by a student's ability to acquire and regurgitate fact. The National Assessment of Education Progress (NAEP) assessments in history serve as prime examples of this trend. In addition, states set out ridiculously detailed standards that list what students should know about history, geography, economics, civics, and other associated topics, and then roll out assessments that target knowledge retention. The intense focus on the answers has left students stranded. They may memorize the order in which Southern states seceded from the Union, but have no idea why this information is important. Facts, absent a question to answer, are quickly forgotten (Bransford et al., 2000; Davis & Luce-Kapler, 2000). Lacking a driving question, students simply aggregate the answers to questions of which they are not even aware and supply those answers. It is nothing but academic bulimia.

A question can be a much more powerful instructional tool than simply having students memorize an aggregation of facts because questions provide the mental structure for students to organize new information. A good question is Velcro for learning, as it helps students to organize and attach information. Because social studies broadly, and history specifically, has always been defined by what answers students should know, students are often left without the questions that led to those answers. For me, one of the most significant reminders of the importance of questions as a basis for instruction is the admonition that "if the content you are expected to teach represents 'answers,'" and most certainly social studies always has, then, McTighe and Wiggins remind us, "what questions were being asked by people who came up with those answers?" (2013). This powerful advice spurs one to consider not the need to have students memorize the order in which the Southern states seceded from the Union, but instead have them explore why they left. "Questions," according to McTighe and Wiggins, are powerful when they help "students make sense of seemingly isolated facts and skills or important but abstract ideas . . . by actively exploring such questions, learners are helped to connect disparate and confusing information and arrive at important understandings as well as more effective transfer of their knowledge and skill" (2013).

ORGANIZING THE MENTAL BEDROOM

The metaphor I use and illustrate in Figure 4.3 is a student's bedroom. Students usually store their clothing on the floor. The clothes are tossed around randomly, and finding what they want to wear—and what is clean—is a challenge. Rather than rooting through the pile on the floor, a hanger helps students quickly and efficiently find what they are looking for. The clothing in this metaphor is the facts provided by teachers to students. Within their brains, facts are randomly stored in long-term memory. We know that the brain is not designed to collect and remember mass amounts of information on a wide variety of topics (Sousa, 2017; Sousa & Tomlinson, 2018). Questions, then—the hanger—can help students connect facts to the broader issue being investigated. Rather than memorizing seemingly random information, the questions, just like the hanger for clothing, help students to aggregate random facts into a pattern that makes it easier to remember, which in turn improves retention (Bransford et al., 2000; Hattie, 2012; Jensen, 2005).

Figure 4.3. Questions Organize Thinking

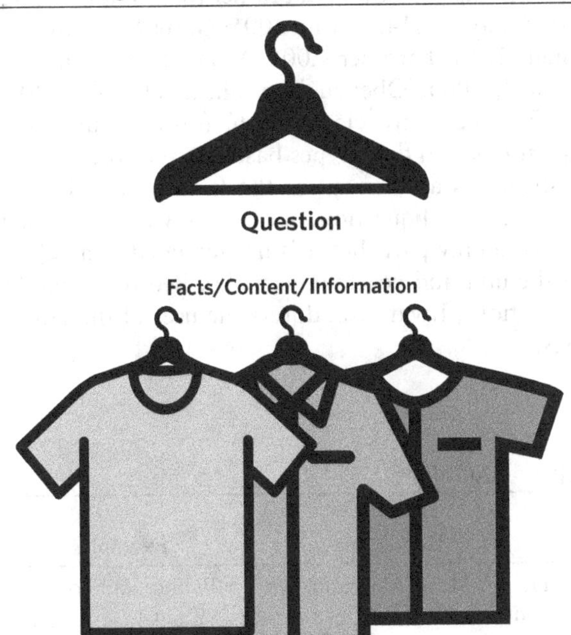

Source: Icons from the Noun Project (https://thenounproject.com)

Thus, questions have the ability not only to focus instruction but also to aid students in organizing, accessing, and applying information they have learned. The reality of this is always cemented for me when it comes to reviewing for unit assessments, midterms, or final exams. When students prepare for these, they often use the investigations we have conducted as anchor points for both memory and review. The examples they harvest for essays are almost always tied to the topics we have investigated though questions rather than random factual recall. "Meaty" questions thus provide a powerful tool that teachers can incorporate into their instructional tool kit (Swann et al., 2018a).

TYPES OF QUESTIONS

While the benefits of using questions as a stepping-off point for instruction has gained significant traction in the last 20 years, there is no agreement on what makes a good question or when it is best for the question to be posed and investigated, or even what to call those questions! Essential questions, overarching questions, key questions, or compelling and supporting questions: Regardless of the nomenclature, they all have the same intent—focus instruction on figuring something out rather than simply telling students the answer (Brush & Saye, 2014; Caron, 2005; Grant & Gradwell, 2010; Grant & VanSledright, 2014; Lattimer, 2008; Monte-Sano et al., 2014; National Research Council, 2005; Obenchain et al., 2011; Riley, 2000; Wineburg et al., 2011). To bring a little clarity to the forest, Figure 4.4 illustrates the division of questions into three types based on purpose.

My investigations are always at the lesson level. They may at times contribute to a unit- level question, but generally they are isolated. That is a conscious choice on my part, but it is not intended as a value judgment on the utility of the unit and yearlong varieties. Before diving deeply into the lesson-level questions, I want to address the uses of the yearlong and unit-long questions.

Figure 4.4. Types of Questions

Type of Questions	Definition	Examples	Source
Yearlong Questions	Help students to organize content over broad swaths of time and geography. Can serve as organizers for review and to assess degrees of continuity and change.	Politics and Power How have different social and political groups influenced society and government in the United States? How have political beliefs and institutions changed over time?	AP United States History Framework
Unit-Long Questions	Broader than a lesson question but narrower than a yearlong question, these help students to consider all of the events, ideas, and people in one unit through a single investigative lens. The questions that drive the investigations on the C3 Teachers website function well as unit questions.	Was the French Revolution successful?	C3 Teachers Inquiries
Lesson-Level Questions	Narrow questions that drive investigations that last no longer than 90 minutes.	Riot, rebellion, or insurrection: How should the urban unrest of the 1960s be remembered?	My Lesson

WE LEARNED THAT IN OCTOBER—YOU MEAN I WAS SUPPOSED TO REMEMBER THAT?

Students are more likely to see math and foreign language as subjects that build on one another from one year to the next. Unfortunately, they do not hold the same beliefs about history. They see history as an episodic collection of photographs rather than a film with a story that builds on itself. Most students walk away from history courses with a broad progress narrative, believing that in the past things were terrible and then they progressively improved (Calder, 2013; VanSledright, 2011). Part of what contributes to this phenomenon is the way in which history is taught. Social studies educators usually aggregate things by unit, give a test, and then move on to the next unit. Rarely do we require students to reach backward and carry content into the new time period. Nor do we ask students to critically assess the changes and continuities across time. As a result, students do not see history as an aggregation, but simply as "one damn story after another," albeit a story with a positive arc and happy ending! In addition, we often sequence courses so that there are large gaps in time between when students study topics. Often students study United States History in 5th grade, 8th grade, and 11th grade, and the gaps between this learning perpetuate the idea that history does not build on previous years like mathematics or foreign language.

To militate against the notion of history as simply a progress narrative and not a cumulative study, I embed themes into my courses. Incorporating specific questions as an organizational structure embedded throughout an entire history course provides connectivity among the content studied throughout the year. For example, having students continually wrestle with questions such as "How has history been affected by the balance between the use of power and the protection of liberty," or "Has the United States been faithful to the promise of *E Pluribus Unum,*" provides a scaffold for students to make links across time and from the past to the present (Endacott, 2011; Good, 2013). These questions can also be utilized to scaffold discussions and to connect "persistent" issues across time (Brush & Saye, 2014). Over the years I have adopted many themes. They usually focus on political, economic, social, or demographic changes within the scope of the course I am teaching. Ultimately, the use of course-long themes pays dividends only when students have some content knowledge from which to pull to make these connections across time and space.

The themes currently provided by the College Board for the AP United States History course, displayed in Figure 4.5, are great tools to utilize at the end of a quarter or semester, or prior to the final exam, and review changes around a topic. Turning the themes provided by the College Board into questions can be a powerful tool.

Figure 4.5. AP United States History Themes

THEME 1: AMERICAN AND NATIONAL IDENTITY (NAT) This theme focuses on how and why definitions of American and national identity and values have developed among the diverse and changing population of North America as well as on related topics, such as citizenship, constitutionalism, foreign policy, assimilation, and American exceptionalism.

THEME 2: WORK, EXCHANGE, AND TECHNOLOGY (WXT) This theme focuses on the factors behind the development of systems of economic exchange, particularly the role of technology, economic markets, and government.

THEME 3: GEOGRAPHY AND THE ENVIRONMENT (GEO) This theme focuses on the role of geography and both the natural and human-made environments in the social and political developments in what would become the United States.

THEME 4: MIGRATION AND SETTLEMENT (MIG) This theme focuses on why and how the various people who moved to and within the United States both adapted to and transformed their new social and physical environments.

THEME 5: POLITICS AND POWER (PCE) This theme focuses on how different social and political groups have influenced society and government in the United States as well as how political beliefs and institutions have changed over time.

THEME 6: AMERICA IN THE WORLD (WOR) This theme focuses on the interactions among nations that affected North American history in the colonial period and on the influence of the United States on world affairs.

THEME 7: AMERICAN AND REGIONAL CULTURE (ARC) This theme focuses on the how and why national, regional, and group cultures developed and changed as well as how culture has shaped government policy and the economy.

THEME 8: SOCIAL STRUCTURES (SOC) This theme focuses on how and why systems of social organization develop and change as well as the impact that these systems have on the broader society.

For example: "How have different social and political groups influenced society and government in the United States?," or "How have political beliefs and institutions changed over time?," could serve as tools to review political change over a United States History course. Some recommend that yearlong questions be exposed at the outset of a course and then used frequently to attach information to them as students progress chronologically through history. I have found that yearlong questions are more useful as periodic postholes when students must consider a larger swath of history before ascribing content to the theme. Yearlong questions are significant tools for helping students organize the sheer volume of material they have studied into an organized pattern (Voelker & Armstrong, 2013). As illustrated in Figure 4.6, these cross-course themes served as the review tool for both my midterm and final exams.

Figure 4.6. Thematic Organizer for Midterm and Final Exam Essays

The midterm and final exam essay questions will be focused on significant changes that occurred between 1865 and 2000 and the people, events, ideas, and factors that drove those changes. As you review for the exam, use the organizer below to help organize the content we studied. The categories below will serve as the themes around which the essay questions will be structured. You will have a choice of completing one of three essays.

Question	Trend	People, events, laws, court decisions, presidential actions, ideas, and factors that drove these changes
How did political beliefs and institutions change between 1865 and 1920?		
How has the United States' connection to, and involvement with, other nations impacted the American people, economy, and reputation between 1865 and1920?	The United States' connection and involvement with the rest of the world increased.	
How has the American economy changed between 1865 and 1920?	A movement to industrialization and mass manufacturing of materials, including the mechanization of farming and the rise of organized labor, created conflict with labor and dislocation of people.	
How has the role of government been defined and modified between 1865 and 1920?	Movement from laissez-faire government role to a greater government role in regulating the changes created by industrialization.	
How has the definition of American and national identity changed between 1865 and 1920?	Discrimination against Indians, African Americans, and some immigrants increased while women gained more political equality.	

Students are provided this organizer on the first day of school. Prior to the midterm exam, we stop and examine the events, people, and ideas we have encountered and organize them to answer the overarching year-long questions that appear in the far-left column. The first decision is to identify what we see as trends over the time period. Then students generate examples that support the trend and could be used in response to the question at hand. This process is again employed at the end of the course to reexamine the questions. The midterm and final exams include questions based around these overarching course-long questions. Students can use the organizers to prepare for the questions and to do some sense-making about how the content they have explored fits together. I have found great utility in the use of the course-long questions, as they aid student learning, facilitate review, and strengthen students' ability to address continuity and change. I highly recommend their use in any course that you teach.

UNIT-WIDE QUESTIONS

My lack of familiarity with using unit-wide questions stems from, more than anything else, my personal desire to increase student engagement at the lesson level. Nevertheless, unit-wide questions can have a significant, positive impact on how students engage with history and how teachers structure the study of a time period. Overarching unit questions help teachers to filter significant content from superfluous and ensure that every lesson within the unit builds student knowledge and ability to eventually answer the question. Unit-level questions, particularly with the advent of the work of Jay McTighe and Grant Wiggins, have become cornerstones in many district curricula (Lattimer, 2008; McTighe & Wiggins, 2011, 2013; Riley, 2000; Swann et al., 2018a, 2018b; "What's the Wisdom," 2020). Linked to their Understanding by Design framework, McTighe and Wiggins have posited that essential questions establish the big-picture ideas that we want students to walk away with after completing a unit of study. They argue that a powerful essential question:

1. Is open-ended; that is, it typically will not have a single, final, and correct answer.
2. Is thought-provoking and intellectually engaging, often sparking discussion and debate.
3. Calls for higher-order thinking, such as analysis, inference, evaluation, and prediction. It cannot be effectively answered by recall alone.
4. Points toward important, transferable ideas within (and sometimes across) disciplines.

5. Raises additional questions and sparks further inquiry.
6. Requires support and justification, not just an answer.
7. Recurs over time; that is, the question can and should be revisited again and again.

The characteristics of good unit-level essential questions share much in common with the lesson-level ones I will discuss momentarily, but the key difference is that unit-level questions require multiple days, multiple lessons, and smaller scaffolded subquestions before students can develop and support an answer, while a lesson-level question can be addressed in 90 minutes or less. The utility of unit-level investigative questions in the social studies classroom is fleshed out by the work of Kathy Swann, John Lee, and S.G. Grant. Using $3 million from Race to the Top federal funding, New York State developed and houses the C3 Teacher Inquiries discussed in Chapter 1. Based on the Inquiry Design Model (IDM), these inquiries are based on compelling questions, analogous to Wiggins and McTighe's essential questions. Swann, Grant, and Lee (2018a) argue that there are 10 types of compelling questions (see Figure 4.7).

After establishing a compelling question, the IDM then guides teachers to develop supporting questions that must be addressed in order for students to ultimately tackle the overarching compelling question. Our friends across the pond in England have made great strides in developing units that have a unifying question as the tendon that connects all topics within a unit. As demonstrated in Figure 4.8 below, the overarching unit question is fed by each of the lesson-spanning inquiry (enquiry if you are British, mate) questions. Although each lesson-level question can and does work in isolation, they each scaffold a student toward the ability to address the overarching question.

For me, the danger in the unit-wide question is, what happens on the days when the compelling questions are being explored? If instruction flattens out and the teacher loses the cognitive tension that the question engenders, then the momentum gained is lost. There is a greater potential for a question to hold students' attention for 90 minutes than it is for a week or 10 days. The intensity and primacy of a unit-wide question could get lost as students wrestle with the supporting questions ("What's the Wisdom,"2020). Those concerns stated, I have seen teachers develop and utilize unit-wide questions and do it incredibly well. Students are engaged, and the overall inquiry can be sustained. I have also witnessed the opposite, where a compelling question at the outset of a unit is lost as daily instruction erases students' interest. My preference is for lesson-level investigative questions that can be explored and put to bed in 90 minutes rather than the overarching unit questions, but there is power to unit-wide questions.

Figure 4.7. Types of Compelling Questions

Type of Compelling Question	Definition	Example
Broad-brush	Appraise big issues, often through a case study	What is justice?
Case Study	Look deeply into ideas, actions, or conditions	Did the printing press preserve the past or invent the future?
Personalized	Offer opportunities to connect with the real world	Why do I have to be responsible?
Analytic	Examine the component dimensions of an idea, event, or phenomenon	Did industrialization make life better for everyone?
Comparative	Analyze and compare multiple components of a phenomena	How could Americans be happier?
Evaluative	Calls for a judgment on an issue	Was the American Revolution avoidable?
Problem-based	Propose potential solutions to a social problem	Should freedom be sacrificed in the name of national security?
Wordplay	Juxtapose different meanings of words and ideas	Is free trade worth the price?
Ironic	Consider meanings below the surface of an idea	Is greed good?
Mystery	Track the elements of an unanswered question	What is the real story behind the purchase of Manhattan?

BUILDING LESSON-LEVEL QUESTIONS

Although yearlong and unit-wide questions have great power, my focus will be on the development of the lesson-level investigation questions. A few key phrases jump out at me when considering designing a lesson-level investigation. "Problematizing" history, exploring substantive historical dilemmas, creating "cognitive incongruity," presenting "cognitive puzzles," and putting students in the "historical problem space" encourage the selection of questions that get at the heart of the interpretive nature of history (Foster, 2016; Havekes et al., 2012; Reisman, 2015a). In the context of history, some questions can inadvertently place the student in a position of having to justify the unjustifiable (defend slavery) conspiratorial (aliens built the pyramids), or not supported by the evidence (President Roosevelt knew the Japanese were going to attack Pearl Harbor on December 7, 1941). We

Figure 4.8. Overview of an Inquiry

Overall enquiry: Who was *really* responsible for bringing an end to the transatlantic slave trade?

Lesson	Main content	Activities	Substantive/ conceptual focus
1. Why was it so difficult to persuade people that slavery was wrong?	Introducing the arguments made for and against slavery.	I. Alphonse the Camel activity followed by students identifying different types of causes. II. Analysing 'Amazing Grace' by John Newton and writing by William Beckford to understand different views within rival camps.	Introduce the class to the idea that causes work in combination to produce change; all historical events are multicausal.
2. Why was abolition possible at the start of the 1800s?	Introduce the wider context of the time – industrialisation, growth of middle classes and non-conformist Christianity.	I. Information-capture activity in which students research different factors. II. Students plot these changes on a graph to explain whether they made abolition more or less likely.	The importance of wider contextual factors in creating the conditions for more immediate change.
3. Why have women's contributions to the abolitionist movement been overlooked?	Emphasise how life changed for certain groups of women. Emphasise the links between this and women's involvement in abolition.	I. Source-carousel activity in which students make inferences from abolitionist chinaware; poetry; badges etc. II. Mapping activity in which students find links between different aspects of substantive knowledge.	The idea that certain types of causes might be overlooked by historians. How causal enquiries might unearth fresh interpretations of the past.
4. Why has history remembered William Wilberforce as the 'hero' of abolition?	Exploring the role of those working in public life to bring abolition – Wilberforce, Clarkson and Equiano.	I. Source analysis using work from Equiano, Wilberforce and Clarkson. II. Exploring interpretations of Wilberforce. III. Selecting evidence to present to parliament.	Understanding the link between underlying conditions and more immediate actions. Understanding the ways in which causes interact.
5. Who was really responsible for bringing an end to the transatlantic slave trade?	Emphasise the role of different groups – women, ex-slaves, politicians.	I. Causal arithmetic activity in which students must find combinations of factors and rate the importance of causes. II. Card sort / linking activity in which students show the relationships between different events using specific vocabulary.	Historical events have numerous causes, and historical causes are part of a complex web. Writing about historical causes well requires precise vocabulary.
6. Who was really responsible for bringing an end to the transatlantic slave trade?	Preparing for a written argument in response to the overall enquiry question.		

Source: From "Beneath the Surface: Unravelling the Complexity of the Causes of British Abolition With Year 8," by E. Marsay, 2020, *Teaching History, 178*, 8–15. Used with permission.

must avoid placing students into these positions. The first way to avoid these conflicts is determining what questions even merit investigation.

COVERAGE DEMANDS CHOICES

You cannot teach all the content about a topic through the lens of an inquiry question. Try, and you will end up with either an investigation with no instructional soul or, at the end of the year, you will be so far behind that you will question why you pursued this path. The sheer volume of content to be covered can cause teachers to get lost in the details, so avoiding what Swann et al. (2018a) refer to as the "content trap" is an essential consideration. This is a benefit, though, of lesson-level questions versus ones that span a unit and have multiple sublevel questions. A lesson-specific question can ease the concerns about trying to cover too much content in one question and also ameliorate concerns about not covering the full scope of the course. I present my unit on Reconstruction as an example. Reconstruction is one of my favorite units to teach. So much of the content sets the stage for much of the 20th century and still has resonance to today's issues. Despite the importance of the content, I cannot spend more than 9–10 days on the time period if I am to make it to the end of the course. Therefore, as outlined in Figure 4.9, I have to choose carefully which lesson(s) within the unit merit a deep dive.

Each lesson is based on a central investigative question, but only two are full-scale 90-minute-deep dives. This ensures that students can focus on applying the literacy skills, and I can still end the year looking at the post-9/11 world. Yes, a unit-wide question could easily be imposed on this time period. The issue for me is less of the efficacy of that structure than its

Figure 4.9. Key Questions in Reconstruction Unit

Reconstruction Lesson	Key Question
Post–Civil War South	What does freedom mean in the postwar South?
Competing Plans for Reconstruction	Why is change so difficult?
The Freedmen's Bureau	Was the Freedmen's Bureau successful?
Southern Resistance	Southern resistance: Counterrevolution, insurgency, or resistance?
Why Did Reconstruction Fail?	Why did Reconstruction fail?
Jim Crow and Disenfranchisement	Can music tell a story?
Competing Views on Racial Progress	Is there one path to equality?
The Lost Cause	The Lost Cause: Myth or memory?

impact on my ability to address the full course and for students to apply their literacy and thinking skills in depth.

I will continue the examination of how to ensure both meeting coverage demands and providing significant opportunities for deep dives in my exploration of what happens between history labs, but at this juncture, it is important to keep this consideration in mind: Select lesson-level questions that best facilitate a deep dive into a question that demands interpretation and promotes argumentation based on evidence. Be careful, though, as not all questions are created equally.

"WOULD YOU HAVE YOUR STUDENTS DEBATE SLAVERY?"

Early in my career, I organized a lesson on the battle for women's suffrage based on a roundtable debate where students represented various opinions on it. Some student's role-played supporters and others those opposed to the movement. The debate went swimmingly as students represented their assigned viewpoints and came to a clear understanding of why this social and political change was so hard to engender. Historical empathy abounded. Later, during a long week of Teaching American History presentations, I was discussing the lesson with Carol Berkin, who asked, "Why do you have students opposing women's suffrage?" Is that really a debatable question? Would you have your students debate slavery? Who is the child that would be defending slavery?" Subsequent to that conversation, I reconsidered the suffrage debate and several other lessons. What I realized is that it was not the topic that I was addressing, because women's suffrage is an essential component of any United States History course, but instead the question posed that created the difficulty. Why people who were so opposed to suffrage had merit was the questions, but there were better questions to ask that would enable students to understand both the arguments for and against the extension of the franchise to women. After my discussion with Professor Berkin, I quickly abandoned the "let's debate suffrage" or "let's debate imperialism"–style lessons and instead moved into adjacent questions that gave greater insight into the historical events being studied without students adopting closed historical positions. This was an important lesson in my evolution toward the use of investigative questions as an element of every lesson.

OPEN VERSUS CLOSED QUESTIONS

Diana Hess's (2009b) exceptional work on teaching controversial issues is enumerated in Figure 4.10 below. It identifies three specific types of questions and can serve as a stepping-off point for the narrowing of what to ask.

Figure 4.10. Open, Closed, and Tipping Questions

Category	Definition
Open	Open questions are ones that are controversial in the historical moment and within the larger societal or national context.
Tipping	Questions that tip move from open to closed or closed to open because of the conditions and context of the moment in which people live.
Closed	Closed questions are ones for which we want our students to believe a particular answer.

In the context of controversial issues, these definitions make sense. The problem is that for a history class, these definitions have the potential to shut down any investigation of meaty historical questions. A closed question that we just want a student to know the answer to is by definition not debatable. A question where we want the students to know one answer is really just catechism. Selecting questions that are simply the identification of facts are neither interesting nor fertile territory for investigation. Historians do not debate if President John F. Kennedy was assassinated. His death on November 22, 1963, despite rumors of him living on in South America with Tupac, is simply a fact. There is nothing debatable about it. By definition, this is a closed question. But historians do debate continually why JFK was assassinated. The Mafia, Fidel Castro, the CIA, Vice President Lyndon B. Johnson, a cabal of wealthy Texans, the Russians, and the lone gunman Lee Harvey Oswald have all been a part of significant historical scholarship debating this question. Thus, whether a question that elicits debate can be supported with evidence on both sides is essential to the success of a lesson-level investigative question.

In history, most questions are never closed because the emergence of new sources and new questions asked of old sources, and the impact of distance on historians' ability to examine events and people within a longer stream of history, reopen questions for renewed debate. By the criteria that Hess establishes, Japanese American internment has moved from open to closed because significant evidence has arisen to demonstrate that the action was not justified and was driven by racial animus (Kennedy, 2001). This is a tough line to walk, because teachers want students to gain historical empathy by seeing events through the eyes of historical actors, but teachers do not want students to have license to argue that Japanese American internment was justified. I caution that if a topic has tipped or even closed, it does not mean that there is not a derivative question that can allow students to investigate that topic. Therefore, recasting the question as what degree racism played in the decision to inter Japanese Americans is still a valid investigative question. Overall, it is important to think critically about how we frame our questions and what we asked students to debate about past actors, actions, events, and ideas.

THE PEOPLE IN THE PAST WERE STUPID

Questions about the past are complicated. In many ways they are more complicated than ones about contemporary issues, civics, economics, or geography. Although we want students to evaluate the actions of past actors, we do not want them to lose the "foreign country" that is the past and simply examine everything through the lens of the present (Lowenthal, 1985). The past is a different place, and seeing historic actors as simply extensions of the present truncates the ability of students to understand why events occurred and why people made the choices they made (Lévesque, 2009; Seixas, 1996; Seixas & Morton, 2013; VanSledright, 2001; Wineburg, 2001). Unfortunately, many students make assumptions that past actors had the same thoughts, motivations, goals, and beliefs as people living today (Barton & Levstik, 2004; Lee & Ashby, 2001). The notion that people in the past were "stupid," or that they had the same information that those living in the present, leads students to make inaccurate evaluations of the past (Reisman & Wineburg, 2008; Shemilt, 1980). To overcome this presentism, students must be able to understand historical perspectives and engage in an empathetic approach to the past through the lens of historical sources (Lee & Ashby, 2001; Levstik, 2001; Seixas & Peck, 2004). Essential to generating this understanding is to set the context for the questions that students are investigating.

Content coverage, presentism, avoiding ahistorical answers, and promoting conspiracy theories are all considerations that impact the development of investigative questions for a history class. Numerous other factors, outlined in Figure 4.11, have also been identified as important criteria to be considered when developing a question.

Each of these criteria is important in its own right, but no question ever developed has even a plurality of these factors. We could make a checklist with the criteria above and set some sort of arbitrary number of the criteria that need to be hit before a question rises to the level of good. Thus, we hit the crux of the problem: A checklist will not lead to a great question. The process is much more art than it is science. Ultimately, the best questions are akin to a carpenter using a level, attempting to find the right balance between student and content, aiming to move that air bubble to the exact middle of the level (Mohamud & Whitburn, 2019). Good questions end up a lot like Supreme Court Justice Potter Stewart's definition of pornography: We know a good question when we see one!

Figure 4.11. Important Considerations for Question Development

- Does the question connect the past to the present?
- Does the question enable students to construct their own understanding of the past?
- Does the question place an aspect of a historical thinking concept at the forefront of instruction?
- Does the question result in a lively, substantial activity through which students genuinely answer a guiding inquiry question?
- Does the question challenge students to examine their own beliefs?
- Does the question represent a reasonable amount of content?
- Does the question hold the sustained interest of middle or high school students?
- Does the question provide an age-, grade-, and subject-appropriate cognitive challenge for the students you are teaching?
- Does the question allow for meaningful exploration of an idea?
- Does the question result in students building an evidence-based summative argument?

THE TUG OF WAR BETWEEN RELEVANCE AND ACCURACY

A question that a historian may like will pull too far away from student needs, interests, or abilities. By the same token, a question that resonates with students may cheapen the content being studied. Striking the "Goldilocks point" ensures a good balance of student and content (Willingham, 2010). As depicted below, Swann, Lee, and Grant instruct us to consider the tension between relevance and rigor. "An inquiry with relevance," they remind us, "is vapid, while an inquiry with only content is just a textbook entry," but the best questions fall in "the common ground between content and students" (Swann et al., 2018a). In addition, teachers developing lesson-level questions must be careful with relevance, because it is usually only a temporary trigger for student engagement (Harris & Girard, 2014; Mohamud & Whitburn, 2019; Mueller, 2017a, 2017b, 2017c; "What's the Wisdom," 2020). Conversely, too much attention on content can lose sight of the developmental level of the audience in front of the teacher. Thus, a great question finds that sweet spot between relevance for students and the demands of content. The document-based question is a classic example of inquiry questions that are widely used to structure instruction but do not strike this balance.

A LITTLE SEX APPEAL GOES A LONG WAY

DBQ questions on the AP exam often skew too far toward rigor and content. Yes, the questions do require consideration of content and facilitate the use of sources, but as worded, they really have no sex appeal for kids. Take, for example, the DBQ question from the 2015 AP United States History exam.

Explain the reasons why a new conservatism rose to prominence in the United States between 1960 and 1989.

This question, or one like it, could have easily populated an undergraduate or graduate history exam and calls for students to pull on content knowledge about domestic politics over a long period. It is a good question that can promote solid writing, unless you are teaching the average high school student. For most students this question lands like the proverbial lead balloon. There is nothing within the question for a student to latch onto to care about. They may care about it because they want to please their teacher, they need a good grade, or even because they love the subject matter, but there is nothing deep driving the investigation of the topic. As a result, the relevance side of the equation is unbalanced in relation to the content side. The issue then becomes not throwing the question out and replacing it with something new, but instead balancing the content and student sides of the equation. Striking this balance could turn this question into:

New Conservatism: Reactionary or Revolutionary?

Both iterations of the question get at the heart of the content students are examining, the rise of conservatism, but the second version has a greater chance of generating some student buy-in. The appeal of iteration two is that students have an entryway that connects them to the topic. Is it a little cheap, yes, absolutely! But as anyone who teaches students will tell you, a little buy-in up front goes a long way to connecting students to the learning process. The first version would be roundly applauded by historians (hell, they wrote it), but not embraced as much by teachers and students, while the second version would cause historians to blanch. It's a balance, but version one is much more aligned with the "textbook entry" than it is with something worth investigating.

HISTORICAL CATEGORIES OF INQUIRY

Beyond sex appeal, an important aspect to consider when developing lesson-based inquiry questions is the historical thinking skills you intend to incorporate into your instructional program. Emphasizing these skills allows you to "build a common language" to structure students' examination of the past" (Mandel & Malone, 2008). In my approach, I refer to these skills as historical literacy skills, although the research calls them metaconcepts or 2nd-order concepts. These are the sort of skills that are asked by historians regardless of the time period or the content being studied. Emphasizing these skills within questions ensures that students are thinking about history in a manner parallel to that of historians (Mandell & Malone, 2008; Seixas & Morton, 2013). For me, the skills I choose to emphasize are:

- Historical Significance
- Continuity and Change
- Cause and Consequence
- Historical Perspectives

If we return for a moment to my re-envisioning of the AP US History question on the rise of conservatism, within that question is the skill of historical perspective as well as continuity and change. No, those words do not appear within the question stem, but they are inherent in the intent of the question. By incorporating these ideas and reinforcing them throughout a course, students can make strong connections to the disciplinary approach of history.

TYPES OF QUESTIONS

Again, there is no tool that can generate questions, but having tried, failed, and succeeded with using questions as the launching point for instruction, I do have some question groups that I have found more successful than not. The caveat is that the questions that I developed were by and large for single-lesson investigations. They were not designed with the precision needed to string a series of investigations into a unit. These question types were organized so students could have a tight investigation and apply the historical literacy skills linked to a thinking concept in 90 minutes or less.

Option Questions

Option questions are one of the earliest types of question that I developed and implemented. These questions are intended to provide some scaffolding for students' thinking. Scaffolding between interpretations is much easier than having students constructing their own interpretations out of whole cloth. It also reduces the cognitive demand on students while they are still gaining facility with the historical thinking skills they are employing while accumulating content knowledge. By providing students with choices about how to consider a historical event, person, or idea, these questions set parameters for the investigation. Sharing these types of questions makes me nervous because they often disappoint the rigor side of the equation in deference to the relevance side. I have received criticisms that the option questions can trivialize or oversimplify important historical figures and events. Although I appreciate the feedback, trivialization or oversimplification is not the intent. Yes, at times they are a tad contrived, but I like these questions because they always work with students. Some examples of options questions I have used include:

- Jacob Riis: Documenting or manipulating the past?
- The Black Power Movement: Was it revolutionary, racist, or reactionary?
- Were the participants in the Chinese Cultural Revolution willing supporters or blind followers?

A key caveat for the option questions is that students are not required to just select one of the options. The intention is not to pigeonhole a historical event or person into one bucket or another. When confronting these types of questions, students can combine, modify, or add other options based on their reading of the evidence. For example, with the Jacob Riis question, students can easily argue that he was manipulating and documenting the past simultaneously. Ultimately, questions organized in this format support the growth of student confidence with making evidence-based arguments about historical events and people and are stepping-stones to more complicated types of questions.

Source-Specific Questions

Source-specific questions allow teachers to set up some sort of straw man to serve as the pivot for an investigation. These types of questions are derived from a historical source that presents a challenge to students, either by the type of source itself or the information provided. Oral history, memoirs, political cartoons, government propaganda, advertisements, old textbooks, and, well, really, just about anything can serve as a stepping-off point for source-specific question-based investigation.

The advertisement depicted in Figure 4.12 touts land available for sale in the post–Civil War American West. Student analysis leads to an understanding that the land, as well as the climate and weather out West, was damned amazing! The source, though, is the launch point for an investigation centered on the question **Settlement of the American West: False advertising?** The investigation leads students to conclusions based on whether you were homesteading or if you took land in the right place at the right time, and its proximity to the railroad. The investigation allows students insight into the complicated and variegated patterns of settlement in the American West.

Figure 4.12. Railroad Advertisement

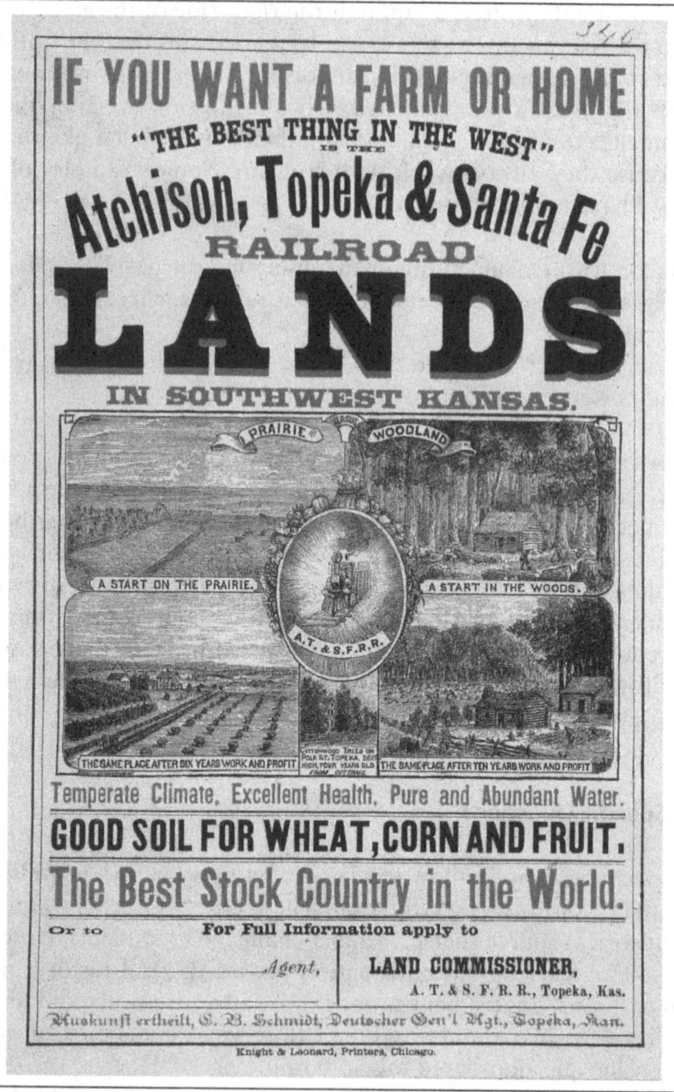

Source: Kansas State Historical Society (https://www.kansasmemory.org/)

Another example of a source-specific investigation would be a photograph I use for exploring busing in the 1970s. The iconic, Pulitzer Prize–winning photograph in Figure 4.13 serves as the launching point for that investigation. I cover the photo, unveil it in sections, and ask students to generate questions about each portion of the image. Students determine the focus of their investigation on three interrelated questions: What led to this

Figure 4.13. The Soiling of Old Glory

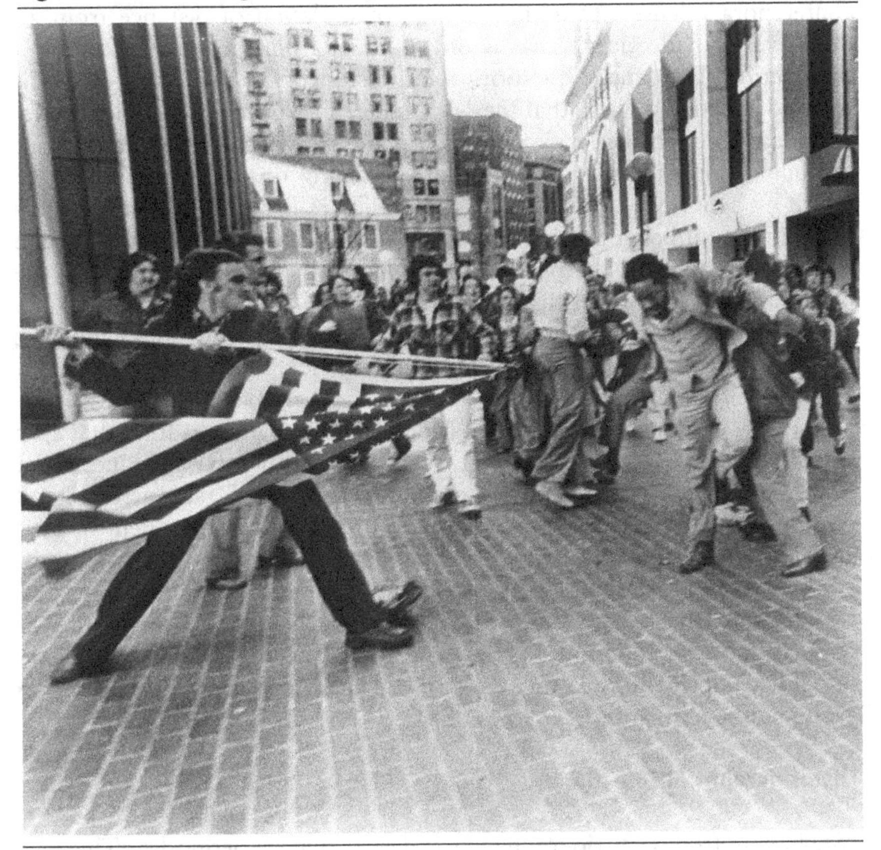

Source: Stanley Forman.

event, what is happening in the picture, and what resulted from the actions? Using a variety of sources, students build the context around the image that helps them understand the impetus for and responses to busing.

In both examples, and other stimulus-based questions, the stimulus itself serves as both a stepping-off point for the investigation and a touchstone to return to as students develop their evidence-based response.

Contextual Questions

A third type of question I have utilized is what I refer to as contextual or empathetic questions. These questions are formulated to reflect problems that people in the past wrestled with during the period when the event occurred or person lived. The intent here is to help students see history through the eyes of the people who were living during that time period (Mandel & Malone,

2008). This is a difficult lift. Students tend to see historical events through contemporary lenses. In addition, the accumulation of distance from an event can provide clarity that is often absent from those living during a time period. Empathetic questions require students to employ both cognitive and affective skills so that they can understand historical people, events, and ideas through the lens of the time period in which they lived and not through a contemporary lens. By understanding the historical context in which an action was taken or a historical figure lived, students can access the source trail being utilized to investigate the central question and make connections between the past and the present by understanding how the past was different. Using historical empathy is a challenge, but it is what makes empathetic questions such rich territory for investigations (Endacott & Brooks, 2013, Harris et al., 2018). Empathetic questions are essential to help students understand an event or person from the perspective of the time period. For example, in my Civil War unit, I have an investigation that asks students to consider: **Was President Abraham Lincoln a tyrant?** Since I hail from Maryland, a state where Lincoln had Democratic leaders arrested and imprisoned at Fort McHenry, the question has resonance. Student investigation into his actions regarding martial law, suspension of habeas corpus, and treatment of "Copperhead" Democrats enables students to understand why he was labeled a tyrant, but also why that may have been more of a political moniker than one steeped in reality. If teachers can avoid overly presentist interpretations, then empathetic questions are a great place to ground an investigation.

Historiographical Questions

"Stay away from historiography—it is deadly with undergrads!" This was advice shared by a history professor one night during dinner while working on a Teaching American History (TAH) grant. Sitting with a younger and older historian sharing advice about teaching, I heard clearly that historiography was best left for actual history majors. Although certainly more challenging than an options or source-specific question, I still think that historiographical questions can be fertile ground in which to plant an investigation, despite remaining a significant challenge (Brown & Hughes, 2018; Fallace & Neem, 2005). Historiography is the study of how and why interpretations of history have changed over time. When engaging in historiographical thinking, students explore how and why historians have constructed divergent or conflicting interpretations of an event or individual from the same evidence, and how new evidence emerged that challenges the interpretation of an event. As a rule of thumb, I do not recommend that teachers wade into really narrow or obscure areas where interpretations have changed, but there are instances when this can be a fruitful opportunity for student investigation. Generally, though, stay broad and attack big topics. Big issues where historical opinion has shifted make the best candidates for these types of questions. Slavery, Reconstruction, imperialism, Andrew Jackson, and the New Deal provide bountiful opportunities to use historiography. A second consideration is to avoid getting into "schools of thought." Students do not need to distinguish progressive historians from psychometric history, from neoconservative or the Annales school. This is what kills these types of questions. Yes, students should understand the context of the historians interpreting the events. But go easy on having kids wade into a Marxist interpretation of the past versus a psychometric view (I am sleepy already!). The Cuban Missile Crisis is one place where I harvest historiography and that can serve as an example of a question influenced by various interpretations of the past.

"Mr. Kennedy . . . You and I Are Like Two Men Pulling on a Rope With a Knot in the Middle—the Harder We Pull, the Tighter the Knot"

We all know the traditional narrative of the Cuban Missile Crisis. President John F. Kennedy established a quarantine around Cuba to block the delivery of missiles and supplies from the Soviet Union. The Soviets demanded that the United States negotiate, and the United States refused. Prior to crossing the quarantine line, the Soviets lost their will and turned around. By "blinking first" when the Soviets turned back, Kennedy's leadership averted a nuclear holocaust. The problem is, as we now know, that the timelines and source trail do not support this narrative. Not only did the Soviet refusal to cross the quarantine line not end the conflict, but there were also more significant events that held the potential to accelerate the crisis to war. There has been a shift in the historiography around this seminal event of the Cold War, and I use that as my entry point into my students' investigation.

After a brief overview of the causes and course of the crisis, my students start their investigation by viewing a short clip from the film *Thirteen Days* (Hardwicke, 2003), which presents the traditional telling of the Cuban Missile Crisis. In this interpretation, President Kennedy is depicted as the calm, cool, and well-informed President who went "eyeball-to-eyeball" with Soviet leader Nikita Khrushchev, and the Soviets "blinked" first (Dobbs, 2009). After viewing the clip, students are asked to list how President Kennedy is depicted. Their descriptions usually fit into the categories illustrated in Figure 4.14.

Students then confront the question: **Did Russia blink first, or is that a myth?** The source trail for this investigation is the timeline in Figure 4.15, based on the work of Michael Dobbs's "Myths of the Missile Crisis" (2008) and *One Minute to Midnight* (2009). Students can either place the icon next to events that either support or challenge the traditional depiction of events, or they can take notes and add specific information to the chart in Figure 4.14e. This sort of scaffolding is essential to help students when they are wrestling with historiographical questions (Swafford, 2022).

Figure 4.14. Cuban Missile Crisis Organizer

Statement	Icon	Myth, Because . . .	Fact, Because . . .
Eyeball to eyeball			
We Knew the facts			
We were fully in control			
We did not negotiate			

After reviewing the events that defined the crisis, students then return to the question: **Did Russia blink first, or is that a myth?** Discussion of the events of the Cuban Missile Crisis makes it clear that there was no moment of Russia blinking. We then explore why and how the telling of the Cuban Missile Crisis has changed over time based on political advantage and expanded access to new documents.

Understanding that our interpretations of history change as more documents become available and/or the initial political and journalistic telling of an event are replaced by more evidence-informed historical narratives is one way to move students toward understanding how historiography works. To gain this understanding, students do not always have to read a series of historians' views, categorize them by school of thought, and then discuss the evolution of the interpretations. In fact, I would generally say NEVER take that approach, but students can use contrasting interpretations to begin to appreciate the idea of historiography and understand that our understanding of history evolves as new evidence, new questions, and new perspectives are introduced.

Figure 4.15. Cuban Missile Crisis Timeline

October 14	• U-2 spy plane detects missile construction in Cuba
October 15	• Pictures analyzed by the CIA, findings reported to President Kennedy
October 16	• President convenes ExComm to discuss options • United Nations Secretary Adlai Stevenson and Kennedy disagree on the missile swap. Kennedy wanted to hold the swap in reserve, while Stevenson desired to put it on the negotiating table from the beginning
October 20	• Kennedy decides on a quarantine of Cuba • Defense Secretary Robert McNamara tells JFK that there were 6,000 to 8,000 Soviet "technicians" in Cuba. In fact, there were 43,000 heavily armed Soviet troops on the island at this point who possessed functioning tactical nuclear weapons.
October 22	• The American people, Soviet Union, and the world are notified about missile construction and American quarantine by a televised Presidential address
October 23	• Soviet Premier Khrushchev blasts quarantine as a violation of international law
October 24	• Soviets conduct rehearsals for missile launches • Khrushchev decides to turn back Soviet ships heading to Cuba • Quarantine begins by American forces fearing the arrival of the Cuban convoy • United States defense forces raised to DEFCON 2: » 24-hour alert for all military » All military leaves canceled » 1/8th of all B-52 bombers airborne at all times » Bombers placed on alert and on runways ready to take off » 90 missile silos uncovered and placed on ready
October 25	• Undercover CIA Invasion of Cuba fails • 500 miles from the quarantine line, Soviet ships turn back from Cuba • Missile construction continues in Cuba • Soviet troops set up to invade American naval base at Guantanamo Bay
October 26	• Khrushchev writes Kennedy stating that he will remove the missiles from Cuba if he promises not to invade Cuba • Soviets deployed nuclear cruise missiles to within 15 miles of the Guantanamo naval base • The United States allows two Soviet ships, the *Vinnitsa* and the *Bucharest*, to pass unmolested through the quarantine line

(*continued*)

Figure 4.15. (*continued*)

	• The *USS Beale* tracks and drops signaling depth charges on the *B-59*, a Soviet submarine that, unknown to the U.S., was armed with a 15-kiloton nuclear torpedo. Running out of air, the Soviet submarine was surrounded by American warships and desperately needed to surface. An argument broke out among three officers on the *B-59*. An exhausted Soviet captain became furious and ordered that the nuclear torpedo on board be made combat-ready. Cooler heads prevailed, and the submarine surfaced and surrendered. • The Soviets deployed nuclear cruise missiles to within 15 miles of the Guantanamo naval base on the night of 26–27 October. The Soviets had sent 80 14-kiloton cruise missile warheads (roughly the size of the bomb that destroyed Hiroshima) to Cuba for local battlefield use.
October 27	• The United States tries to find the *Grozny*, a Soviet ship approaching the quarantine line • Four Soviet submarines, two inside the quarantine line and two just outside, were located by the U.S. Navy • The Soviet Union detonates an atomic bomb in a Siberian test • The U.S. detonates an atomic bomb over a Pacific Ocean test site • U-2 spy plane shot down over Cuba • U2 pilot Captain Charles Maultsby accidently flies over the Soviet Union while on a mission to the North Pole to monitor Soviet nuclear tests, spending 74 minutes in Soviet air space, causing the Russians to scramble half a dozen fighter jets in response. The Air Force fails to inform the President of what had happened until half an hour after he left Soviet air space. • Khrushchev writes Kennedy again, demanding the removal of U.S. missiles from Turkey • U.S. spy plane shot down over Cuba • Attorney General Robert F. Kennedy meets with the Soviet ambassador and reveals that the United States missiles in Turkey are outdated and plans had been made to remove them, but they would deny this if the Soviets made their removal part of the agreement. • President Kennedy only responds to Khrushchev's letter of October 26th, ignoring the letter of the 27th
October 28	• At 6:30 a.m. the Soviet ship *Grozny* stops just short of the quarantine line and turns around • Khrushchev orders the missiles in Cuba to be "crated and returned"
April 1963	• United States begins dismantling and removing Jupiter-class nuclear weapons in Turkey

Source: Michael Dobbs, "Myths of the Missile Crisis" (BBC), and *One Minute to Midnight*

Check Out Receipt

Northeast
https://www.lfpl.org

Monday, October 13, 2025 3:03:14 PM
96286

Title: Developing historical thinkers : supporti
ng historical inquiry for all students
Material: Book
Due: 11/3/2025

Title: The milepost : all-the-North travel guide
. 2025.
Material: Book
Due: 11/3/2025

Total items: 2

You just saved $83.21 by using your library.
Since 2021, you have saved $1,336.19.

The Louisville Free Public Library supports educ
ation and lifelong learning at our 17 locations
and online at www.lfpl.org.

946

IT IS ITERATIVE AND RECURSIVE AND FRUSTRATING (BUT ALSO EXCITING)!

An effective investigative question, be it lesson-level or unit-level, is "a moving target" (Mueller, 2016, 2017a, 2017b, 2017c, 2018). They are frustrating, challenging, maddening, and rewarding all at the same time. Unfortunately, they are also time-consuming. Developing a good question takes time. This is not pulling down a worksheet to accompany the book or designing a graphic organizer to assist students with note-taking, because, as Rebecca Mueller (2017b) reminds us, ". . . teachers may have a sense of where they are headed but become disoriented along the way." There is rarely a straight path to a great question.

In an effort to map the process of developing a question for an investigation, I took notes during the development process. Outlined in Figure 4.16 below is the cognitive path I undertook.

Ultimately the path begins with a curriculum guide or a set of state standards and the identification of what needs to be taught, or it could start with a singular historical source. Sometimes it is with a question that you want to

Figure 4.16. Question Development Map

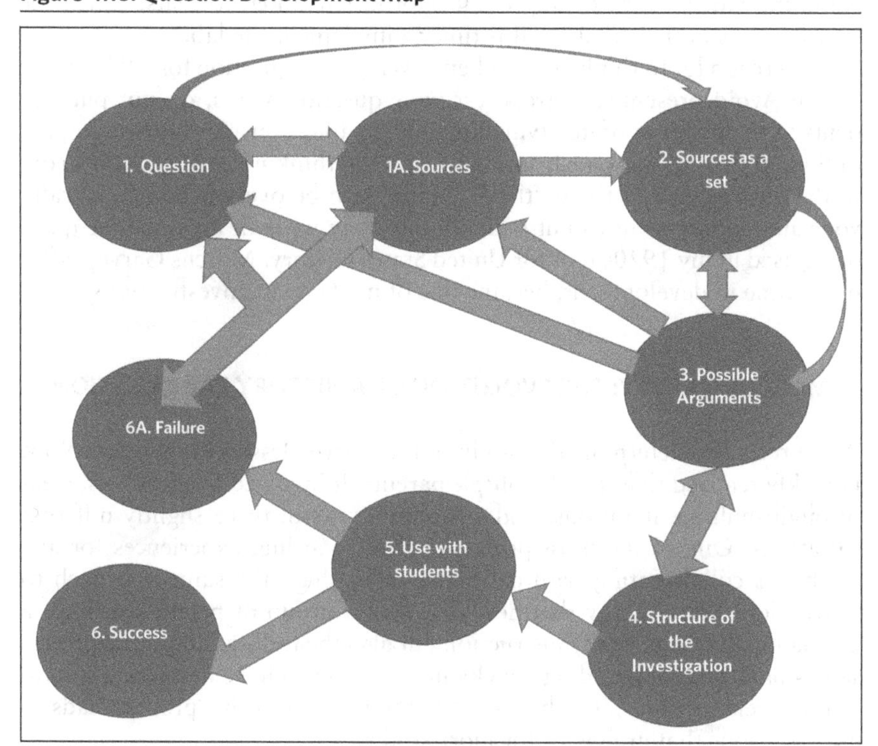

explore, and oftentimes you move back and forth among the topic, the question, and possible sources as you revise, and re-revise the investigative question. Sometimes you start with the sources and then develop the question and move back to replacing other sources. Regardless of the exact starting point, the initial stages of question development are the most challenging.

Beyond Step 3 in the diagram, teachers must determine if the path they are sending students on for the investigation can lead to a fruitful end. Stress testing, as Swann, Lee, and Grant refer to it, occurs in Step 4 when teachers must assess if students can develop legitimately different answers to the overarching question from the sources provided (2018a). Since an inquiry must lead students to constructing an argument centered on an unsettled question, it can only be effective if it can lead students to several evidence-based answers. Stress testing the question ensures that the questions and sources work well together. If there is only one answer to the proposed question, or there is not much that is debatable, then you are headed back to revise the question and alter the universe of sources utilized.

Once the question arrives in a satisfactory form and the sources are selected, teachers must then decide the organizational structure for the lab. There are a multitude of options for structuring an investigation. Investigations could be in the form of a jigsaw, a trial, a hearing, a gallery walk, individual work or any number of instructional formats. When the structure has been settled on, it is time to implement the lab.

There is a lot to think about when developing a question for a 90-minute lesion: Avoid presentism, stress test your question stems, do not put students in the position of justifying the unjustifiable, consider historiography, options-style questions, or fronting a historical thinking concept, and so on. In the abstract, all of these "think abouts" can be overwhelming. To calm your anxieties, I want to put them all into play with an investigative question I used in my 1920s unit for United States History. Marcus Garvey, after much time in development, became one of my favorite investigations.

MARCUS GARVEY: THE EVOLUTION OF A HISTORY LAB QUESTION

When trying to determine the origin of the Garvey lesson I highlight below, I quickly realized that it had multiple parents. It involved five teachers, went through multiple iterations, and currently exists in three slightly different variations. One of the most professionally rewarding experiences for any teacher is collaborating with colleagues who share the same approach to instruction. The synergy that develops with a group of people can have a lasting impact on not only instruction but also the feelings about the profession. I have been astoundingly lucky in my career to have developed several of these relationships. The back-and-forth inherent in this process leads to investigations that are better for more students.

Figure 4.17. Marcus Garvey

Source: Library of Congress.

The need for this investigation was driven by the fact that Garvey always appeared on the county-wide final examination. In addition, we saw a significant gap in the weaving of the African American story into the greater narrative arc of American history. The African American experience between the rise of Jim Crow and the emergence of the post-Brown Civil Rights Movement was not addressed very well. African American history was explored either through the window of Jim Crow oppression or through efforts to escape segregation via the Great Migration. Garvey became a unique window into both the 1920s and the evolution of the African American experience.

The question formation for this History Lab, outlined below in Figure 4.18, began with a listing of questions on what we wanted to know about Garvey. Most of these questions establish the background information that would need to be understood before a significant investigation of Garvey could take place.

These types of questions served as an important reminder for the background information students would need before they could adequately dive into the Garvey investigation. Unfortunately, but not surprisingly, these early questions left us with a list of content but certainly not anything worth investigating. What followed, as illustrated in Figure 4.19, was the generation of higher-level questions that revolved around significance. In addition, the questions began to play with some ways to frame Garvey's actions.

The evolution of the Marcus Garvey question is a perfect example of how wading through the sources leads to looping back and revising the question. Our initial question, **Marcus Garvey: Racial Visionary or Enemy of the State?**, led us to the relationship between Garvey and the Ku Klux Klan. This led to the discovery of an article penned by W. E. B. Du Bois in *The Crisis* magazine where he asked whether Garvey was a "lunatic or a traitor" (Huggins, 1986). With that source, we headed back to the question to tweak it in a new direction. The ultimate ending point for the question was not actually authored by us but instead Du Bois (so much for all of that work!). In 1924, Du Bois, reflecting on Garvey's meeting with the leadership of the Ku Klux Klan, stated that Garvey was the "most dangerous enemy of the

Figure 4.18. Evolution of Marcus Garvey Investigative Question, Part 1

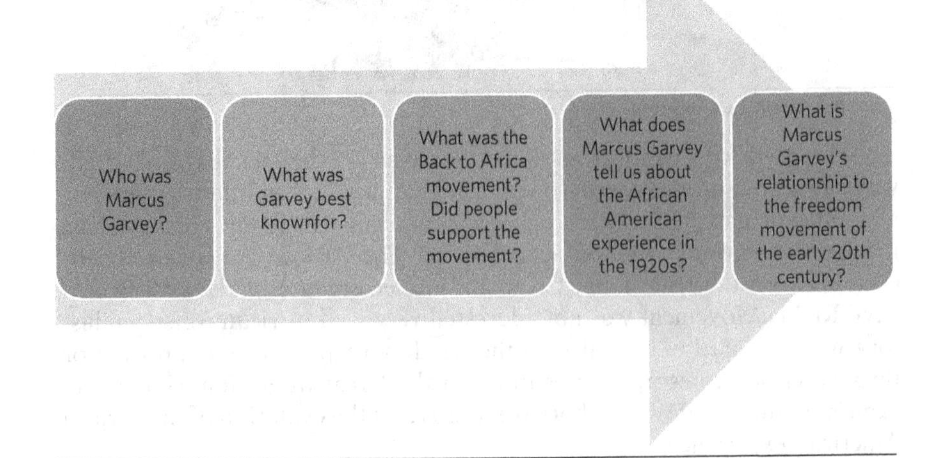

Figure 4.19. Evolution of Marcus Garvey Investigative Question, Part 2

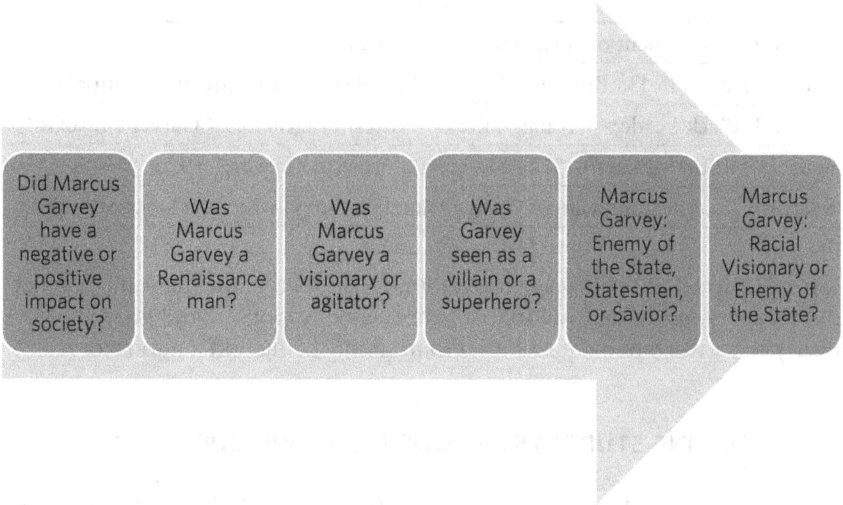

Did Marcus Garvey have a negative or positive impact on society?	Was Marcus Garvey a Renaissance man?	Was Marcus Garvey a visionary or agitator?	Was Garvey seen as a villain or a superhero?	Marcus Garvey: Enemy of the State, Statesmen, or Savior?	Marcus Garvey: Racial Visionary or Enemy of the State?

Negro Race in America and the world." And there it was. The question was provocative, focused, and contextually relevant.

Was Marcus Garvey the "most dangerous enemy of the Negro Race in America"?

We settled on this version of the question because it opened Garvey and his efforts to a full examination. In addition, the fact that Du Bois asked the question about Garvey has significant impact on how students substantiate their response to the question. When we stress tested the question against the sources, it held up well and allowed students to develop and support several evidence-based responses to the overarching question.

The subsequent investigation allows students insight into the career and eventual deportation of Marcus Garvey. Through the sources identified in Figure 4.20 below, students discover the efforts of the United States Department of Justice to undermine and discredit Garvey, as well as both the passionate support of his followers and the antipathy of the mainstream elements of the early 20th-century freedom movement.

Students are drawn into the racial politics of the 1920s and can see a continuum from Booker T. Washington to W. E. B. Du Bois through Garvey and eventually to Malcolm X and Martin Luther King Jr. The investigation always generates great discussion and debate and has served all of us well over the

Figure 4.20. Marcus Garvey Sources

Source
Source 1: Department of Justice secret document
Source 2: W. E. B. Du Bois, *The Crisis,* May 1924, "A Lunatic or a Traitor"
Source 3: Black Leaders Writing to the U.S. Attorney-General—"Garvey Must Go"
Source 4: Robert Bagnall, "The Madness of Marcus Garvey," 1923
Source 5: Excerpt from Marcus Garvey's autobiography, written in September 1923

years. The heart of the investigation, though, is found in the question. It generates curiosity, promotes multiple evidence-based responses, and gives students agency to investigate the past rather than simply being told a good story.

HAVING STUDENTS DEVELOP THEIR OWN QUESTIONS

All the discussion above is predicated on the teacher designing the question that structures an investigation. Although student development of compelling questions has been a significant push since the advent of the Common Core literacy standards, due to the demands of time, content coverage, and other extraneous factors that can impact instructional time, teacher-designed questions are the more frequent path to question development. Teacher-designed questions shift the time spent with students developing questions to students wrestling with the question. This saves time over the course of a semester or year. Ultimately, teacher-developed questions need to be viewed as the first step in the gradual release of responsibility from teacher to student.

The work of the Right Question Institute (RQI) is the strongest tool currently available to foster student development of inquiry questions (Melville & Minigan, 2018; Minigan & Beer, 2017; Minigan et al., 2017; Rothstein & Santana, 2012). Initially developed to empower communities that were disaffected from communicating with government, it has found a home within the education community. The approach dovetails nicely with inquiry, historical investigation, and phenomena-based science instruction. To develop their own questions, the RQI process teaches students to utilize the Question Formulation Technique (QFT). QFT asks students to do the following:

- Generate as many questions as possible about an image, writing, song, or other initial stimulus.
- Do not judge or evaluate anyone's questions.
- Change statements into questions.
- Identify and label questions as open-ended or close-ended.
- Change close-ended questions into open-ended ones.
- Prioritize questions.

With the questions prioritized, students then seek resources to support an evidence-based response to the question.

Periodically I employed a modified version of this process. I do not use the full process because of the previously stated concerns about time and coverage. An additional issue is with the step after the student formulation of a question. If students generate the questions, it makes it superdifficult to select the source set to support their research. Therefore, the default is to have the students move from the question formulation to their own research. On its surface, you think, of course, that's what historians do! The problem is time. Students heading online or to the library to select sources eat up classroom time. Then there is the need to narrow down the sources and separate the legitimate sources from Internet garbage. By the time you realize it, you are a week into a topic that does not merit that much time. In addition, the student-created questions have a greater chance of leading to undebatable questions than do teacher-developed ones (Minigan & Beer, 2017). I simply cannot afford more than one or two of these deep-end inquiry experiences per year.

The analogy I use to explain how I justify the use of more teacher-designed questions than student ones is that of the historian and the archivist. An historian who has developed a research question heads to an archive, but the historian does not start on the first floor and start reading everything until she arrives at the top floor. Instead, they rely on the archivist, who has a strong understanding of the sources available and can select and suggest sources for the historian to utilize. In the classroom, the teacher assumes the role of the archivist so that time is used efficiently.

This sounds like I am poo-pooing real inquiry, research, and the kind of civic online reasoning skills that are so essential to success in today's information-rich environment. In a perfect world, I would want this format all the time, but the reality is that teachers live in highly structured environments. We must comply with pacing guides, assessment, and accountability demands. These demands do not allow time for even infrequent meanderings into the deep end of inquiry. As a result, I graft the QFT into my lesson-level inquiry approach. That said, the development of questions is an important skill for students to develop, and by selecting the initial stimulus material, it is possible for a teacher to turn over to the students the development of the question and still preselect the sources to support their investigation. As the school year progresses and my students' abilities grow, student-driven question creation can serve as a pathway to more authentic inquiry and set the stage for the ultimate inquiry: student research projects.

Dust Bowl Migrants

A part of Dorothea Lange's work as a photographer for the Resettlement Administration during the Great Depression, the image in Figure 4.21, is my stepping-off point for a look into the Dust Bowl migration. It also serves as

Figure 4.21. Dust Bowl Migrants

Source: Library of Congress

an example of how I can graft the QFT to the need for shorter, lesson-level inquires. I initiate the lesson by asking students to examine the image and generate a list of the questions they have. Students then move into pairs and then small groups to share and prioritize their questions. Next, we generate a class list of potential questions. Student-generated questions include:

- When did this happen?
- Where did it happen?
- Who is she?
- Where is she going?
- Where did she come from?
- Why does she have all her stuff with her?
- Is it just her and the baby?
- Why is she dressed so nicely?
- What happened?

Eventually the student/class-generated question for this investigation is some variation of:

Where Is She From and Where Is She Going?

The question sets up students to investigate a range of sources and develop a contextual chronology around the image. Forming the question empowers students and gives them a greater stake in the investigation because it is their own curiosity that is being satisfied as they mine historical sources.

Ultimately, for students to become proficient in the development of meaty questions to investigate, teachers must first develop the same capacity and model these types of questions for students. Exposed to investigations driven by good questions, students will eventually be able to be released to develop their own questions. This will pay great dividends as they take on individual research.

CONCLUSION

"My students cannot do this" is not the appropriate concern when it comes to question formulation. Instead, the anxiety surrounding this aspect of historical investigations is on teachers. Developing good questions is time-consuming and cognitively exhausting, but by the same token, it is exciting, rewarding, and revitalizes our love for our discipline. I hope that this chapter fills in a significant gap that existed in the first book and helps promote confidence on the part of teachers seeking to have students investigate questions about the past. Alas, although there is no database of questions or magic algorithm that generates them, there are many tools that teachers and curriculum supervisors can utilize to move away from history as an aggregation of answers to the study of questions that provide a reason to learn the content about the past. The most important thing to remember is that not having students investigate the past through the lens of a question is more detrimental than having them investigate through an imperfect question that may need revision.

CHAPTER 5

"Discussion Is for Classes Like Foreign Language"

Expanding Discussion in the Classroom to Deepen Student Facility With Historical Thinking

We don't discuss in this class. That is more for a class like foreign language.

—My Son's Advanced Placement United States History Teacher

During a parent–teacher conference I inquired about whether my son was engaging in discussion and was making thoughtful, fact-based contributions, tuning out, or acting the class clown. To my shock, which I know I did not hide well, my son's Advanced Placement United States History teacher informed my wife and me that "discussion was not something that occurred in history class." Yup, none. Zip. Zero. Nada.

In defense of the teacher, when you force a course like Advanced Placement United States History into a single semester, lots of good instructional practices get thrown overboard in deference to the demands of coverage and the cudgel of accountability, but really, no debate or discussion at all—none?!! I was speechless but was reminded of one of my favorite cartoons, which depicts a teacher addressing a classroom of students by saying, "This class will stimulate your ideas and thoughts. And remember—no talking."

Historians argue perpetually. Generally, that discourse is conducted through their writing or lectures, but if you are an attractive historian, you can go on PBS and make an argument! Whatever the format, discussion is a key disciplinary skill for history and social studies because the heart of the discipline is the collision of evidence-based interpretations (Hess, 2004a, 2004b). The discussions that take place in the context of a historical investigation range from informal and unassessed to formal and assessed. Structured academic discourse allows students to explore the question, interrogate the evidence, develop an answer to the overarching historical question, defend their answer orally, and serve as a form of pre-writing. Discussion is an essential element when engaging students in the process of investigating history and cannot be removed from the pedagogical tools employed in the classroom.

Some of my strongest memories of students are centered on class discussions. I have fond recollections of debates over how to end the war in the Pacific, mock congressional hearings on post–World War II espionage, mock Supreme Court hearings on the civil liberties cases during World War I, and numerous one-on-one paired debates where students represented opposing historical figures. Various discussion formats allow students to emerge as leaders, for their personalities to shine, for humor and relationship-building, and for the teacher to hear students interacting with content and engage in formative assessment. With discussion, there is no need to wait to read a student's paragraph or grade a student's test. Instead, be it partner, small-group, or large-group conversations, classroom discussion enabled my students to engage one another daily in the content of my course, and I was able to listen. Sometimes I am listening intently to provide feedback, sometimes just to ensure the line of conversation is relevant, and sometimes I just sit back and let the words flow. Unlike my son's teacher, I have always found conversation to be one of the essential components of my instructional approach. Conversation, a tool so essential to our humanity, must be part of instruction, especially in a history class, and even more so in one that intentionally has students confronting the past through the lens of questions.

When I share the history lab process with preservice and practicing teachers, I am often hit with the refrain, "My kids cannot do this." When I ask why, these teachers often identify the fact that their students do not like to talk about content-related topics in class. Kids not liking to talk about content-related topics in class, I get that, and although some would prefer to listen or engage in another task, many students do love to talk if the topic is compelling, the environment is a safe space that encourages discussion, and they are taught how to be effective in discussions.

My intention in this chapter is to explore how to infuse substantive academic discourse into instruction so that we teachers can grow student comfort and capacity for content-focused conversation. I will use the Pullman strike of 1894 as a case study for the healthy integration of a variety of discussion formats and strategies into historical investigations.

PLEASE, NOT ANOTHER STRIKE!

Anyone who has taught United States History with me knows that I have a deep affinity for the period from the end of the Civil War to the Great Depression. Within 50 years, industrial growth catapulted the United States from a second-tier power of Germany and England to the economic engine of the world. In particular, the evolving relations between capital and labor during this period fascinate me. The contested space that was the factory floor, steel mill, coal mine, or assembly line challenged the relationship between capitalism and the Constitution, and if there is a strike that occurred, I have a lesson for it! The rail strike of 1877, Pullman, Haymarket, Homestead, Ludlow, Bread and Roses, the Flint Sitdown Strike of 1936 . . . I have one for each of them. This fetish for capital–labor conflict forced me to have to pick one strike that could be used as a window into the issues of the time period. My final choice was usually the Pullman strike of 1894 (and sometimes a few others if I had the time and my peers were not looking!).

It is important for students to understand where the labor movement in the United States came from, how it impacted the economic growth in the late 19th and early 20th centuries, and how it significantly expanded the size of the middle class. With the American labor movement now in significant decline and generally seen as an impediment to economic growth, students have at best little knowledge about how unions function, and at worst a sense that labor is a tool that is more negative than positive. Textbooks often downplay or make invisible the significant role played by labor. Historical perspective is important for students to develop so that they can understand the evolution of the labor movement as a force in 20th-century American history and appreciate how its decline has impacted American life in the late 20th and early 21st centuries (Cole, 2011).

But what is debatable about the Pullman strike? We know it occurred, we know when it occurred, we know how it was resolved. These are all facts surrounding this important event, and there is not anything debatable about facts. It is not the events of the Pullman strike, which are neither contested by historians, nor on the surface much different than any other Gilded Age strike that make it such a wonderful opportunity for discussion. Instead, it is the way in which causality and perspective collide around Pullman and Debs that makes this a worthy exemplar to highlight in the chapter. George Pullman, his eponymous town, and the Debs-promoted strike that occurred there in 1894 present a fantastic forum for fostering "intentionally planned talk" about the contested relationship between capital, represented by George Pullman, and labor, symbolized by Eugene Debs (Larson, 2022).

My interest in Pullman stemmed from the famous cartoon displayed in Figure 5.1. The image displays Eugene Debs as the sole destroyer of commerce. Clearly the cartoonist was taking a position relative to the relationship between capital and labor. There was a story here and, as I discovered, a rich one that historians still debate.

Before I use the Pullman strike as a case study on how to infuse discussion into inquiries, we need to consider what we know about discussion as a pedagogical strategy and explore some tools to increase its effective use in the classroom.

Figure 5.1. King Debs

Source: Image by W. A. Rogers from Library of Congress (https://www.loc.gov/item/92515992/)

NOT GOING TO DO IT

Sadly, there is a plethora of reasons not to conduct classroom discussions, from the use of faulty analogies by students, to the dissemination of false information, to dominant voices drowning out the quieter ones. During professional development sessions I have conducted, preservice and practicing teachers have offered other potential barriers to legitimate academic discourse:

- Kids are reluctant to participate either due to shyness, lack of trust in how their peers will react, or being uncomfortable with their understanding of the content.
- Opinions often rule over facts.
- Discussions are assessed in a very visible arena, raising student anxiety.
- Students do not complete the preparatory work needed to participate from a position of knowledge.
- A small group of students often monopolize the conversation.

- Students' background knowledge is limited and thus limits the depth of the discussion.
- Time to teach required content is limited and thus discussion can knock teachers off their coverage calendar.
- Discussions can devolve into shouting matches.
- Discussions can range into topics that are too controversial and thus lead to parent complaints to administrators.
- Students offering misinformation can promote misunderstandings about content.
- You just don't know what students are going to say!

Inadequate training, the need to maintain control, combined with the teacher holding low expectations of students' cognitive or social abilities, also emerge as reasons that militate against the implementation of discussion in most social studies classrooms (McAvoy & Hess, 2014). Although each of these explanations is rooted in practical classroom experience, none of them are insurmountable, nor do they offset the deleterious effects of teacher-driven, discussionless classrooms. Yes, teaching discussion is a difficult task, and that may explain why it is so hard to find in classrooms (Dillon, 1994; Larson, 2000, 2022; Parker & Hess, 2001), but the benefits are so significant for student engagement, motivation, and learning that everyone should incorporate discussion into their instructional repertoire.

Unfortunately, substantive and sustained discussion in the social studies classroom is hard to find. Research consistently indicates that there is little to no discussion taking place in most classrooms (Cazden, 2001; Hess, 2004a, 2009a, 2009b; Nystrand et al., 2003; Saye & SSIRC, 2013). During classroom instruction, only 10% of instructional time involves student discussion (Nystrand et al., 2003). The majority of what is labeled as discussion in the classroom is actually recitation, where students answer teacher questions and the teacher provides feedback (Wilen, 2004). Where discussion does occur, it is dominated by teacher talk, as "teachers talk between 70 and 80 percent of class time" (Hattie, 2012, p. 80), and teacher talk increases as the students' age level rises and as the class size decreases. The bottom line is that what is called discussion in classrooms is often a game of chicken. Teachers ask a question, then patiently wait for a student response. Absent a response, the teacher answers their own question and then asks another question. This one is answered by one student and then the process restarts. Rarely does discussion involve students responding to one another, with the teacher retreating to the edge of the conversation (Hess, 2004a, 2004b). The trend toward limited student discussion has implications for the achievement gap.

In classrooms with higher numbers of students living in poverty, teachers talk more and students talk less (Gamoran & Nystrand, 1992; Lingard et al., 2003). Teachers of high-achieving students spend 55% of class time talking, compared to 80% for teachers of low-achieving students (Flanders, 1970). Student engagement is also higher when teachers talk less, and this is especially true for at-risk students. In a nutshell, the substantial academic benefits of a consistent and substantive use of classroom discussion far outweigh the costs.

LET'S TALK

An essential component of building preservice and practicing teacher capacity for investigating history is breaking the trends around discussion that define most history classrooms. The justification for doing so are many. Promoting consistent, student-driven, and content-rich discussion teaches "students how to articulate their understandings of a question, explain their arguments, listen to others think through the same question, and challenge others' responses" (Hess, 2004a, 2004b). Perhaps the most significant reason to include discussion is the simple fact that it leads to increased student achievement (Hess & Posselt, 2002; Nystrand et al., 1998).

Besides simply being a highly effective instructional strategy to promote deep learning, many of the benefits of infusing discussion into the classroom are civics-based (Hattie et al., 2020). Discussion of controversial issues is a significant predictor of civic knowledge, support for democratic values, participation in political discussion, and political engagement, while students regularly report that discussions in classrooms increase their interest, engagement, and understanding (Andolina et al., 2003; Engle & Conant, 2002; Hess, 2009a, 2009b; Levinson, 2012; Nystrand et al., 1997). Political tolerance, growth of knowledge about issues, and increasing the likelihood of engaging in political conversations are all direct benefits of structured discussion of controversial issues (Avery, 2002a, 2002b; Avery et al., 2013; Knowles & McCafferty-Wright, 2015). Both small- and large-group discussions can promote the development of historical empathy (Ashby & Lee, 1987; Bartelds et al., 2020; Brooks, 2011; Doppen, 2000; Harris et al., 2018; Kohlmeier, 2006; Lee & Shemilt, 2011; Wilschut & Schiphorst, 2019). So, yes, teachers have practical and pragmatic concerns about using discussion as an instructional tool in the classroom. The bottom line, though, is that none of these factors is insurmountable. The benefits far outweigh the costs.

IT IS NOT JUST DEBATES

As a new teacher, the terms *debate* and *discussion* immediately made me think of the most formal (and time-consuming) versions. Formal debates with opening and closing statements, rebuttals, and so on were what I thought I needed to be facilitating. Sure, there is a place for these types of activities, but right out of the gate in my career, or even at the start of a school year, this is not the best route to integrating discussion into the classroom successfully. As my career progressed, I completely moved away from that structure and never returned. I found the highly structured debates to be too formal, too time-consuming, and less engaging for students than other discussion structures that I borrowed from other teachers. Instead of thinking you need to re-create a scene from *The Great Debaters*, it is more productive to consider discussion as a menu of options: each effective given your goals, time demands, and content being discussed. By moving from the definition of discussion as a classical debate and instead into one that focuses on students engaging students through the content, then you will have more success, greater engagement, and fewer headaches.

There is a plethora of structures to facilitate discussion, and teachers should seek to use a variety of structures rather than just the same structure over and over again (Russsell & Byford, 2009). In Figure 5.2, I present nine options that demonstrate the range of discussion from one-on-one to full class.

"I DON'T FEEL COMFORTABLE"

"Please come see me during your planning period." These words in an email from a principal are never an indication that something good has happened. Too frequently it means a parent has called to register a complaint, but the concern over parent complaints and moving onto an administrator's radar is the single biggest deterrent to classroom discussion. I have had my share of phone calls and administrative conversations. What I discovered as a result of conversation with both parents and administrators is that they both want to ensure all voices are heard, all sides are represented in classroom discussions, and students are not attacking one another for their viewpoints. These conversations always reminded me that the culture of my classroom went a long way to ensuring that students were comfortable and parent phone calls did not happen.

Sitting and listening or taking notes during a lecture, answering questions while watching a film, completing a worksheet while reading a textbook—all of these activities have one thing in common: Student anxiety is low. Students are not worried about saying the wrong thing, not knowing the answer, or the myriad other concerns that manifest themselves when some kids hear that they are going to be discussing a topic. A classroom that does not create an atmosphere that anticipates these

Figure 5.2. Classroom Discussion Formats

Technique	Description	Benefits
Think-Pair-Share	This is the most basic conversation format. Students are asked to think about a question, image, reading, excerpt, or other stimulus, and then discuss their thoughts with a neighbor.	Requires students to think before they respond; because of the low stakes and low visibility of the conversation, it increases the likelihood of student participation.
Read-Write-Pair-Share	A derivation of think-pair-share. The process starts with a common reading, a quick-write to help students think through what they read, and then the pairing and sharing.	Helps students who may struggle with a reading to organize their thoughts in writing prior to discussion and then to unpack their thoughts when discussing it in a low-stakes, low-visibility setting.
Paired Debate	Students are assigned a role, person, source, or side different from their partner. Pairs prepare for the conversation by reading materials from a different perspective than their partner's. Then students engage in a one-on-one discussion. Students must maintain their role/side/person/source and may not interrupt the other person. Each stage is timed so that each side gets 60–90 seconds to address the question provided by the teacher.	The low stakes and low visibility of the conversation increase the likelihood of student participation. Because students are representing a role, person, or side, they feel more confident because it is not "their ideas" they must verbally articulate. In addition, the short duration of each round of the conversation reduces student concerns over filling a large amount of time with conversation.
Four Corners	The discussion portion of this format can occur in a number of ways. The premise is that students confront a question, consider four (or more responses), and then either move their bodies to the corner that represents a response or hang a sign with their name in that corner. The students can either discuss their answer choice with the classmates in the corner (in pairs, triples, or small groups), or the teacher can facilitate a discussion. Students should switch corners if someone presents an idea that causes a change of mind.	The visual representation of opinions allows the teacher to quickly see where every student is on the question at hand. It also ensures that every student has at least thought about the question because either their body or their name tag has to be placed in one of the corners. The format encourages student-to-student interaction.

Technique	Description	Benefits
Continuum/ Philosophical Chairs	Students confront an overarching question and are asked to represent their thoughts about the answer along a spectrum. Students place a Post-it with their name along the spectrum where it best represents their response. Then students can ask other students: Why did you place your name there; What evidence supports your argument, and so on.	The visual representation of opinions allows the teacher to see quickly where every student is on the question at hand. It also ensures that every student has at least thought about the question. The format encourages student-to-student interaction.
Small Group	Students discuss the question at hand in groups ranging from 3 to 8.	This allows for some visibility for students but not as much as a full-class discussion. Allows students to hear their peers and provides more opportunities for all students to participate. If the groups increase (3, then 5, then 7), students can carry ideas from the smaller groups into the larger ones.
Inside-Outside Circle	Students take turns either participating in the discussion or listening, and either taking notes or writing feedback for their partner on the inside circle. At a set time, the inside circle becomes the outside circle, and the outside the in.	This format increases the number of students who can participate because the size of the full group is half the full class.
Structured Academic Controversy	Students work in pairs to understand one side of a topic, then debate with another pair that researched the opposing side. Groups then switch sides, conduct more research, and debate from the opposing position.	Encourages students to gain an understanding of both sides of an issue.
Full Group: Simulations, Trials, Congressional Hearings, Socratic Seminars, Café Conversations	These structures require the most preparation on the part of both teachers and students and have the highest degree of visibility for students when participating, and often the highest stakes in terms of accountability. The distinctiveness of each format is less important here than the fact that all students are involved in the conversation.	If run well, the main benefit is that the teacher can remove oneself and allow the discussion to flow organically.

legitimate worries carried by many students will be unable to promote substantive discussion.

To ensure a reduction in student anxiety, teachers must build a classroom culture that promotes civil academic discourse. This foundation must be well-established before a discussion occurs. Setting groundwork can be difficult, as the teacher is often pushing back against cultural norms that reward the loudest and most obnoxious voices over the most reasoned and polite. From Jerry Springer to *Crossfire*, *Hannity* to Rachel Maddow and the nightly assault of numerous cable political shows, students see discourse that generates ratings but is not productive for learning.

Instead of a free-for-all, students should have some clear baseline for what you expect during discussions. One of the best tools for communicating the culture that you desire to create is to videotape students in the previous year's or semester's class having a productive discussion. As students evaluate the short video clip, seeing their peers helps to personalize the message and solidify the expectations you have for a culture that supports positive and civil discussion. This visual representation is also complemented by sharing specific expectations for student–student interaction. I have found that the fewer number of "rules" presented, the greater the chance of students internalizing them. The guidelines that I establish are ones that undergird my overall classroom climate:

- Do not interrupt someone until they have finished speaking.
- Shoot the message, not the messenger.
- Listen actively while not actively talking.

Regardless of the rules I impose, my actions as a teacher have the greatest impact on establishing a classroom culture that promotes discussion. If I make fun of student comments, am dismissive, or allow other students to be rude when peers respond, then the rules will not matter. Students look to the teacher to set the expectations. Eighty percent of students reported that they would speak less in a classroom discussion if they felt that their ideas were not valued (Hess & Posselt, 2002). It is the most powerful tool we have as teachers to influence students' academic behaviors. How much a teacher talks is a teacher action recognized as an impediment to building a strong discussion culture (Simon, 2001). If the students know that the teacher will take over and talk, most will simply wait until this happens. I have watched myself do it when I have a small class, a preponderance of non-talkers, or I allow my enthusiasm for sharing my knowledge to outweigh the need for students to share theirs. By limiting our voices, we create space for student voices and send a strong message that we want conversation. "Never say anything a kid can say" is great advice for any teacher who wants to build a culture that sustains substantive conversation (Reinhart, 2000). Much of student apprehension about engaging in conversations in the classroom can be ameliorated by establishing a culture that promotes confidence, safety, and accuracy.

TEACHER TALK MOVES AND HISTORY

In addition to a classroom culture that facilitates discussion, preservice and practicing teachers can also model good questioning and discussion behaviors when they are leading instruction. One of the most effective tools I have used in professional development to increase teacher capacity for integrating discussion is the use of Talk Moves. The purpose of Talk Moves is to help the teacher focus on the questions that he or she poses to students so that students are required to surface their thinking, expose misconceptions, listen to one another, and engage other students. In the context of mathematics, the Talk Moves are often employed to help students who are stuck without providing them the answer or to expose thinking employed when solving a problem so that other students can benefit from that explanation. Although Talk Moves are really centered on teacher-driven or -assisted discussions, they help to promote a culture of discussion in the classroom and can model for students the kind of moves they can and should be utilizing when they are conversing. Figure 5.3 was not my invention, but instead a repurposed tool that I discovered my peers in mathematics utilizing.

When practicing these Talk Moves during professional development sessions, I provide teachers with a silly, content-free topic to discuss, such as:

- Is a hot dog a sandwich?
- Are cats better pets than dogs?
- What is the best French fry shape: thin and straight, crinkle-cut, waffle, or steak fries?
- Should cell phones be banned in schools?

The PD participants then conduct either a full-class or small-group discussion where the teacher presence is more pronounced (Schmidt & Pinkney, 2022). While the other teachers role-play students engaging in a discussion, the teacher employs the Talk Moves to guide the discussion. After a short 5- to 10-minute discussion, the "students" evaluate the teacher's use of various Talk Moves, and the teacher does the same for the students. I have found that as teachers engage in these role-plays, it strengthens their confidence to facilitate discussions in their own classrooms and pushes back on the "my kids cannot do this" reflex.

Figure 5.3. Talk Moves for Social Studies

Talk Move	Potential Teacher Statements	When and Why to Use It
Purpose: Helping Individual Students Clarify and Share Their Own Thoughts		
Wait Time	• *In 30 seconds, I'm going to ask you for your definitions. Think quietly about what you want to say.* • *What do you think the cartoon is communicating? (Wait 10 seconds.)*	✓ Use anytime you've asked a question to the whole class or whenever you've called on a particular student (e patient). ✓ Allows students time to organize and rehearse their thoughts.
Writing as Thinking Time	• *Take 60 seconds and write out your thoughts regarding the question I just asked.*	✓ Teacher poses a question and asks students to write for a minute to help get their thoughts on paper.
Turn and Talk	• *Turn and talk with your partners about that.* • *Okay, Deva just shared with us her strategy. Turn and talk with your neighbors about it—why does it work? What questions do you have?*	✓ Use if wait time doesn't increase the number of students willing to talk during whole-class discussion. ✓ Students can say aloud what they may want to say to the whole group. ✓ Works best for brief periods of time. ✓ Ask students to report on what their partner said.
So, Are You Saying . . . ?	• *Are you saying that . . . ?* • *Are you saying you think 24 is odd? Is that right?* • *So, it sounds like you're agreeing with _____. Is that what you're saying? Why?*	✓ Use when a student's response shows a lack of clarity. ✓ Buys thinking time. ✓ Helps other students keep track of what is going on. ✓ Allows teacher to model precise vocabulary.
Say More	• *Can you say more about that?* • *What do you mean by that?* • *Can you give an example?* • *Tell us more.* • *I'm not sure I understand yet. I need you to say more.* • *Why do you think that?* • *What is your evidence?*	✓ Use when a student gives a very short response. ✓ Shows the student that you value their thinking. ✓ Helps the teacher understand what a student is thinking.

Talk Move	Potential Teacher Statements	When and Why to Use It
Purpose: Helping Students to Listen Carefully to One Another		
Who Can Repeat?	• *How did you arrive at that conclusion?* • *Who can repeat what ____ said?* • *Who can say again what _____ just said?* • *Who can put what ____ said in their own words?* • *_____, can you repeat what _____ said in your own words?* (Teacher may ask the person who made the original statement for verification.) *_____, is that correct?* • *Could everyone please turn to the person next to you and repeat what ____ just said?*	✓ Asking students to restate what has been said. ✓ Use when an important point has been made or hinted at. ✓ Use to practice respectful listening. ✓ Provides another version of an important point in kid-friendly language. ✓ Especially valuable for ELL. ✓ Encourages students to be clear in their communication. *Do not use in a punitive way to catch a child who is not listening.
Purpose: Helping Students to Deepen Their Reasoning		
Why Do You Think That?	• *Why do you think that?* • *What convinced you that was the answer?* • *Why did you think that strategy would work?* • *What is your evidence?* • *How did you get that answer? Can you prove that to us?*	✓ Use any time a student gives an answer without explaining what they were thinking. ✓ Allows for misconceptions to surface so that you can clear them up in a respectful way. ✓ Enhances metacognition. ✓ Allows you to make a student's thinking explicit for the benefit of the rest of the class.
Purpose: Helping Students Engage With Others' Thinking		
What Do You Think About That?	• *Who agrees or disagrees with _______'s conjecture?* • *What do you think about _____'s strategy?* • *Will it always work?* • *Did someone think about it in a different way?* • *______, do you agree or disagree with what ___________ said? Why?*	✓ Use when students are wrestling with new ideas. ✓ Be sure to use this talk move with both correct reasoning and faulty reasoning. ✓ Encourages students to reflect on and evaluate what is being said and see how it fits in with their own understanding.

(*continued*)

Figure 5.3. (*continued*)

Talk Move	Potential Teacher Statements	When and Why to Use It
		✓ Respectfully disagreeing needs to be modeled. ✓ Teacher should not support one idea or the other.
Who Can Add On?	• _______ *got us started. Who can pick it up from there?* • *Who can predict what they think* ______ *did next?* • *Would someone like to add on?* • *Does anyone else have an idea to add?* • *Does anyone have a different way to solve it?*	✓ Asking other students to share related ideas. ✓ Use when a discussion has stalled, and other ideas probably exist and could be shared. ✓ Encourages multiple solution processes to be shared. ✓ Encourages students who are slower at processing to add their ideas.
Explaining what someone else means.	• *Who can explain what* _________ *means when she says*_________*?* • *Who can explain how/why* _______ *came up with that answer?* • *Why do you think she said that?*	

Source: Classroom Discussions With Math, by C. O'Connor, N. C. Anderson, & S. Chapin, 2013, Math Solutions Publications; *Talk Science Primer*, by S. Michaels & C. O'Connor, 2012, TERC (https://inquiryproject.terc.edu/shared/pd/TalkScience_Primer.pdf).

BUILDING STUDENT CAPACITY FOR DISCUSSION

Although Talk Moves can pay dividends for students as well as teachers, I find that building and supporting student capacity for classroom discussions benefits from a slightly different approach. For a variety of reasons we have already discussed, students are reticent to engage in academic discourse.

The first route to building student comfort with discussion is to provide a variety of structures for conversation. Running right to a full-class debate with desks in a circle and hashing out a topic will simply reinforce the reticence that emerges when students hear "discussion." Instead, consider discussion as a continuum that runs from students talking to themselves (often on paper, but out loud is okay, too!), to talking in pairs and in small groups, to larger groups, to finally a full-class discussion (Wassermann, 2010).

Keep in mind that as the size of the forum increases, the number of students who can and want to participate decreases. If you have a class of 35 and you are set to debate for 30 minutes, that is less than one minute for every student. If, though, you divide the conversation into phases with 5 minutes for think-pair, 5 minutes for small groups of four, and 10 minutes for groups of 8, and then 15 minutes for full-class discussion, the occasion for everyone to have participated increases dramatically. Discussion groups of seven or fewer students dramatically increase participation (Cohen & Lotan, 2014). The way in which you structure the opportunities for conversation will go a long way toward building student confidence, trusting their peers, and increasing the quality and quantity of conversations within the classroom.

What to say is also an important capacity to build with students. The resource in Figure 5.4 is something that I provide to students to utilize during discussions. The intent behind the sheet is to provide some crutches that students can use to wade into discussion when they may be reticent to do so on their own. It helps students not to just participate but to also allow them to participate in a productive manner. In addition, the sheet is predicated on the belief that the best classroom conversations revolve around student-to-student interaction, with the teacher speaking little if at all (Hess, 2004a). The center column identifies statements that students can make when they are seeking a classmate with whom to elaborate and clarify. The far-right column then provides other students with stems for how they could respond to a student who has posed a question to them.

I allow students to have a copy of this cheat sheet with them during discussions. For some students, it is just the push they need to jump into a conversation and participate. It is not a panacea, but combined with a variety of discussion formats, student confidence can grow.

The ultimate goal of intentionally building students' capacity around discussion is to engender in the classroom what is referred to as "accountable talk." A classroom that has fostered this capacity among students will witness students asking other students for evidence (Michaels et al., 2008). Accountable talk classrooms combine conversation with active listening. The dialogue occurs between students rather than between the teacher and students. The conversation is cumulative, as students not only harvest the readings for information but also utilize information they have heard from peers. This is the goal, and while sometimes we fall short, with discussion it is important to not let perfection be the enemy of the good. "Good discussions," as Abby Reisman so eloquently put it, "have little to do with magic

Figure 5.4. Student Placemat to Promote Discussion

Conversation Skill	Statements to Make	Responses
Elaborate and Clarify	• Can you elaborate on . . . ? • What do you mean by . . . ? • Can you tell me more about . . . ? • What makes you think that . . . ? • Can you clarify the part about . . . ? • How so? • How/why is ________ important? • How does ________ connect to . . . ? • I am a little confused about . . . ?	• I think it means that . . . • In other words . . . • I believe that . . . • An analogy for this might be . . . • It is important because . . . • It's similar to when . . .
Support Ideas With Examples	• Can you give me an example from the source? • Can you show me where in the source it says that? • Are there more cases of ____ happening? • What is the evidence that supports your argument?	• For example . . . • In the source it said that . . . • One example was . . . • For instance . . . • According to . . . • On one occasion . . . • In this situation . . . • To demonstrate . . . • In fact . . . • Indeed . . .
Build On/ Challenge Someone's argument	• What do you think about the idea that . . . ? • How does this connect to the idea that . . . ? • I agree with your argument that . . . but how do you deal with the fact that . . . • I think your argument about . . . is wrong because . . . • How can . . . be true . . . if you consider . . . ?	• I would add that . . . • I want to expand on your point about . . . • I want to follow up on your idea that . . . • Then again, I think that . . . • Another way to look at this could be . . . • Yet I wonder also if . . . • What struck me about what you said was . . .
Paraphrase	• So you are saying that . . . • Let me see if I understand you . . . • Am I right in hearing you say that . . . ? • In a nutshell, are you arguing that . . . • In other words . . . • What I am hearing is . . . • Essentially you think that . . . • It sounds like you are saying that . . .	• No, I am saying . . . • Yes, I am saying . . .

and everything to do with careful planning and pedagogical savviness . . . substantive discussions occur because teachers have a clear sense of how they want students to engage with the text, with one another, and with the content." By providing effective scaffolding, all students can engage in productive, evidence-based, historical discussions (Reisman, 2017; Reisman et al., 2019).

SCORING AND FEEDBACK

Scoring and providing feedback to students during discussions is a difficult task, especially with what has happened to class sizes over the last 30 years. I struggled with this particular aspect of classroom discussion. Early in my career, I would use the scoring aspect to motivate participation in discussion. "You must participate at least twice during today's discussion to receive full credit," I would say to my classes. Students would dutifully say something twice and then fall silent—both orally and cognitively. Grading, I learned, does not motivate anything other than compliance. My takeaway was that feedback is a more useful tool to sustain the discussion culture I had created and in helping students to become better contributors. Too much emphasis on scoring a student's participation can suppress the willingness to engage in conversation. This does not mean that I gave up grading participation. Because my district did not allow participation to be part of the calculation of a student's grade, I shifted things. I provided feedback on each discussion, and simply kept a tally of participation. At the end of the quarter, if a student had a 77 and participated in every discussion, I would have no problem boosting their grade to a B. If they went silent, then they could keep the C. By focusing on the feedback and turning the scoring into a positive tool, most of my students were more willing to join in and talk.

With an emphasis on feedback instead of scoring, the question came back to, how does a teacher listen intently to discussion and take notes to provide substantive student feedback? The key is to remember that quality is more important than quantity when it comes to feedback. Too much feedback, and the student either does not read it or they cannot separate one aspect from another. In addition, you cannot provide feedback to all students in every discussion (Barton, 2019; Havekes et al., 2017). Dividing and conquering will help focus the teacher on the quality of feedback provided to the students. This is a difficult challenge, as some students who were provided feedback on a previous discussion may reduce their participation, assuming that they will not receive feedback again, while other students who have not yet heard from the teacher may press. A rubric can help to ensure that no student goes without some feedback for every discussion, but also allows you to alternate the in-depth feedback you provide to students on a rotating basis.

The tool in Figure 5.5 evolved over time but provided a mechanism to share feedback with students. Over time I isolated the kinds of discussion characteristics that I felt students should exemplify. The score was to reflect how well they employed a particular tool. If there were either serious issues or the opportunity for praise, I could address that quickly in the Notes section. The intent was not to sum it all up into a grade but to recognize, reward, and redirect student discussion behaviors.

One note: *Popcorning* is when, during a discussion, a student makes a point, then another student says something unrelated, and the next student says something unrelated to what either of the previous students said. It is a clear indication that students are not listening to one another and simply saying something so they feel like they have participated. It is my least favorite student discussion behavior, and so it is one of the only negative behaviors I include on the rubric.

Although the drive to hold students accountable for participating is a strong one to overcome, feedback goes much farther toward supporting and growing a culture of discussion than does grading.

By laying out the benefits of embracing academic discourse in a history classroom, constructing a culture that is supportive of discussion, building teacher and student capacity, and making decisions about providing effective feedback, I hope to address the concerns that teachers have expressed regarding students who cannot engage in historical investigations because they do not like to talk in class. Moving forward, I want to put some flesh on the bones and provide an example of classroom discussion through the lens of an actual lesson. It is one of my favorites: the Pullman strike of 1894.

THE PULLMAN STRIKE OF 1894

I organize the investigation of the Pullman strike of 1894 into a mock congressional hearing. In this format, students are subpoenaed to testify in front of the United States Congressional subcommittee on labor disturbances. When testifying, because they are under oath, they must answer the questions posed to them as if they were the person who created their source. This ensures that students understand not only what the source says, but who created the source, when, and why. When not testifying, the students assume the role of a committee member. Although this is not a historical recreation, a congressional hearing did take place after the events at Pullman in 1894.

Figure 5.5. Discussion Feedback Tool

Discussion Trait	Feedback
Takes a position/makes a claim	
Supports position/claim with details, examples, explanations, and evidence	
Reasoning is logical and does not use irrelevant analogies or metaphors	
Elaborates and clarifies when presented with counter-arguments	
Appropriately challenges the accuracy or logic of others' statements	
Asks pertinent, purposeful, and penetrating questions of others	
Paraphrases other arguments	
Acknowledges the positions of others	
Responds to the statements of others	
Statements are relevant to the flow of discussion	
Statements exhibit preparation/ accuracy	

(*continued*)

Figure 5.5. (*continued*)

Discussion Trait	Feedback
Makes eye contact with group, even when not speaking	
Listens actively while not actively talking	
Respectfully allows others to finish; did not interrupt	

Discussion Scoring Guide

Discussion Trait	Score
Takes a position/Makes a claim	0 1 2 3 4 5
Supports position/claim with details, examples, explanations, and evidence	0 1 2 3 4 5
Reasoning is logical and does not use irrelevant analogies or metaphors	0 1 2 3 4 5
Elaborates and clarifies when presented with counterarguments	0 1 2 3 4 5
Appropriately challenges the accuracy or logic of others' statements	0 1 2 3 4 5
Asks pertinent, purposeful, and penetrating questions of others	0 1 2 3 4 5
Paraphrases others' arguments	0 1 2 3 4 5
Acknowledges the positions of others	0 1 2 3 4 5
Responds to the statements of others	0 1 2 3 4 5
Statements are relevant to the flow of discussion	0 1 2 3 4 5
Statements exhibit preparation/accuracy	0 1 2 3 4 5
Makes eye contact with group, even when not speaking	0 1 2 3 4 5
Listens actively while not actively talking	0 1 2 3 4 5
Respectfully allows others to finish; did not interrupt	0 1 2 3 4 5
NO POPCORNING	0 -1 -2 -3 -4 -5
NOTES	

SOURCE-BASED TESTIMONY

There are a ton of sources available for the Pullman strike. As the lab evolved, I moved away from just testimony in front of the actual Strike Commission and, reflected in Figure 5.6, added some from others who had visited and commented on the town of Pullman. Because the congressional hearing format is different from a jigsaw, I do violate my "rule" about limiting investigations to six sources. You could certainly conduct the lab with fewer sources and get to the same end, but increasing the sources to nine ensures a greater number of students "testifying" than would six.

The sources provide a great deal of opportunity for sourcing, contextualizing, and corroborating. In addition, the contradictions between the sources provide fertile ground for debate and discussion.

SETTING THE STAGE

I do solemnly swear that my testimony will be based on the perspective of my source and nothing but the perspective of my source, even if it has an overt point of view, so help my first-quarter grade.

After taking their oath, students prepare for the hearing. I establish some background on Pullman, the railcars, and the town, as well as the economic decline. This background can be established through the debriefing of a common homework reading, watching a quick video introduction, or a mini-lecture. Whatever the format, students need a common background before they dive deeply into the sources.

Background established, students prepare for their testimony. If they have read their source for homework, they can immediately group with students who read the same source. If they have not read the source prior to class, they will need to do so before they can be grouped. After reviewing the sources, I remind the class that when testifying:

- All team members will be asked questions.
- Testimony must be based on information found in your source.
- Members of Congress (everyone in the audience) must take notes on the testimony.

Usually I prefer only one overarching question for an investigation. In this instance, I have expanded to two questions. The hearing must determine:

- **Who bears the greatest responsibility for the events at Pullman?**
- **Should Eugene Debs have been sent to prison for his role in the Pullman strike?**

Figure 5.6. Pullman Strike Sources

A	Reverend William H. Carwardine, *The Pullman Strike.* Charles H. Kerr and Company, 1894.	Carwardine was a Methodist minister who served the workers in Pullman. The author lived in the town, and he actively tried to aid the workers during negotiations.
B	Richard T. Ely, "Pullman: A Social Study." *Harper's Magazine* 70 (February 1885): 452–466.	Ely was a strong supporter of labor union strikes and government regulation of the workplace, including ending child labor. He was strongly opposed to laissez-faire economics.
C	*Statement of the Pullman Strikers,* June 15, 1894.	This statement from a Pullman striker was delivered at the June 1894 Chicago convention of the American Railway Union (ARU).
D	Testimony on the Part of Striking Employees: Theodore Rhodie	This statement from a Pullman striker was provided to a Congressional committee investigating the causes of the strike.
E	George Pullman, Open Letter in the *Chicago Herald,* June 1984	In this open letter, written as the strike began, George Pullman explained his motives for cutting wages during the economic depression of 1893.
F	*United States Strike Commission Final Report: Information about the Pullman Company*	From the final report of the United States Strike Commission report on the 1894 strike at Pullman. The commission was made up of three members, none of whom represented labor.
G	*United States Strike Commission: The Congressional Perspective on the Causes of the Strike*	From the final report of the United States Strike Commission on the 1894 strike at Pullman. The commission was made up of three members, none of whom represented labor.
H	Grover Cleveland, *The Government in the Chicago Strike of 1894.* Princeton University Press, 1913.	Written by the former president 19 years after the strike.
I	Eugene V. Debs, "The Federal Government and the Pullman Strike: Eugene V. Debs's Reply to Grover Cleveland's Magazine Article." Written circa July 7, 1904. Published in *Appeal to Reason* (Aug. 27, 1904), pp. 1–2.	This article was written for *McClure's Magazine* in reply to Cleveland, but the editor of that publication refused to publish it. The first paragraph that appears in this edited version was omitted from all subsequent reprints of this document dating back to 1908.

Based on years of implementation of this hearing with students, I have found that sticking to the first question about responsibility, the class inevitably ends up discussing Debs. As a result, I now implement the investigation using both. I know, another rule broken, but flexibility is the key to surviving in the classroom, and if the decision allows for greater exploration of an event, person, or idea, then break the rules!

A HEARING IS NOW CALLED TO ORDER!

After the administration of the oath and a quick review of the guidelines, our hearing is off and running. Student groups representing each of the sources take the stand in front of Congress. I play the role of committee chair and pose questions to each sworn witness. The questioning strategy is twofold: first, to ensure that students are sourcing, contextualizing, and closely reading the documents. The second is to encourage the audience—my members of Congress—to consider how the multiple testimonies corroborate one another and begin to build their answers to the overarching investigative questions. To achieve this level of student-to-student conversation, discussion must be built into this scenario in a manner not consistent with an actual Congressional hearing. Between each testimony, students need to unpack their thinking without teacher mediation.

DISCUSSION AND PULLMAN

During the Pullman exploration, there are at least six distinct opportunities for a variety of discussion strategies to be employed, as outlined in Figure 5.7.

Discussion Opportunity 1

This phase of discussion is initially structured by the teacher but is ultimately driven by students. Brought together with the 4–5 other students who read the same source, students are asked to do the following:

- Compare notes.
- Make sure they understand what the source is saying.
- Understand who wrote the source and how that might impact the information provided.
- Understand when and why the source was created and how that might impact the information provided.

What actually occurs in this discussion is more along the lines of information transfer, but as students move into the sourcing and contextualizing,

Figure 5.7. Pullman Strike Discussion Opportunities

	Opportunity for Discussion	Discussion Tools
1	Discussion with other students who read the same source when preparing testimony.	Small-group discussion
2	Student–student questioning during each testimony	Student-to-student questioning
3	Conversations about individual sources after each testimony.	Think-pair-share
4	Student-generated questions posed to sources testifying.	Individual to individual
5	Discussion after all sources are presented.	Small groups of 3, then 4, and up to 5 students
6	Discussion regarding answer to overarching question.	Full group

there is more challenging of others. This kind of conversation can go off the rails quickly if students either just copy one another's notes or allow one person to tell everyone else what to think. To avoid these traps, teachers need to set up clear guidelines and model these conversations. Providing students with a clear example helps them to hear what they should be talking about and limits the tendency to keep the conversation at the "just the facts, ma'am" level. At the outset of every school year, the first time these kinds of sharing/low-level conversations take place, I always either model one with some students or show a filmed conversation on previous years' students. This goes a long way to ensure on-task and productive talk.

Discussion Opportunity 2

During one iteration of the hearing, students asked the group who presented Source I, "You are looking back at the Pullman strike in hindsight. How might that impact your thoughts on the event?" Another year, after the testimony of Source F, student-generated questions focused on issues related to the sourcing of the document. Members of Congress asked those testifying: "There was no labor representation on the congressional committee investigating the strike. Doesn't that undermine the legitimacy of their findings?" Later, when George Pullman testified, student-generated questions focused on how his profit motives might have impacted what he was choosing to share with the audience. These examples are exactly the kind of thinking and dialogue I want to encourage between students in this phase of the discussion, but it only works if it is student-initiated and student-led. That student-led action does not occur naturally—unless it is about something inappropriate to the classroom—so it needs to be encouraged for it to become natural. When students get to the comfort level where they question the evidence being presented by the other students, they are clearly reflecting their understanding of sourcing, contextualizing, and corroboration.

Discussion Opportunity 3

After each group testifies in front of the subcommittee, students turn to a partner in Congress and discuss the testimony. Student discussion can range from reactions to what was stated, questions they may have and would like to ask, and, as the testimony progresses, corroboration or lack thereof between various sources. These discussions are intentionally timed (1 minute), and then students are asked to turn to another partner and continue to discuss (1 minute). The truncated time frame requires students to focus their thoughts and keeps them from "discussing" non-Pullman related topics. The first time these kinds of conversations occur, the teacher can seed them with conversation starters such as

- What struck me the most about that testimony was . . .
- What ________ said seems to agree/disagree with what ______ said because . . .
- I am starting to think that . . .
- What most confuses me is _______ because . . .

Because these conversations happen after each testimony, the discussions serve to break up the flow of the lesson and enable students to progressively build and substantiate their arguments. In many ways the conversations function as a pre-writing activity where students can test their prospective answer to the overarching question and weigh the evidence that might support or challenge that claim. Students are often heard discussing problems with the evidence.

Discussion Opportunity 4

An important element of speaking is listening. Often, when other students make presentations, other students check out. The mock Congressional hearing eliminates that as an option, as students are held accountable for asking questions of those who are testifying. Students pose such questions as

- To the member of the United States Strike Commission a student asked, "Wouldn't the lack of labor representation on your committee mean that you are anti-labor?"
- To President Cleveland, students inquired how "looking back in hindsight might change your opinions?"

This phase of conversation will not spontaneously occur. Unless students are taught to ask questions and given guidance on the types of questions they should be asking of historical sources, they will struggle. The questions from these students indicate that they have begun to internalize the ideas of sourcing and contextualization. The questions are not perfect, but they drive conversation between two students rather than between the teacher and students, and that is essential for the growth of students' capability with classroom discussion.

Discussion Opportunity 5

At the conclusion of the testimonies, students quickly move into small groups of 4 or 5 to discuss the overarching question. These conversations can evolve from teacher-seeded questions to completely student-driven opportunities. If the conversations stall, or wander off-task, a bell can be rung, and a new question offered to help focus students. The purpose of this discussion is to synthesize all of the evidence presented and allow students to apply the evidence to developing an answer to the overarching question.

Discussion Opportunity 6

I transition from discussion opportunity 5 to 6 by having students record their thoughts in either a four corners format or via a continuum. The focus is to surface all of the thinking that has occurred in the previous five discussion opportunities and link it back to the overarching focus question for the lesson. Emphasis at this phase should be on students utilizing multiple pieces of evidence to support their answer to the overarching question. It is here that students make their claims, support them with evidence, and challenge the claims of others. Essential, though, is that all discussion be linked back to the sources. Too often students in this phase will revert to statements like "I think," or associate their reasoning with statements like "personally I feel." Although there should be a significant amount of student-to-student interaction and little to no teacher intervention in the conversation, it is imperative that teachers intervene to remind students to couch their responses in the evidence. The building and supporting of claims and the challenging of others makes this the highest-risk and highest-reward aspect of the lesson.

The lesson concludes with a student self-evaluation. The emphasis in this assessment, illustrated in Figure 5.8, is on their listening to others' claim-making and use of evidence. It is best to let students know prior to Debate Opportunity 6 that this is how they will be assessed. The foreknowledge reminds students to be good listeners and to take notes on what they are hearing.

Figure 5.8. Pullman Strike Assessment

Based on our discussion of Who bears the greatest responsibility for the events at Pullman? /Should Eugene Debs have been sent to prison for his role in the Pullman Strike? React to what you heard from other members of your class. Select one of the following and answer in 4-6 complete sentences. Be sure to reference the author of the information or the source(s) they cited by name. You may not be narcissistic and cite yourself!

- The most persuasive claim/argument I heard was . . . because . . .
- The least persuasive claim/argument I heard was . . . because . . .
- The source(s)/evidence that most influenced my decision was . . . because . . .
- The source(s)/evidence that least influenced my decision was . . . because . . .

CONCLUSION

I have yet to meet a teenager who did not want to feel that their opinions are valued and heard. I have met plenty of students who are reluctant to share those thoughts, and at times shy away from opportunities to share, but all teenagers want to be heard. The key, as I have outlined in this chapter, is the intentionality with which the teachers go about integrating discussion into their repertoire (Reisman, 2015a; Reisman et al., 2020; Segall et al., 2018) Essential is to help students align their discussions with evidence and to distinguish between opinion and evidence-based interpretations. "My students cannot do this," as a comment regarding students and discussion, is often best understood as a teacher saying, "I am not sure how to structure discussion so my students can do it." By embracing the obvious pedagogical value of discussion, teachers can address and grow their own skill set and leverage this high-value practice to the benefit of student motivation and learning.

CHAPTER 6

"My Kids Felt More Seen Today"

Teaching Hard Histories

> *[This lesson] generated some really rich conversation and I know some of my kids felt more seen today. And hopefully some bad ideas got dispatched along the way.*
>
> —Adam Laye, Gilder Lehrman Teacher of the Year, Maryland, 2021

Russell's mom was mad. It was the kind of meeting all teachers dread: an angry parent whose irritation is directly tied to some instructional decision that I made. Russell's mom scheduled an appointment with me to discuss an assessment that she found "offensive." I could not blame the county curriculum guide or some random source I got from the Internet. Nope, my instructional choices were on trial, and anxiety was high as we sat down. Thankfully, Russell's mom approached it with a level head rather than the "you are an idiot" approach that sometimes dominates the tone of parent–teacher conversations.

Her concern was that she found an assessment that her son had been assigned to be offensive to Catholics and Jews, and a tacit promotion of torture. The assessment was "The Inquisitors' Datebook" that students completed after exploring the motivations, tools, impacts, and reactions to the Inquisition. In the lesson summative assessment, students were asked to take on the perspective of an inquisitor and to enter various activities into their datebook. Cute, right? Students found the assessment accessible because they could apply what they had learned about the Inquisition in a creative manner. Plus, it wasn't an essay!

From Mom's perspective, the teacher was asking her child to support the use of torture directed at religious minorities. Essentially, the assessment had turned her child into an inquisitor. She wasn't wrong. I felt horrible. My intentions, although pure, clearly led to unintended consequences. My curricular choices led to unplanned, yet significant, negative consequences. I had committed "curricular violence" before the term had even been invented (Jones, 2020).

All teachers make mistakes in the classroom. We mischaracterize a topic, person, or event; we overgeneralize or misspeak in a way that causes confusion or even anger among students. The past is a place of immense emotions:

exhilarating highs and devastating lows. It is the home of victories and defeats, successes and failures, the well-intended and the misinformed. The past is also the home to violence, ignorance, hatred, and grief. As the gatekeepers to the past that students access (Thornton, 1991), teachers can open the gate to beauty and ugliness, nationalism and jingoism, narratives of progress and exceptionalism, or those of colonization and inequity. Classroom teachers can also, intentionally or unintentionally, ignore actions and consequences, or we can place greater emphasis on some aspects of past actions. Other times it is our silences that send messages. Who we leave out of the narrative is sometimes more telling than who we include or how we address those people, events, or ideas. The invisibility of certain people, events, or ideas can cause students to feel minimized or to question the fullness of the history they are learning, but as the opening quote illustrates, making marginalized groups visible pays dividends for students and teachers.

Compounding these choices is the fact that sometimes our unintentional actions may speak less to sloppiness or trying to jazz up our instruction and instead to unconscious biases. During classroom instruction, unintended microaggressions can manifest themselves in ways that we do not recognize. If not arrested and addressed, these microaggressions can accumulate into curriculum violence "when educators and curriculum writers" develop and implement "a set of lessons that damage or otherwise adversely affect students intellectually and emotionally" or a lesser manifestation has already occurred (Jones, 2020). Too often it is topics around race, gender, and sexuality where these types of curricular and instructional decisions occur. A paradigm-shifting report published by the Southern Poverty Law Center on the teaching of American slavery coined the phrase "hard history" and set some parameters for understanding the implications for the classroom:

> Slavery is hard history. It is hard to comprehend the inhumanity that defined it. It is hard to discuss the violence that sustained it. It is hard to teach the ideology of white supremacy that justified it. And it is hard to learn about those who abided it. We the people have a deep-seated aversion to hard history because we are uncomfortable with the implications it raises about the past as well as the present. We the people would much rather have the Disney version of history, in which villains are easily spotted, suffering never lasts long, heroes invariably prevail, and life always gets better. We prefer to pick and choose what aspects of the past to hold on to, gladly jettisoning that which makes us uneasy . . . (Shuster, 2018)

Slavery is without a doubt a hard history, but I have co-opted the term to serve as a broader umbrella for hard history around not only slavery but also topics regarding race, religion, immigration, gender, sexuality, xenophobia, Islamophobia, and misogyny. Social studies and history classes are full of these hard histories that must be taught if students are to be prepared to understand the world in which they will live and work.

These hard histories, even before the onset of the manufactured crisis of critical race theory and attendant laws restricting the discussion of topics that "make students feel uncomfortable," were challenging for teachers. Race, gender, sexuality, and the often-violent repression involved in upholding restrictive laws and in defending these restrictive status quos present pedagogical challenges. When making presentations to preservice and practicing teachers, the concern is rarely that "kids cannot do this," but instead, "How do we [teachers] conduct these investigations without generating parent phone calls, causing student emotional responses, and/or alienating groups of students?" The teaching environment in many states in the post-COVD world is even more fraught. I fully respect that, but this chapter reflects implementation of a series of lessons on the LGBTQ+ community during the tail end of the pandemic and the onset of the critical race theory kerfuffle, and thus may not reflect the post-COVID reality for many teachers. That said, this chapter will explore teaching hard histories through the inquiry process. I will use three lessons on the origins of the LGBTQ+ movement as examples to model how to avoid doing curricular damage while providing a deep understanding of what some consider a "controversial" topic to teach, and doing so through the historical investigation lens.

WHY HARD HISTORIES?

Race, religion, immigration, gender, sexuality, xenophobia, Islamophobia, misogyny: These and other topics are as central to the teaching of history as are capitalism, nationalism, constitutionalism, and diplomacy. The reality, though, is that the first list is more likely to result in a phone call from an angry parent than the latter. My perspective has always been that students need to understand a full, unvarnished history. Race, religion, gender, and sexuality cannot be ignored. Doing so actually does harm to students, as they will enter a world where those historical forces have impacted the construction of their world and continue to be influential today. A filiopietistic recounting of exceptionalism, progress, and shiny happy people does not help students to appreciate fully where we came from, nor does it prepare them to understand the world they will occupy as adults. By the same token, a history that condemns everyone and everything and overemphasizes the negative does nothing but breed cynicism.

My approach has been to center students and take on the contested issues and hard histories rather than ignoring the difficult topics. From my perspective, history that makes us uncomfortable has power. It provides perspective, develops wisdom, teaches tolerance, and promotes understanding. It also runs counter to the whitewashed history that I was fed in my K–16 education. Take, for example, lynching. In my education, Jim Crow started and stopped with water fountains. The use of extrajudicial terror to enforce

Jim Crow and disenfranchisement was not part of the historical narrative to which I was exposed. As I came to understand this phenomenon and its use as a tool to consign African Americans to a social, economic, and political place in post-Reconstruction America, the more I understood that it needed to be a part of instruction. My intent in addressing these topics was not to generate cynicism or to condemn those in the past, but to ensure that my students could understand how the world in which they live is linked to the past. We cannot send students into a world that is populated with issues around race, gender, ethnicity, violence, and inequality without arming them with an understanding of how history contributed to those current issues. The approach also fosters skills that are essential for productive citizenship, as students who explore these difficult issues feel more comfortable discussing them in the future (Avery et al., 2013; Hess & Posselt, 2002).

As demonstrated in Figure 6.1, recent public polling indicates that a vast majority of Americans want to learn the hard histories that confront their previously held beliefs, even if it makes them uncomfortable (Burkholder &

Figure 6.1. Survey Data on Teaching Difficult Topics

Survey Respondents' preference for history that challenges or reinforces extant knowledge

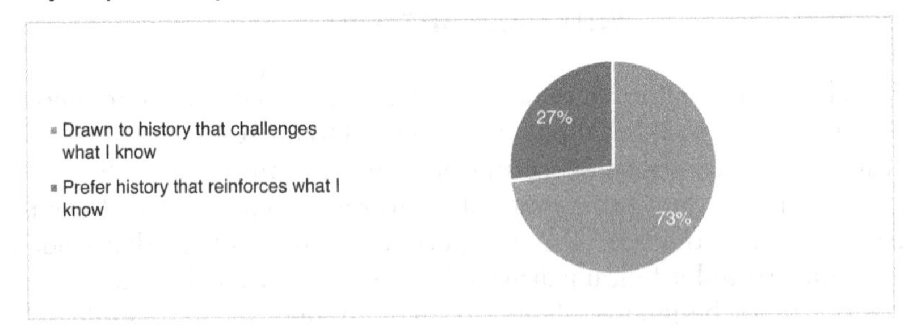

Survey Respondents' views on uncomfortable history

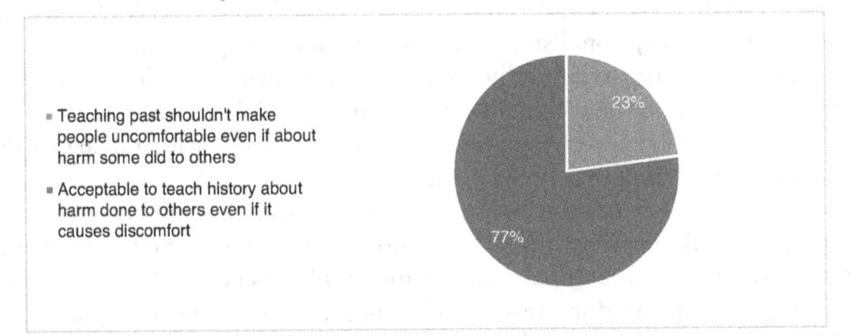

Source: Reprinted from *History, the Past, and Public Culture: Results from a National Survey*, by P. Burkholder and D. Schaffer, 2021, American Historical Association. Used with permission.

Schaffer, 2021). This speaks clearly to the need to incorporate slavery, racism, xenophobia, gender, and sexuality histories into the narrative so that students can learn a fuller and more accurate telling of history.

This is telling, but it does not mean that support for the study of hard histories is universal or that there will not be pushback. Clearly the politicization of critical race theory (CRT) and the unfounded fears that resulted and were legislated upon indicate that a portion of the country does not want to confront any past that makes them uncomfortable (Sawchuk, 2022). If anything useful came out of the 2021 debate over CRT, it is a reminder that teachers do not work in a bubble, and we must be cognizant of the communities in which we work and the milieu of the time in which we teach (Polikoff et al., 2022). There needs to be intentionality behind the instruction that supports wrestling with these hard histories so that students are comfortable and adults are accepting. More on how to achieve that intentionality in a moment.

Unfortunately, the research is clear that while I was teaching current and contested issues within my curriculum, I was more the exception than the rule. Research shows that these difficult histories are not being taught, and if they are, they are not taught with much facility (Goldberg & Savenije, 2018; Kitson & McCully, 2005; Mitchell, 2021; Rosado et al., 2022; Shuster, 2018). The reasons for the timidity toward dealing with these types of topics parallel those that limit the use of high-quality instruction outlined in Chapter 3. Teacher confidence in their knowledge about the content, hesitancy regarding their ability to handle the topics, concerns over how students will react and interact, and the potential for these issues running counter to the values and mores of a local school community all hamstring efforts to address race, religion, gender, sexuality, and other controversial issues and "hard histories" (Byford et al., 2009; Camicia, 2008; Journell, 2011; Linter, 2018; Philpott et al., 2010). None of these factors is insurmountable, but they do require teachers to prioritize and grow to ensure a thoughtful inclusion into their instructional toolbox.

CONTROVERSIAL ISSUES AND HARD HISTORIES

Current and contested issues are not fully synonymous with hard histories, but in many ways, it is a distinction without a difference. Both tap into values and emotions, both can make students and parents uncomfortable, and both are essential to a well-rounded social studies education that prepares students to participate in a democracy. Both generate discussion and debate and draw students into instruction that is engaging, but hard histories around topics like slavery, gender discrimination, racism, xenophobia, and others that are approached from a historical rather than a contemporary lens are different in that they are closed for debate. "Open issues are ones that have multiple reasonable positions, and when taught, all reasonable positions should be given a fair hearing," but in the United States, we are no longer debating if slavery should be abolished or if women should have constitutionally protected suffrage. Historically, when these issues were being debated, they were open, but in the context of a history course, they are settled, and "settled issues only have one reasonable position, and viewpoints that run contrary to the settled position should not be presented as legitimate within the classroom space" (Journell, 2020). This does not mean that the teaching of the topics of slavery or gender and sexuality are not controversial.

Unlike controversial issues, controversial topics are no longer open for debate. "Controversial topics refer to elements of the curriculum that could be seen as inappropriate or objectionable by parents, administrators, or the larger public," while "Controversial issues are questions that require students to investigate, evaluate, or deliberate multiple and competing views. These questions ask students to make a judgement about a public policy . . . once the issue has been identified, the teacher will design inquiry activities that help students learn about competing views and decide for themselves what to think" (Ho et al., 2017; McAvoy & Ho, 2020). Recently Islam, a central part of any World History or World Geography curriculum, has become a contentious topic. The role and influence of Islam on global history is a fact and not open for debate, but the events of September 11, 2001, made Islam a source of consternation among a small, reactionary group of parents and pundits. As a result of this politicization, the teaching of Islam became controversial (Department of Justice, 2011). Thankfully, teachers and school leaders resisted the effort to suppress teaching about the role of Islam in history.

The work of the Southern Poverty Law Center's Teaching Tolerance's *Teaching Hard History: American Slavery* illustrates well the challenges of teaching these topics. Slavery is neither contested, nor is it controversial, but it certainly makes people uncomfortable and has the potential to be taught in a manner that both distorts its historicity and can do damage to those studying it. Children of color who only see their contribution to the historical narrative as the recipient of discrimination, hatred, and/or violence struggle with the dissonance between the historical narrative they hear at home and the one perpetuated in school history (Woodson, 2015). The debate over critical race theory that dominated the headlines in 2021 and 2022 hinged on the concerns that learning about slavery might make students feel guilty or bad about themselves. These misinformed views led to legislation that limited the ability to teach about any topic that might make someone feel uncomfortable (*Map*, 2021; Ray & Gibbons, 2021). Both the post-9/11 attempts to limit the teaching of Islam and the post–George Floyd protests effort to limit the teaching of slavery serve as a stark reminder that events outside of the curriculum can impact the ability of educators to address essential topics.

HARD HISTORIES AND INQUIRY

With a few caveats, the inquiry approach to history instruction that I advocate aligns well with the teaching of hard histories. At its heart, inquiry asks students to confront challenging questions about topics; consult and weigh a variety of sources; and develop, defend, and refine an evidence-based response to those questions. Hard histories are ripe for this type of approach, but not without guardrails. The three most significant warnings are around the question posed to guide an investigation, the resources used to support the investigation, and the instructional techniques employed.

Inquiry questions around hard history topics like slavery, gender discrimination, immigration, and others should not open discussion that allows students to justify racism, violence, or prejudice. This forewarning is not meant to imply that students should not confront the justifications that were proffered to explain enslavement, support discrimination, or perpetuate inequality in the past. Students need to understand how systems of oppression, inequality, and discrimination are constructed so they can appreciate the challenges facing those who tore down those systems and the lingering connections between the past and the present. That said, students should not find sanction in past racist/sexist/homophobic arguments to support these systems of oppression, either historically or in a contemporary context. Questions such as Was slavery bad? or How bad was slavery? are not effective questions to structure an investigation simply because there are not two legitimate, evidence-based answers. The ownership of another human being is not now, nor was it then, a good thing. It was justified through the creation of racist laws, beliefs, and tools that attempted to justify the ownership of another human being. Having students even entertain that slavery was "good" or wasn't that "bad" will only lead to bad history, bad feelings, and bad consequences for teacher and student (Swann et al., 2022).

When dealing with hard histories, it is important to center the difficulty. This is not done best through inquiry. Because hard histories often deal with significant acts of dehumanization, violence, and oppression, allowing the lived experiences to speak for themselves is often the best route to addressing these stories. Close off anything debatable about these topics and instead allow these events to speak for themselves. By removing inquiry, teachers are able to address the emotional reactions that can sometimes be evoked by topics that center injustice, suffering, and violence (Harris et al., 2022).

Instead of developing an inquiry question that argues about the institution of slavery, shift the focus of the questions about these hard histories to decenter the institution and examine instead the impacts of the institution on such things as political division, the rise of abolition, or on enslaved families; or shift to centering questions on factors that impacted the growth of slavery such as the cotton gin or westward expansion. Other rich areas of examination would be on factors that influenced the elimination of the institution like resistance by enslaved persons or self-emancipation. For example, when dealing with the topic of slavery, an inquiry question such as, Does it matter who ended slavery?," outlined by Swann et al. (2018b), allows students to confront slavery through the lens of the debate over whether slaves self-emancipated and pressured the system or if governmental decisions led to emancipation. This question can structure an investigation that centers the views of the enslaved, as well as free Blacks, and can use both contemporary and current resources, but it does not put students in the position of having to justify or defend slavery. Another take might be: How did different perspectives on slavery cause the Civil War? With this shift, students must understand the institution of slavery, but the focus becomes on the institution's political impact and not the brutalization of the enslaved. By targeting the question, teachers can avoid justifying the unjustifiable but still allow students to understand how difficult histories impacted everyone.

A second warning on successfully merging inquiry with hard history topics is regarding the types of resources that are utilized during an investigation. The selection of resources is always precarious, but when investigating an issue like slavery, immigration, or LGBTQ+ history, even more caution is advisable. Teachers should immerse students in the historical sources that allow students to hear the voices of those who experienced these events. In addition, ensuring that students see those enslaved, persecuted, and discriminated against not as victims, but as possessing agency, is an important goal when selecting the sources that students examine. The voices of oppressors, the deliverers of violence, and the justifiers of discriminatory systems should not be the sole lens through which students see a historical issue, event, or person. Too many of these sources can put students in the "position of defending and/or identifying with the oppressors," which should not be the point of any investigation ("Why Simulation Activities," 2018). Students should understand the ideologies and justifications that were used to discriminate, enslave, or persecute, but license should not be provided to sanction or perpetuate these views.

If we use lynching as an example, there are numerous resources that could humanize the experience through newspaper articles describing lynching, such as the writings of Ida B. Wells and the haunting lyrics of Billie Holiday's "Strange Fruit." These are excellent resources that can be mined for material to support an investigation. What about visual images that might quantify lynching via maps, charts, and graphs, or pictures? These sources pose a more delicate challenge for teachers.

James Allen's (1999) book and website collection of lynching postcards, *Without Sanctuary,* provide a unique challenge when studying the hard history of lynching in America. The postcards are gruesome, evocative, and emotionally devastating. They also speak clearly to the way whites normalized these extrajudicial murders and perversely disguised them as justice. The notion that there would be a market for these images as post-cards, let alone that they were sent to others with messages on the back, was unreal to me, but should they be used instructionally? The postcards could be used to push back against the "but they also lynched whites" argument that I heard every year from white students, but could also be scarring for students of color, or any student who has difficulty with brutality or violence. Training provided by the United States Holocaust Memorial Museum around the use of graphic materials is illustrative here:

> Graphic material should be used judiciously and only to the extent necessary to achieve the lesson objective. Try to select images and texts that do not exploit the students' emotional vulnerability or that might be construed as disrespectful to the victims themselves. Instead of avoiding important topics because the visual images are graphic, use other approaches to address the material. ("Guidelines for Teaching About the Holocaust," 2022)

Using these guidelines as a rubric, the postcards help achieve the lesson objective if the lesson focuses on efforts to eliminate the practice and not a perseveration on the violence. Their misuse could easily exploit students' emotional vulnerabilities and existing fears and prejudices.

Thus, having students examine the website collection of the sources would not be advisable, but there is power in the use of one postcard. Providing a trigger warning and an opt-out for students, along with mediation by the teacher to provide context, can harness the power of the image to set the stage for an investigation into the anti-lynching movement, the life of Ida B. Wells, or the tools utilized under Jim Crow to erode the successes of Reconstruction. The same logic applies to other images. Unstructured and non-teacher-mediated examination of concentration camps or brutal passages from slave narratives, anti-LGBTQ+ violence, or other hard histories is not a sound instructional practice. Judicious, intentionally mediated, and limited use can allow for the use of images without leading to detrimental impacts on students.

A final word on resources is necessary. Although they play no role in a legitimate investigation, "word scrambles, crossword puzzles . . . do not encourage critical analysis but instead [lead] to low-level types of thinking" and thus have no part in the resource trail used to support investigations into inquiries about hard history topics ("Guidelines for Teaching About the Holocaust," 2022). There is a rich repository of historical sources for most hard history topics and a thoughtful selection, aligned with a focused question to structure the investigation, can seed the ground for a fruitful investigation, but if the instructional strategy is not selected with the same intentionality, that ground will not remain fertile.

The final guardrail for successfully integrating inquiry with hard histories focuses on the instructional techniques employed. Topics like slavery, immigration, LGBTQ+ discrimination, lynching, and others should not be conducted in a way where there is limited adult participation to mediate concerns and provide stability when, or if, student emotional vulnerabilities are exposed (Sabataso, 2020). Open-ended debates and especially simulations should not be used when inquiring about hard history topics ("Why Simulation Activities Should Not Be Used," 2018).

As explored previously, discussions are an excellent way to allow students to dialogue about important topics in history and social studies (Teaching Tolerance, 2019). The goal of a good discussion is to allow students to drive the dialogue and the teacher to retreat to the edges of the conversation. For many topics, this is effective pedagogy. For hard history topics, it is problematic. Because of the emotional nature of the Holocaust, chattel slavery, gender discrimination, and misogyny, a discussion that has the teacher off to the side and places students in the driver's seat does not allow for the mediation necessary to provide context, clear up misconceptions, or guarantee the safe space needed to wrestle with these topics. Having a discussion component in an inquiry about a hard history topic is important, but it is not recommended that teachers remove themselves from the dialogue.

Simulations also have their place in history instruction, but not when it comes to emotionally fraught issues of exploitation, brutality, and discrimination (Gonzalez, 2019). Unfortunately, simulations continue to be employed by teachers, especially around topics like the Holocaust and slavery (Drake, 2008; Schwartz, 2019). Having students simulate a slave auction or "reenact scenes from the Holocaust," including "digging their classmates' mass graves and simulating the shooting of victims," manipulates students emotionally in hopes that they will connect with events from the past (Asbury, 2021). These dreadful, and sadly all too frequently occurring, pedagogical decisions perpetuate an oversimplification of horrific events, minimize the actual trauma experienced by the participants in the past, recreate racist power dynamics, and can cause emotional hurt for students (Schwartz, 2019). Bottom line: Do not use simulations when investigating difficult histories; they trivialize "the experience of the victims and can leave students with the impression at the conclusion of the activity that they actually know what it was like to experience these atrocities" ("Why Simulation Activities," 2018).

Absent simulations and open-ended discussions, teachers should select structured instructional strategies that immerse students in the historical sources that allow students to hear the voices of those who experienced these events. Source evaluation either individually, in small groups, or utilizing a grouping strategy like a jigsaw or think-pair-share lend themselves to investigations on hard history topics, including those involving LGBTQ+ people.

LGBTQ+ HISTORY

LGBTQ+ students have always been in my classes, but as I worked to incorporate the voices of African Americans, immigrants, religious minorities, Latinos, and others, the realization hit me that my LGBTQ+ students never had an opportunity to see themselves as part of the American narrative. In addition, all my students were being denied the opportunity to see the full complexity of the American experience and how the LGBTQ+ struggle for rights fits into the overall American story. An effective curriculum should serve as a window and a mirror, and in terms of the LGBTQ+ historical experience, mine was only partially meeting this admonition (Berman, 2022; Styles, 1996). When teachers do not know about a topic, person, or time period, their usual reaction is to avoid teaching it. When a lack of knowledge is paired with a lack of resources, the chance of a topic being taught decreases even more. Mix in the notion that a topic is controversial, and it is rare that it will be part of an instructional program. This was my reality when I realized that my United States History course was deficient when it came to the voices and experiences of LGBTQ+ people.

A recent study by GLSEN demonstrates that the most significant issue is that LGBTQ+ stories are simply absent from the narrative. Sixty-six percent of the representative national sample of LGBTQ youth surveyed indicated that there was not any representation of LGBTQ+ people in the curriculum, and for the small percentage who did encounter LGBTQ+ people, the representation was negative (GLSEN, 2019). This critical American history must be integrated into existing units so as to normalize the study of LQBTQ+ people (Berman, 2022; Collins & Ehrenhalt, n.d.; Fleming et al., 2019). Essential to broadening the historical narrative being investigated is to include LGBTQ+ stories, but not remarginalize them through inclusion at the end of a unit. When examining my course, I looked for opportunities where I could capitalize on historical eras during which LGBTQ figures played a prominent role, leverage LGBTQ movements within the context of different social movements, and "eradicate the erasure" of these stories that existed within my course and cover LGBTQ+ rights history by beginning with the 19th and 20th centuries (Maguth & Taylor, 2004). My goal was clear, but I was lacking several tools in my pedagogical toolbox to make it a reality.

Lack of personal knowledge, lack of instructional resources, and the fact that some community members considered this a controversial topic presented themselves as barriers to my own growth. In this respect, I was no different from most teachers (Berman, 2022). Nevertheless, I knew that I needed to push the instructional envelope and provide a richer, more accurate representation of the American past. It was time to lean into the work.

My first step was to expand my own limited knowledge. Like most teachers of my generation, my high school, undergraduate, and graduate educations did not provide any foundational knowledge on the LGBTQ+

experience (Thornton, 2002, 2003). Randy Shilts's *And the Band Played On* (1987/2007) was the first book I read that centered LGBTQ+ experiences, but it was far from a comprehensive history. Thankfully, Amazon and Google focused their algorithms in the right direction, as I was able to verse myself in this history. John D'Emilio's work, *Sexual Politics, Sexual Communities: The Making of a Homosexual Minority in the United States* (1983), opened my exploration. Also helpful were some library reference books that compiled primary sources about the LGBTQ+ experience in the United States. Like most teachers, my learning was autodidactic, but the knowledge barrier was quickly overcome.

Concomitant to growing my personal knowledge, I also sought instructional resources to facilitate the development of investigations. Sadly, it was a short and fruitless exploration: There was nothing. It was the early 2000s when I started this work, and even the growing reach of the Internet could not provide anything around LGBTQ+ history. Textbooks at best mentioned Stonewall, supplementary sources were nonexistent, and the digitization of resources was just starting (Mayo, 2011; Thornton, 2002, 2003). Anything I used instructionally would have to be self-authored. The good news is that at the time of publication of this book, the quantity and quality of instructional resources, accessible online archival materials, and teachers who have incorporated these topics into their instruction has exploded. This explosion has allowed more teachers to bring these topics into the classroom.

The final barrier was the concern over how students, colleagues, administrators, and parents would react to the inclusion of these stories into my course. By the early 2000s, Ellen was out, Will was living with Grace, "don't ask, don't tell" was under attack, *The L Word* was on cable, and the Internet was providing more access to information about homosexuality. My students were coming of age in a popular culture that promoted acceptance and understanding of LGBTQ+ people (Fowler & LaBoiunty, 2019; Jennings, 2006; Mayo, 2017; Thornton, 2003). The younger age cohort was showing a greater level of toleration and acceptance of same-sex marriage and people, and in 2011, the percentage of Americans who supported same sex-marriage surpassed those opposed and never looked back (https://www.pewresearch.org/politics/2017/10/05/5-homosexuality-gender-and-religion/). I quickly realized that most of my students were not only expecting to learn these stories, but were disappointed by their absence (Snapp et al., 2015).

GETTING BY WITH THE HELP OF SOME FRIENDS!

In 2015, all my preparation was ready to go live, and then I left the classroom. After 22 years of teaching high school, I moved into a state-level position overseeing K–12 social studies. Sadly, I was never able to execute my work around the incorporation of LGBTQ+ history into my United States History course. Thankfully, I have been able to work with two amazing teachers who picked up this work, incorporated the lessons into their classrooms, and shared student work and their personal reflections.

I have known and worked with Adam and Nicole since they entered the profession. They have a strong understanding of historical thinking, of teaching students with diverse needs, and also of the work ethic needed to focus on continual growth as professionals. They were also aided by the addition of state and local curricular requirements that required coverage of these topics. Adam and Nicole teach in a large urban school system that is socioeconomically and demographically diverse. Adam teaches in a school that has a significant English Language Learner population, and Nicole teaches in a school that is predominately African American. I am grateful for these teachers continuing work that I was unable to bring across the finish line.

The lessons I share in this chapter were envisioned as unified investigations to be taught in the last three units of my United States History course. Although separated by other lessons within each unit, the unified arc of the three investigations was to help students move from the mistreatment of LGBTQ+ people in the 1950s through the Supreme Court's decision in *Obergefell v. Hodges* (2015). I wanted students to understand the goals, tools, and outcomes of one of the most effective political movements of the late 20th and early 21st centuries. The focal point was how LGBTQ+ people used the tools of democracy to gain political and economic rights and social acceptance, and for students to understand the barriers that needed to be overcome to achieve these goals.

WHY THE LAVENDER SCARE?

The first lesson in this three-lesson arc focused on the Lavender Scare of the early 1950s. The selection of this event aligns well with the recommendation that when integrating LGBTQ+ history into courses, teachers should look for places where the LGBTQ+ experience intersects with subjects already taught (Collins & Ehrenhalt, n.d.). In this case, the Lavender Scare occurred simultaneously with the rise and fall of McCarthyism, a topic already woven into the structure of the existing course. The additional examination of the Lavender Scare deepens students' understanding of McCarthyism and allows students to see LGBTQ+ people as part of the broader historical narrative being studied.

Starting the deep dive into the LGBTQ+ fight for legal rights with the Lavender Scare also provided an opportunity to go back to move forward. Often teachers do not teach every event in chronological order. Sometimes it is better to wait to teach a topic until it can provide the context for a deeper dive later in time. For example, when teaching immigration, teachers often do not address immigration with a full lesson until after they teach the 1924 Immigration Restriction Act until they get to the 1965 Immigration Act. This does not mean that changes, both subtle and substantive, did not occur to immigration policy between 1924 and 1965, but instead, that those changes are contextually more important when setting up the examination of the reforms of 1965 than they are to teach a lesson on each immigration action between 1924 and 1965. In the case of the Lavender Scare, students needed the context for the events of the 1950s by going back to examine how the treatment of LGBTQ+ people has evolved since the 1920s. I do not teach a lesson on the LGBTQ+ experience in each unit, nor do we, say, teach economic history in each unit. Instead, when information becomes relevant, we go back to pick up a topic and bring it forward so that it aids our understanding of the topic being investigated. In this case, students needed to see how homophobia had become more mainstream and gay life more marginalized.

The change in the public understanding of homosexuality, the term used in the 1950s to describe gay men and lesbians, is best exemplified by the 1952 decision by the American Psychiatric Association to define homosexuality as a "sociopathic personality disturbance" in the publication of the first *Diagnostic and Statistical Manual of Mental Disorders*. Defining homosexuality as a medical malady led to efforts to repress, stigmatize, and persecute LGBTQ+ persons throughout society. The United States Post Office kept names on a list to monitor any homosexual "paraphernalia" being received, so they could tip off the police and have LGBTQ+ persons arrested, while the U.S. military would dishonorably discharge, the Federal government would fire, and local school systems would dismiss anyone suspected of being LGBTQ+. In addition, police officers would often solicit sex in areas known to be gay-friendly, and then entrap suspected gay men and lesbians and arrest them for soliciting sex. By the 1950s, the legal effort to marginalize gay and lesbian men and women was centered in the nation's capital. Drawn by employment opportunities due to government jobs expanding under the New Deal and by the federal expansion during World War II, Washington, DC was home to a gay community that was being harassed and entrapped by police (Johnson, 2006).

Simultaneous with the panic over same-gender relationships was the emergence of the Red Scare. Ignited by Senator Joseph McCarthy, the Red Scare set off a furious investigation for communists who were purportedly infiltrating the United States government and threating the security of the nation. Both scares shared the fear of being undermined by something that was considered "un-American" or unnatural: Communism on the one hand and sexual orientation on the other.

The later-named Lavender Scare found form through two congressional investigations. These investigations discovered that the military and federal government had already been accusing individuals of homosexuality and had fired and discharged almost 5,000 people, but:

> . . . the committee had discovered little evidence to back up the claim [that homosexuals were vulnerable to blackmail and thus were security threats]. It had never found a single example of a homosexual American citizen who had been blackmailed into revealing state secrets. And it had uncovered considerable difference of opinion within the U.S. Government over whether foreign governments attempted to blackmail homosexuals. (Johnson, 2006)

Despite the lack of any evidence, the McCarthy-inspired paranoia induced a fear-driven effort to purge gay people from government service and was institutionalized in 1953 when President Eisenhower issued Executive Order 10450, which added "sexual perversion" to the list of employment regulations that could lead to someone being dismissed from federal government employment. Between 1953 and 1974, upwards of an estimated 10,000 LGBTQ+ persons lost their jobs because of this executive action. Yet, amid this public persecution, people like Frank Kameny emerged to push back and set the stage for the events at the Stonewall Inn in 1969.

My Lavender Scare investigation thus is intended to allow students to understand how multiple causes led to this event. In turn, the persecution that occurred during this scare becomes the context for the second lesson that examines the origins of the gay liberation movement. To facilitate this, students investigate the question:

Why the Lavender Scare?

From my perspective, this lesson is important so that students can understand the context in which the gay liberation movement emerged. Students needed to understand the depth of discrimination encountered by LGBTQ+ people. This lesson was a potential land mine because it could give sanction to students in my class who were uncomfortable with same-sex relationships to latch onto specious homophobic arguments made in the mid–20th century to discriminate against LGBTQ+ people. In addition, there was the risk that LGBTQ+ students in my classroom could feel emotional revulsion to what they were learning. I knew that leaving "queer history out of the curriculum" was as detrimental to students as it was to teach it in an irresponsible manner (Jones, 2020). I wanted to surface this history for all my students but needed to do so in a manner than would not simultaneously traumatize teenagers who may or may not have become comfortable with their own sexuality.

The first way to navigate this fine line is to ensure that whenever in the scope and sequence of your course you surface the voices of the LGBTQ+ community, you initiate the lesson with a discussion of appropriate language. The language around sex, gender, and sexuality has evolved. When I was growing up in the 1970s and 1980s, the term "queer" was considered derogatory. Now the term has been reclaimed by some within the LGBTQ+ community and in some circumstances—but not all—is now considered appropriate (Perlman, 2019). Helping students to understand what terms mean, and how and why they have evolved, can create a sense of community, and set guardrails for historical investigations of the LGBTQ+ experience (Collins & Ehrenhalt, n.d.).

The second way to avoid curricular violence is to consider deeply the resources you use in the lesson. Like slavery, LGBTQ+ history requires that teachers employ a stronger oversight of the materials of instruction. *Teaching Hard History* makes it clear that one of the issues with teaching and learning around slavery is that too often students are taught the topic without context. To sidestep the violence, racism, brutality, and dehumanization that occurred under chattel slavery, teachers and curriculum "shield from [students] the reality of slavery in American History." In many cases, "students learn about liberation before they learn about enslavement" (Shuster, 2018). We do not want to glorify the violence and racism that were created to justify the institution of chattel slavery, but we do want students to understand the institution in order to contextualize the efforts to destroy it. The same holds true for the discrimination and ugliness that defined historical reactions to LGBTQ+ peoples. We do not want to glorify discrimination faced by LGBTQ+ peoples, nor do we want instruction to relive the violent acts perpetrated against them. Students do need to understand the injustice and oppression that gave rise to moments, leaders, a movement, and significant changes to American life. The question that teachers must wrestle with is not: How do I avoid the ugliness associated with slavery or immigration, or gender and sexuality? Instead, the question is how to provide historical context for the freedom movements associated with these hard histories while not fetishizing the violence and hatred. Much of that comes down to timing, emphasis, and the resources selected.

In 2015, a high school history teacher in Missouri shared a clip from a 1959 film, *Boys Beware*. Jointly produced by the Inglewood, California Police Department, and the Inglewood Unified School District, the film depicts "homosexual men as stalkers who gain the trust of young boys with offers of soda pop and pornography before tricking them into having a homosexual relationship" (Kaufman, 2015). The teacher's intention was to use the film to demonstrate how attitudes and beliefs about same-sex relationships have changed over time. But the openly anti-gay themes of the film upset some students in the class. The teacher was suspended and pushed into retirement for violating district policies regarding the promotion of discrimination (Zimmerman & Robertson, 2017). When developing this lesson, I discovered the same resource. It offers a clear insight into the prejudicial views of the time period, but it also perpetuates negative stereotypes and harmful depictions of LQBTQ+ individuals. I decided against using it for these reasons. Explaining the change in historical attitudes over time is

Figure 6.2. Lavender Scare Sources

Source	Source the Document: How might this information and the context potentially impact the information provided by the source?	Why the Lavender Scare?
Source A: "Problem of Homosexuals and Sex Perverts in the Department of State." Memo from Carlisle Humelsine to Undersecretary of State James E. Webb, June 23, 1950.		
Source B: Interview with Helen James, 2018. **OR** **Source B:** Interview with Joseph C. Walsh, Director of the Security Office, 1989.		
Source C: "The Theory and Practice of Soviet Intelligence," Alexander Orlov. Declassified and released on September 22, 1993.		
Source D: Letter from Senator Ben Cardin to Secretary of State John Kerry, November 29, 2016.		
Source E: Extension of Remarks of the Honorable Katharine St. George of New York in the House of Representatives, May 1, 1952.		
Source F: Executive Order 10450-Security Requirements for Government Employment, President Dwight D. Eisenhower, April 27, 1953.		

important, but it should not be done in a way that inadvertently perpetuates negative stereotypes.

For this lesson I landed on six sources, described in Figure 6.2, that enable students to explore the multiple factors that coalesced into the Lavender Scare and to do so within the context in which these events unfolded.

The final and very lesson-specific strategy I employ to ensure that I strike a balance with this lesson is to teach it within the context of my Domestic Early Cold War unit. Students would enter the lesson having studied McCarthyism, the Rosenberg Trial, atomic espionage, and the Cold War hysteria that impacted the United States in the late 1940s and 1950s. Placing this lesson in its historical context allows students to investigate the Lavender Scare with an understanding of the events, people, and ideas that defined life during that time period. The past is a foreign country, and thus placing the Lavender Scare in the historical context in which it unfolded helps students to see the event not through contemporary lens, but instead as an event steeped in its own time period.

THE INVESTIGATION

Beginning with the end in mind, the intention of the lesson is for students to build a historical argument that contextualizes the Lavender Scare and allows students to associate multiple causes with the actions of the federal government. To facilitate construction of the argument, students utilize hexagonal thinking. At the midpoint of the lesson, students are provided a bag of laminated hexagons and washable pens. They are asked to construct a claim and then build a visual representation of their argument about how the multiple causes of the Lavender Scare worked to facilitate that event. The variety of the sizes of the hexagons, displayed in Figure 6.3, indicates the importance of the cause in relationship to the other causes.

The arrows are used to demonstrate the connections and relationship between the causes (Chapman, 2003; Potash, 2020; Weibe, 2020). I also provide students labels for the hexagons. Students must consider sourcing and contextualization issues when they are weighing evidence and building their arguments. Non-causes can be unconnected to the overall argument chain. There are several ways to differentiate this tool. You can allow students to cut out the hexagons and glue them to a larger sheet as they construct their argument; you can have students work independently or in small groups; you can allow students to develop the causes that will populate the hexagons; and/or you can use online tools rather than traditional paper. With this end in mind, how do we get students into this difficult period of American History?

Structuring the Investigation

The lesson begins with students viewing the trailer for the documentary *The Lavender Scare* to introduce the events (https://www.youtube.com/watch?v=Y_Dui2YxEO4) and establish the question that drives this

Figure 6.3. Lavender Scare Hexagons

McCarthyism	Fear of Communism
Political Gain	Homophobia
Fear	Other:

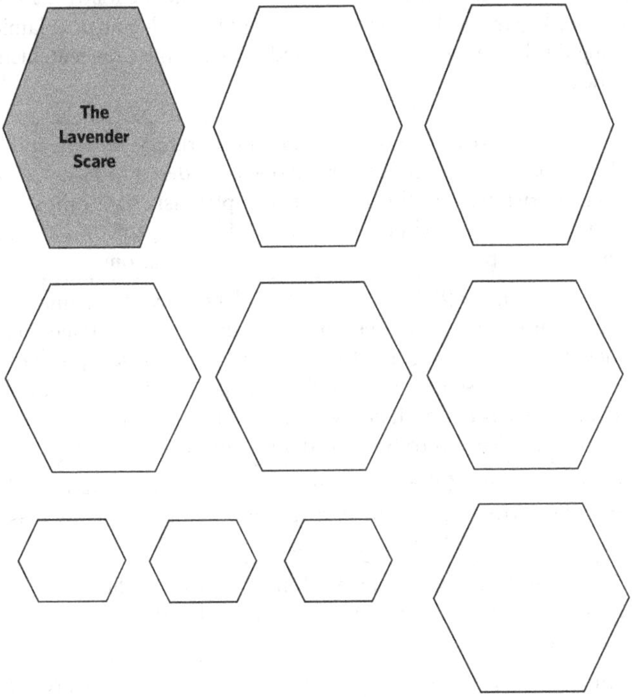

The
Lavender
Scare

investigation: **Why the Lavender Scare?** Next, I provide students with examples of how gay people were discriminated against, including by the American Psychological Association; local, state, and federal laws; and the enforcement of these laws. This discussion leads to a debrief of the reading in Figure 6.4.

Students often want terms such as "security risk," "deviate," or "loyalty" explained either because they are unsure of the definition or they see the term as antithetical to language used today, or because they think that the words as they were applied in the mid–20th century create issues for LGBTQ+ peoples. This is an important teachable moment to help students to understand how and why language around LGBTQ+ individuals has changed over time.

The discussion of the words serves as an entryway into discussing the actions taken by the federal government that facilitated the execution of the

Figure 6.4. Lavender Scare Reading

"These People Are Frightened to Death": Why the Lavender Scare?

The Lavender Scare was an effort by the federal government to investigate, identify, and dismiss all government employees suspected of being homosexuals. Between 1953 and 1975, upwards of an estimated 10,000 LGBTQ+ persons were fired as a result. Various events contributed to this effort. Examine the following timeline of events and circle key terms that seem to be important to defining/explaining/understanding this historical phenomena, and then complete the statement at the bottom of the chart.

1946	Congress approved a law that gave the secretary of state and defense the "broad discretion" to fire anyone considered to be a "security risk." Security risk was, in this instance, a euphemism for homosexual. Starting in 1950, a similar rider was added to provide 11 other federal agencies the power to conduct similar investigations.
1947	Executive Order 9835 issued by President Harry S. Truman allowed the federal government to investigate and dismiss government employees if they were members of the Communist Party, a fascist, or had "sympathetic associations" with either group. The order established loyalty boards to conduct these investigations and recommend dismissal for anyone deemed to be a loyalty risk but not a security risk.
1950	Senator Joseph McCarthy alleged that communists were working in the State Department, and the two specific examples he provided were also homosexuals he claimed were "security risks."
1950	Deputy undersecretary of state John Peurifoy testified in front of Congress that the State Department had already fired 91 homosexual employees deemed "security risks."
1951	FBI director J. Edgar Hoover established the "Sex Deviates" program, which required investigators to investigate fully any allegations that a federal employee might be a homosexual. In addition, he required that local police departments should indicate on a fingerprint card any time a federal employee was arrested for homosexual acts.
1950	Senators Wherry and Hill conducted an investigation. They heard from the Washington, DC, police, government officials from the State and Defense Departments, military intelligence, and the Civil Service Commission. The Committee produced a report that made the argument that homosexuals were a threat to national security. The report was sent to U.S. embassies and foreign intelligence agencies.
1950	During the Hoey Committe investigation, Congress gathered information from federal agencies, law enforcement, judicial authorities, and the medical community to determine the number of suspected homosexuals investigated or removed from employment and to determine the government's policies and procedures regarding the "suitability" of hiring homosexual employees. The committee reported that an estimated 5,000 homosexuals had been detected in the military and civilian government workforces.

Figure 6.4. *(continued)*

1952	Executive Order 10450 issued by President Dwight D. Eisenhower, ended the Loyalty Review Board and ordered all federal agencies to investigate employees to determine if they were "security risks."

An important term to understand/define/explain is ____________________
because____

____

____

____

____

____

____

Lavender Scare. This portion of the lesson ends with students speculating on possible historical justifications for the Lavender Scare. Prior to transition to the document work, I explain and model for students the hexagonal thinking activity that will serve as both formative and summative assessment for the lesson. This portion of the lesson ends with students considering, discussing, and labeling their hexagons based on their initial understanding of the Lavender Scare.

The concern, as with any sort or prediction strategy such as an anticipation guide, is that students will arrive at a claim and then never alter it. In this instance, the concern was that students would weigh one of the factors to the exclusion of the others. This is a possibility because this is an evidence-based investigation: Students only fall back to their first thoughts about causality if they see the evidence as strongly reinforcing their predictions. If they try to argue that they were right in their preliminary prediction, then it is incumbent on the teacher to require students to link to the evidence and not just instinct. In post-instruction interviews, both Adam and Nicole indicated that students did not simply rely on their initial instincts, but instead altered their causal maps based on the evidence and discussion. As depicted in Figure 6.5, you can see how two different groups altered their claims and the evidence that supported their argument. One student group initially felt that the Lavender Scare was driven by needs for political gain, McCarthyism, and the concomitant fear of Communism. As we will see momentarily, exposure to the source trail alters their claim.

The source work in the lesson hinges on two factors. First, students wrestle with the relationship between homophobia and fear of Communism. Students' discussion pivots around questions like: Does one have a stronger influence on the other? Was the fear of Communism used as a cover for

Figure 6.5. Group A Lavender Scare Hexagons, Pre-Sources

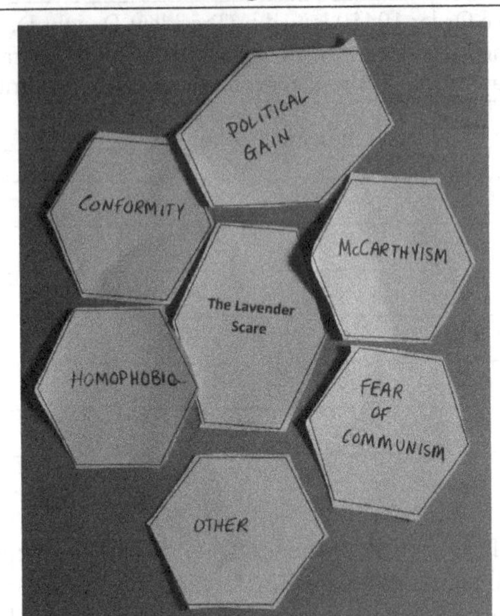

homophobia? Second, students raise significant questions about the validity of the argument that being gay or lesbian made someone a "security risk." They come to realize that sexual relationships of any kind make someone potentially vulnerable to committing acts of espionage, but that ascribing this risk just to gay people is homophobia defined. While these discussions are taking place, students are toggling back and forth between the discussions and the organization of the hexagons. A pencil or dry-erase/overhead markers enables students to change their minds and relabel hexagons as their claim takes form. As the images below illustrate, students build, change, and revise their claims and the relative weight of each factor. Once students arrive at a consensus regarding their claim, they share those claims with classmates and explain why they assigned the numerous factors to the differently sized hexagons. As depicted in Figure 6.6 below, the group from above changed their thought processes.

Central to their discussion were both contextual and evidence-related factors. Contextually, students considered how suburbanization and the milieu of the 1950s reinforced notions of conformity and perpetuated a fear of anything "different since we saw how important the idea of the nuclear family was during this time." This knowledge was gained from previous lessons on suburbanization and the domestic culture of the Cold War. They saw evidence in this embracing of conformity and the fears within

Figure 6.6. Group A Lavender Scare Hexagons, Post-Sources

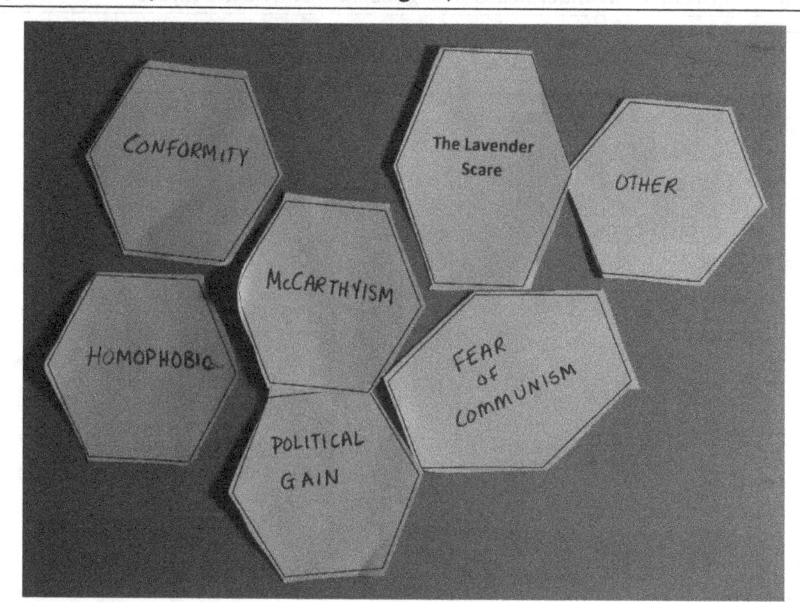

the language of President Eisenhower's executive order that connected the context to the evidence.

In the second group, depicted in Figure 6.7, you can also see an evolution in student thinking. In this case, prior to the evidence examination, students determined that homophobia and conformity were unrelated to the fear of Communism, McCarthyism, and political gain in causing the Lavender Scare. After their examination and discussion of the evidence, the group built more of a clumped causal chain that reduced political gain and instead gave more weight, or in this instance size, to the fear of Communism and McCarthyism.

The unpacking of group decisions was punctuated with questions about the sourcing and context for the evidence utilized in the investigation. Students drew serious concerns about the weight that they could ascribe to the arguments made by sources C and E. Deep consideration of the sourcing and context of those sources led to students giving more credence to homophobia and fear of Communism than to any arguments about the "security risks" presented by government employment of gay people. In Figure 6.8, you will see that students who unpacked their thinking at the conclusion of the lesson gave primacy to McCarthyism and a generalized "fear" of things that did not conform to traditional norms.

One of the most significant things I learned in early iterations of this lesson is that students did not appreciate how ingrained homophobia was

Figure 6.7. Group B Lavender Scare Hexagons, Pre- and Post-Sources

Before Evidence Examination	After Evidence Examination
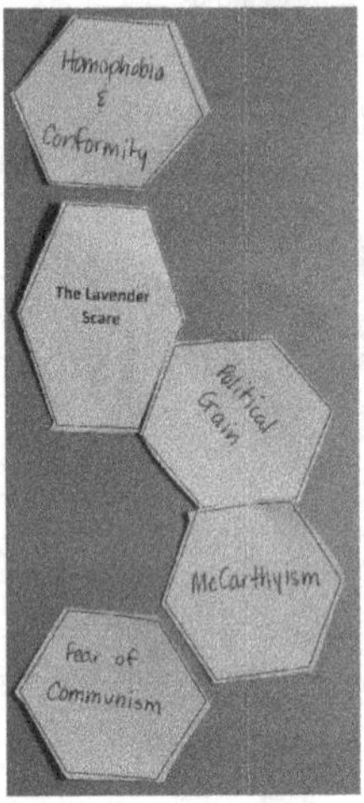	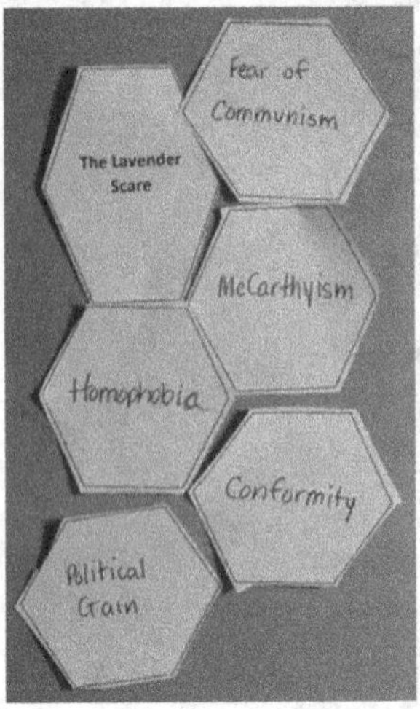

in American culture prior to the 1950s. This was a direct result of my own instructional choices. Students needed to understand LGBTQ+ history as it existed prior to the Lavender Scare. By introducing the fight for gay rights in the 1950s, I had unintentionally reinforced both the invisibility of LGBTQ+ peoples and created a misconception among students as they considered the causality of the Lavender Scare. As David K. Johnson reminds us, "we should not forget that the Lavender Scare was a reaction to an earlier time of openness and visibility for the gay community. Such periods of progress are always subject to a backlash" ("Interview with David K. Johnson," 2004). Clearly, I needed to provide more insight for students around gay life in the 1920s through the 1940s to help set a stronger foundation for them to investigate events in the 1950s. As good teachers do, my partners in this endeavor were able to think on their feet and help to reinforce the way homophobia had manifested itself well before the 1950s, and help students to contextualize that causal factor. In the long term, the initial teaching of this lesson will lead to the inclusion of other lessons that surface the LGBTQ+ experience within the broader American narrative so that students are better armed to wrestle with the causes of the Lavender Scare. Lessons on the 1920s and the Harlem Renaissance, inclusion into discussions of impacts of World War II on the home front, and others will help to bring greater visibility to the LGBTQ+ experience prior to the deep dive into the Lavender Scare.

Figure 6.8. Student Responses

The lavender scare is caused by the fear of being different which is connected to McCarthyism. The fear of communism is apart of the McCarthyism because it relates to fear of something different leading to homophobia. McCarthyism made it so it was okay for these witch hunts for a specific group of people like Communist which then extended to homosexuals. This all relates to homophobia causing executive order 10450 by eisenhower, baring homosexuals from being employed from the federal government.

The fear of communism along with fear of bombs in the 1950s started the causes of the lavender scare. with hightened fear of anyone being a communist, Mccarthyism was born along with the investigations of supposed communists in hope of political gain. Then, erupting the lavender scare which support belief of homophobia, which was later an important cause of the lavender scare. By spreading McCarthyism and fear of communism, homosexuals were targeted even more which led people to be skeptical and support homophobia. Overall, the lavender scare was driven by the fear of communism to justify homophobia / hide it in to support political gain during the 1950s.

The causes relate to one another because most of them are people acting out of fear. People were scared of communism and things like homosexuals which they didn't understand. For example, in source A, they mentioned how not much was known about homosexuals, so because they were scared of communists and McCarthyism, they probably tried to put the blame on something they didn't know about. This influenced my thinking because I realized that they were mostly acting out of fear and that even though they are still probably homophobic, they just didn't know about homosexuals and were already very on edge which could be a reason why they targeted homosexuals. Source B says that different was associated with communists which kind of backs that up.

These causes relate to one another because the fear of communism made people, like Joseph McCarthy, famous and gave him more political power. Because of his political power, he could make wild accusations and used McCarthyism, which made people not want to look like communists. Because of this conformity, people were looking for people who were different which caused homophobia and the stigmatization of gay people. The evidence influenced my thinking because in Source E, St. George said, "... members of one conspiracy are prone to join another conspiracy." This shows that the fear of communism made people homophobic.

Ultimately, the investigation allowed students to understand that a perverse soup of homophobia, political gain, McCarthyism, fears of communism, social forces reinforcing 1950s conformity, and other factors congealed and led to the disruption of both public and private lives of over 10,000 LGBTQ+ persons in public service. These student interpretations aligned well with the arguments made by David K. Johnson in *The Lavender Scare: The Cold War Persecution of Gays and Lesbians in the Federal Government* (2006), who presents a nuanced argument about multiple factors coalescing to manifest this event. Most importantly, the Lavender Scare investigation also allowed for the introduction of Frank J. Kameny, a pivotal bridge from the persecution of the 1950s to the slow revolution that exploded on the evening of June 28, 1969.

IT WASN'T JUST STONEWALL

The second investigation in this lesson arc focuses on the question: **When was the modern gay liberation movement born?** This investigation is taught within the context of the broader rights revolutions on the 1960s and in a separate unit for the Lavender Scare investigation. Prior to initiating the investigation, students have already examined the civil rights fights for African Americans, women, Latinos, and Native Americans. From the Lavender Scare lesson, students will know about the Mattachine Society, Frank Kameny, and some of the early efforts that emerged in resistance to the scare.

I initiate the lesson by projecting the following image and asking students to determine what is happening and if the image and/or the events depicted in Figure 6.9 are spontaneous or staged. The image was taken in 1966 at Julius's bar in New York City. Inspired by the sit-ins utilized by the civil rights movement, members of the Mattachine Society sought to draw attention to the discrimination that gay patrons encountered in New York bars. The intention was to order a drink, identify themselves as homosexual, and, when denied, use this as a launching point for a lawsuit about anti-gay discrimination. The press had been notified beforehand that the sip-in was to take place. The first bar that the protesters patronized closed after they were tipped off by the media, and the second two visited served them drinks. Fred McDarrah of the *Village Voice* newspaper was at the bar to cover the event and snapped the photograph the students examine at the outset of the lesson.

When analyzing the image, students focus on several things: the way people are dressed, the fact that they are all white and all male, and in particular, the bartender's hands over the glass. What tips students off to the fact that the image was staged and not spontaneous was the location of the person shooting the picture. The position is perfect to capture both the Mattachine Society protesters and the bartender and thus helps students to

Figure 6.9. The Sip-In

Source: Fred W. McDarrah via Getty Images

understand that the image was not staged, but also not as spontaneous as it may appear. Instead, it was an effort by a political group to gain attention and news coverage for an example of discrimination based on sexuality.

After establishing that protests against legal, political, and economic discrimination were occurring in ways similar to the other rights movements they have studied, the lesson shifts to a debrief of the homework assignment found in Figure 6.10. The intent of the homework is to paint a picture of organizations, methods, and goals of the gay liberation movement and to set up the central question that students will be investigating.

The point of this homework is not to determine if students correctly label the efforts as led by organizations or individuals, or if they determined the correct number of medium-sized impacts. Instead, those labeling actions serve as a reading strategy that exposes students to the actions taken across time and geography to push back on the discrimination faced by LGBTQ+ persons. I debrief not by checking the A's and O's, but instead with a series of questions:

- Was there a gay rights movement before 1969?
- How do you know it was a movement?
- Did it effect change?

Figure 6.10. Stonewall Reading

Gay Liberation Pre- and Post-Stonewall Riots

The Gay Liberation Movement focused on gaining the legal, political, and social rights of full citizenship for all LGBTQ+ individuals. Examine the following and label them as **organizations** (O) or **actions** (A), and assess their impact as **small** (S), **medium** (M), or **large** (L).

	1924	The Society for Human Rights is founded by Henry Gerber in Chicago. The first gay rights organization publishes the first American publication for homosexuals, *Friendship and Freedom.*
	1948	Biologist and sex researcher Alfred Kinsey publishes *Sexual Behavior in the Human Male.* Kinsey concluded that homosexual behavior is not restricted to people who identify themselves as homosexual.
	1950	In Los Angeles, gay rights activist Harry Hay founds America's first sustained national gay rights organization. In an attempt to change public perception of homosexuality, the Mattachine Society aims to "eliminate discrimination, derision, prejudice and bigotry," to assimilate homosexuals into mainstream society, and to cultivate the notion of an "ethical homosexual culture."
	1955	In San Francisco, the Daughters of Bilitis become the first lesbian rights organization in the United States. The organization hosts social functions, providing alternatives to lesbian bars and clubs, which are frequently raided by police.
	1956	American psychologist Evelyn Hooker shares her paper "The Adjustment of the Male Overt Homosexual," which concludes homosexuality is not a clinical entity and that heterosexuals and homosexuals do not differ significantly.
	1958	In *One, Inc. v. Olesen,* the United States Supreme Court rules in favor of the First Amendment rights of the lesbian, gay, bisexual, and transgender (LGBT) magazine *One: The Homosexual Magazine.*
	1959	Furious that LAPD officers were arresting their friends purely for legally congregating in Cooper's Donuts, a popular gay meeting place, a group of LGBTQ+ persons fought police officers at the donut shop in downtown Los Angeles. A large group pelted the officers with donuts, coffee, and paper plates forcing the police to retreat and return with larger numbers.
	1962	Illinois repeals its sodomy laws, becoming the first U.S. state to decriminalize homosexuality.
	1964	A small group of LGBTQ+ persons picketed the draft office in New York City after they discovered that the confidentiality of gay men's draft records was violated.

Figure 6.10. *(continued)*

	1965	Seven men and three women picketed the White House. The first of a series of pickets held throughout the summer, targeting the Civil Service Commission, the State Department, and The Pentagon.
	1965	At Independence Hall in Philadelphia, picketers begin staging the first Reminder Day to call public attention to the lack of civil rights for LGBT people. The gatherings continue annually for five years.
	1965	Approximately 150 people participated in a sit-in when the manager of Dewey's restaurant refused service to "a large number of homosexuals and people wearing non-conformist clothing." Members of the society also leafleted outside the restaurant the following week and negotiated with the owners to bring an end to the denial of service.
	1965	Activists picketed the White House on April 17 and the United Nations on the 18th after learning that Cuba was placing homosexuals in forced labor camps.
	1966	After transgender customers become raucous in a Compton's 24-hour San Francisco cafeteria, management calls police. When a police officer manhandles one of the patrons, she throws coffee in his face and a riot ensues, eventually spilling out onto the street, destroying police and public property. Following the riot, activists established the National Transsexual Counseling Unit, the first peer-run support and advocacy organization in the world.
	1966	A coalition of homophile organizations across the country organized simultaneous demonstrations for Armed Forces Day. The Los Angeles group held a 15-car motorcade and activists picketed in the other cities.
	1967	A police raid on the Black Cat bar led to a demonstration of 400 people that garnered evening news coverage. That demonstration played a role in the founding of the leading national LGBTQ magazine, *The Advocate*.
	1968	The Student Homophile League of Columbia University in New York City picketed and disrupted a panel of psychiatrists discussing homosexuality.
	1969	Gay activist and journalist Gale Whittington was fired by the States Steamship Company after coming out in print. A small group of activists operating under the name "Committee for Homosexual Freedom" (CHF) picketed the company's San Francisco offices every workday between noon and 1:00 for several weeks.

(*continued*)

Figure 6.10. (*continued*)

	1969	Tower Records fired Frank Denaro, believing him to be gay. The Committee for Homosexual Freedom picketed the store for several weeks until Denaro was reinstated. The CHF ran similar pickets of Safeway stores, Macy's, and the Federal Building.
■	1969	Stonewall Riots in New York City
	1970	Christopher St. Liberation Day commemorates the one-year anniversary of the Stonewall riots. Following the event, thousands of members of the LGBT community march through New York into Central Park, in what will be considered America's first gay pride parade. In the coming decades, the annual gay pride parade will spread to dozens of countries around the world.
	1973	The board of the American Psychiatric Association votes to remove homosexuality from its list of mental illnesses.
	1974	Kathy Kozachenko becomes the first openly gay American elected to public office when she wins a seat on the Ann Arbor, Michigan, City Council.
	1977	Harvey Milk wins a seat on the San Francisco Board of Supervisors and is responsible for introducing a gay rights ordinance protecting gays and lesbians from being fired from their jobs. Milk also leads a successful campaign against Proposition 6, an initiative forbidding homosexual teachers. A year later Milk is assassinated.
	1979	An estimated 75,000 people participate in the National March on Washington for Lesbian and Gay Rights. LGBT people and straight allies demand equal civil rights and urge for the passage of protective civil rights legislature.
	1982	Wisconsin becomes the first U.S. state to outlaw discrimination on the basis of sexual orientation.

Students discuss each question in pairs, then quartets, and then as a full class. Students often pointed to the 1962 Illinois law that decriminalized homosexuality and sodomy because they felt it "set the example for other states to follow." The discussion is an opportunity to introduce historical figures and movements like Harry Hay, The Mattachine Society, the Daughters of Bilitis, and Frank Kameny.

Ultimately, the discussion leads to the unveiling of the central question for this investigation:

When was the modern gay liberation movement born?

To attack this question fully, students must understand the events around the Stonewall riots. I provide this via a short video clip describing the Stonewall riots and ask students to identify what happened. This background information on the Stonewall riots facilitates the first effort by students to "cast their vote" for when the movement was born as they move to a corner of the room that best represents their current thinking about the central investigative question. Options include: before the Stonewall riots, at Stonewall, because of Stonewall, other, and not sure (yes, I know, rooms have four corners, but work with me here!). When students arrive at the corner of their choice, they conduct a quick pair-share to unfold their argument and the evidence that they feel best supports their claim. From pair-share the conversation moves to a full-class discussion with each corner making their argument. This is intentionally a quick effort to ground students in the question and for them to consider the events of the time period, but it is not intended to be the definitive conclusion of the lesson. Instead, students need to examine evidence so that they can support their claims with more than just gut instinct.

The investigation is structured with six sources, listed in Figure 6.11, that represent a range of historians, journalists, and movement members reflecting on Stonewall as well as movement participants illuminating their efforts prior to Stonewall.

Students examine their source and then jigsaw with other students to gain a full understanding of the views brought forth about the events at Stonewall. From group discussion, I debrief student thinking by again asking students to vote with their feet by moving to a corner of the room that best represents their current thinking about the central investigative question.

When students arrive at the corner of their choice, they engage in a quick pair-share to unfold their argument and the evidence that they feel best supports their claim. From pair-share, the conversation moves to a full-class discussion with each corner making their argument, substantiating it with evidence, and responding to the arguments made by the other corners. The trick of the discussion is to make sure students root their arguments not only in the events depicted in the homework timeline, but also in the arguments outlined by the various sources examined. After debriefing each of the sources and discussing how they influence the central question, students are often struck by how many of the arguments they had initially posed are aligned with those made by the journalists, historians, and movement participants. This discovery is empowering and creates an alignment between the information they gleaned from the homework and video clip, with the evidence drawn from the historical sources. Students often want to use the names and dates irrespective of the historical sources, and this phase of the lesson allows them to see the how content and argument align to make claims stronger. Win-win!

Figure 6.11. Stonewall Sources

"Watch out. The Liberation is underway." : Were The Stonewall Riots the Birth of the gay liberation movement?

Source	Source the Document: How might this information and the context potentially impact the information provided by the source?	According to the source, when was the modern gay liberation movement born?
Source A: Simon Hall (2010), "The American Gay Rights Movement and Patriotic Protest." *Journal of the History of Sexuality*, *19*(3), pp. 536–562.		
Source B: Interview with Barbara Gittings, 1980s: https://www.youtube.com/watch?v=l5kk81AGcBI		
Source C: Mark Krone (2018). "Stonewall Was Important But Not Because it Was First": https://facingtoday.facinghistory.org/author/mark-krone		
Source D*:* Screaming Queens: The Riot at Compton's Cafeteria, 2005: https://vimeo.com/1667849		
Source E:. Interview with gay liberation movement leader Franklin Kameny, 1982: https://digital.wilcoxarchives.org/islandora/object/islandora%3A155		
Source F: The Mattachine Society, Inc., "In Case You Didn't Know," Tri-fold Brochure, 1956: https://www.campbooks.biz/archive/2019/8/30/the-mattachine-society-in-case-you-didnt-know		

An interesting phenomenon during the discussion of the central investigative question was some students' desire to distinguish between "birth" and "conception." In what is actually a fairly nuanced argument, students parsed out the difference. In their opinion, the more important question is when the seed was planted rather than when the baby was born. These students generally saw the birth of the movement occurring with the high-profile, media-covered events at Stonewall, but that the efforts of numerous people and organizations in the 1950s and 1960s are more important than the birth. As one student wrote, "[The Modern Gay Liberation Movement] was conceived in the 1950s. This is because there is much evidence of some of the first gay liberation groups forming in the late 1950s. An example is the Mattachine Society . . ." In many ways this argument aligns with the intent of the question, opens up discussion, and puts students in the position of supporting their claims with evidence from the sources.

The lesson concludes with one of my old standby assessments: a birth certificate, as illustrated in Figure 6.12. Students complete the birth date and time and the historical "mothers and fathers," and then I give them a choice between two summative questions to surface their thinking.

The student responses in Figure 6.13 show that not only do students use information gleaned from the sources, but they also meld them with interpretations of the events prior to, during, and subsequent to the events at Stonewall. In addition, they even make connections to other information like the relationship between the Black civil rights movement and the gay liberation movement. The assessments reflect the rich discussions, the sources, and previous learning. They also, as student work often does, reflect unclear understandings, misunderstandings, and/or factual errors. None of these distract from a clear pattern of thinking and an attempt on the part of many students to make a claim, support that claim with evidence, and consider significance.

Important to the Stonewall lesson is that it allows students to see LGBTQ+ people possessing agency. In each instance, although obviously targets of de jure and de facto discrimination, violence, and harassment, LGBTQ+ people fought back. Through organizations, protests, petitions, and open resistance, the effort to secure rights for LGBTQ+ people run parallel to the efforts of British colonists to win American independence, suffragettes to win the ballot, and African Americans to destroy Jim Crow. Centering the focus on their agency allows students to see LGBTQ+ people as similar to anyone else they have studied that marshal the tools of democracy to demand and win rights. The emphasis on agency is also at the forefront of the final lesson in this arc.

"NO UNION IS MORE PROFOUND THAN MARRIAGE"

The last lesson in the sweep examines the federal decision to legalize same-sex marriage via the Supreme Court. This is an odd lesson for me because it feels

Figure 6.12. Stonewall Assessment

"Watch out. The Liberation is underway." : Were the Stonewall Riots the Birth of the Gay Liberation Movement?

Based on your knowledge of the events, ideas, organizations, and personalities that associated with the Gay Liberation Movement, you must decide when the movement actually was born and the events, ideas, organizations, and personalities that should be considered the "parents" of the movement. Decide when the movement was born and explain why you selected that time period **OR** who/what gave birth to the movement and why you give them credit. Be specific in your justifications (**5–7 SENTENCES**) and be sure to point to specifics from source analysis and class discussion.

Certificate of Birth

This Certifies that the Gay Rights Movement was born to

____

Mother Father

On

____

Date Time

At

____

____

____

Location (City/State)

Who or what should get credit for giving birth to the Modern Gay Liberation Movement and why?	When was the Modern Gay Liberation Movement born and why?

Figure 6.13. Stonewall Student Responses

Student Responses

The Movement was born after the Stonewall Riots in 1969 as it was the first time the movement received attention, members, and unification. As mentioned in Source C the riots got widespread and even worldwide media attention which caused the movement to become mainstream. With the movement being mainstream it came into the consciousness of the American public including gays, lesbians, openminded people, and politicians making the movement a key issue and one of great importance as now it was relevant thanks to Stonewall. The movement also received a surge in members as seen with Source A how there was an explosion in the number of gay organizations, newspapers, businesses, etc. after Stonewall. Stonewall also granted unification for the movement with source C explaining how gays become united wanting equality both socially and political, and source E notes how it turned the movement from small to grassroots with organizations for gays also increasing over tenfold. The Stonewall riots gave the attention, members, and unification that gave birth to the Modern Gay Liberation Movement, without it the movement would of needed another decisive and emotional event that may of never occurred.

The Mattachine Society and the civil Rights movement should recieve credit for giving birth to the modern day Gay liberation movement. Harry Hay wanted to assimilate homosexuals into mainstream society and eliminate discrimination, bigotry, and prejudice for ethical homosexual culture. This ties into the goals of the civil rights movement, which sparked a time of anti-discrimination activism and paved the way for expanded liberation

The modern gay liberation movement was born in 1950 when the mattachine society was founded because it's one of the first LGBTQ+ rights organizations that spread the homosexual movement publically. In the 1950s, organizations acted as the foundation for advocation and allowed the promotion of such events to occur. The stonewall riot was the first event that converted the gay rights movement into something bigger but wasn't the moment because such actions occured before as well.

Figure 6.13. (*continued*)

Harry Hay should have credit for the Modern Gay Liberation Movement. Hay formed the Mattachine Society and partcapated in the movement and even after he left, the Society stuck around. The Mattachine Society, even after investigation by the FBI, still stood to unify the community and did so successfully. It started in the early 1950's with the creation of the Mattachine. They were still working together to push for gay rights but on a small scale. When Stonewall happened, the media focused it's attention on the movement making it bigger but not the start of it.	1969. After the Stonewall riots gay culture and political activism grew quickly which led to many gays finally speaking out and joining/creating groups. Also it helped transform the previously small and non-impact gay movement into a large and explosive one. People could argue that before the Stone wall riots gays were still fighting for rights but it wasn't as explosive as mentioned in Source A.

less like history and more like current events, because not only did it happen while I was alive, but it happened while I was teaching. In fact, during my career the topic of same-sex marriage transitioned from a current events exemplar in my United States Government and Politics class, to a lesson in my United States History course. For students today, the Supreme Court decision on same-sex marriage is history, and when we plan courses, we must keep this reality at the forefront of planning. Teachers often do not plan backward, and as a result they end up teaching the early material in great depth and fail to end the course as adjacent to students' birth. The cumulative effect is that as time passes, more history accumulates, and the distance between the end of the course coverage and students' lives widens. Since the birth of seniors in the class of 2020, we have witnessed the social, political, and military impacts of the 9/11 attacks, the Great Recession, the explosion of social media, the longest war in American history, the election and administration of America's first African American president, and Russian interference in American elections. These topics also assume that our courses adequately covered the events of the 1990s or, for that matter, the 1980s. Anecdotally I can tell you, they do not (Brow & Schell, 2016). Nevertheless, it is incumbent on us as teachers to ensure that every 5 years or so we trim topics from earlier units to ensure that our courses cover important events, people, and ideas that occurred after the birth of our students (Fischer, 2022). In the case of same-sex marriage, the lesson migrated from current events to American history in 2017–2018.

The end goal for students is to make a claim about the relationship among cultural change, political activism, and government action in facilitating the federal legalization of same-sex marriage as they wrestle with the question:

What won the day for marriage equality: cultural change, political activism, or government action?

As discussed in Chapter 3, these kinds of options questions can help focus student investigation, discussion, and use of evidence.

This lesson follows a predictable pattern. I utilized a photo of the AIDS Memorial Quilt display in Washington, DC, to initiate the investigation. Students are asked to examine the photo in Figure 6.14 and list what they see, think, feel, and wonder.

Figure 6.14. AIDS Memorial Quilt in Washington, DC

Source: Library of Congress

From the discussion of the image, we debrief a homework reading that outlines events that undermined and promoted equality for LGBTQ+ persons in the 1980s and 1990s. The AIDS crisis, Don't Ask, Don't Tell (DADT), the Defense of Marriage Act, and legislation to overturn DADT, as well as court decisions in *Lawrence v. Texas* (2003) and *Obergefell v. Hodges* (2015) are all topics addressed to set the context for the deep dive into same-sex marriage. At this point, students understand that the right to marry and the elimination of the DADT policy have occurred. What they do not know is why. On the surface, it looks like enlightened politicians and noble Supreme Court justices provided these rights, but is that the accurate telling of this phase of the LGBTQ+ rights movement? Clearly, laws and precedents had changed, but as Molly Ball argued in 2015:

> . . . What changed . . . wasn't the Constitution—it was the country. And what changed the country was a movement. [The *Obergefell v. Hodges*] decision wasn't solely or even primarily the work of the lawyers and plaintiffs who brought the case. It was the product of the decades of activism that made the idea of same sex marriage seem plausible, desirable, and right . . . But that didn't happen organically. The fight for same sex marriage was, above all, a political campaign—a decades-long effort to win over the American public and, in turn, the court. It was a campaign with no fixed election day, focused on an electorate of nine people. But what it achieved was remarkable: not just a Supreme Court decision but a revolution in the way America sees its gay citizens. (Ball, 2015)

This investigation tests the notion that change is always made by politicians. The intention of this lesson is for students to convey clearly and concisely, but with depth, the key information gleaned from their source and how that information informs the development of a claim about the overarching investigative question. When they examine their source, students identify the factor(s) that impacted the legalization of same-sex marriage; how that factor impacted the legalization of same-sex marriage: and whether their source supports the claim that cultural change, political activism, and/or government action had more influence on the legalization of same-sex marriage. They first investigate the source independently, then in groups of students who examined the same source, and finally reach consensus on what information the source brings to bear to the overarching question.

As illustrated in Figure 6.15, the source trail includes the kind of visual sources that are only available to topics being explored from the 1950s forward: recorded interviews, videos, public opinion polls, and television advertisements. Students love the diversity as well as a break from so many text-dominant sources. The sources also reflect both allies and gay and lesbian activists. Because this lesson was a holdover from my AP Government and Politics course, the sourcing and contextualization are less important than the corroborative value of the respective sources. Nevertheless,

Figure 6.15. Same-Sex Marriage Sources

Source	Source Information
Source A: Public Opinion Polls	These are a series of public opinion polls conducted by reputable polling firms. They all show changes in public attitudes toward issues related to same-sex marriage.
Source B: Interview With Evan Wolfson	In 1983, Evan Wolfson wrote his Harvard Law School thesis on the freedom of gay people to marry. From 1989 until 2001, Wolfson worked full-time at Lambda Legal Defense and Education Fund, the nation's preeminent advocacy group working on behalf of lesbian, gay, bisexual, and transgender people and people living with HIV/AIDS. In 2001 he created the organization Freedom to Marry, which developed a national strategy called the Roadmap to Victory to push for marriage equality. The interview was conducted by Richard Socarides, an attorney and longtime gay rights advocate who served in the White House during the Clinton administration. The interview was conducted in 2013, two years prior to the *Obergefell* decision.
Source C: Hollywood and LGBT Visibility	The video is part of an online exhibit based on the original material exhibit "Speaking Out for Equality: The Constitution, Gay Rights, and the Supreme Court" held at the National Constitution Center in Philadelphia, PA., on the 50th anniversary of the first Annual Reminder Day demonstration at Independence Hall in Philadelphia, PA.
Source D: Vermont Historical Marker	In 2017, the historical marker was placed on the lawn of the Vermont State House to commemorate Vermont's role in promoting marriage equality.
Source E: Prop 8 Television Advertisements	California Proposition 8, the Same-Sex Marriage Ban Initiative, was on the ballot in California on November 4, 2008. Approved by the voters, Proposition 8 added language to the California Constitution that defined marriage as between one man and one woman. Proposition 8 had the effect of reversing the state court's ruling that protected marriage equality, and thus it banned same-sex marriage. Proposition 8 was upheld under state constitutional law but not federal constitutional law. These videos were shown on television channels in California. **Watch any three of the "vote no" videos.**
Source F: Freedom to Marry Television Advertisements	Freedom to Marry was founded in 2003 by Evan Wolfson and was dedicated to winning marriage equality for same-sex couples. The organization focused on winning marriage equality in a critical mass of states, growing national majority support for marriage, and ending marriage discrimination by the federal government. These videos were part of a public campaign to win marriage

(*continued*)

Figure 6.15. *(continued)*

Source	Source Information
	nationwide. Freedom to Marry produced dozens of online videos and TV ads to tell emotionally powerful stories of couples, families, allies, and unlikely messengers to build a critical mass of public support and drive the media narrative. **Watch any three of the videos**
Source G: Mary L. Bonauto Video	Mary L. Bonauto is a civil rights lawyer and the Civil Rights Project Director at GLBTQ Advocates & Defenders (GLAD). Bonauto and her GLAD colleagues pursued an incremental, state-based strategy to secure government marriage licenses for same-sex couples in the New England states. She was part of court cases in Vermont and Massachusetts that provided marriage equity. The video is a recognition of Bonauto's work by the MacArthur Foundation. This program recognizes people of extraordinary talent and provides them funds to support their work. Bonauto was recognized in 2014, one year prior to the Supreme Court's decision in *Obergefell v. Hodges*.

students must consider historical perspective and significance in addition to corroborating across sources, and thus the lesson employs significant historical literacy and thinking.

Beware the Student Presentation!

The structure of this investigation is around mini-student presentations. Beware the student presentation. Student presentations can be a great complement to any teacher's instructional toolbox. They can also be as dull as watching paint dry. Many students love to have center stage and share information with their classmates, while other students blanch at the thought. Neither will be as effective as they can be making a mini-presentation unless the teacher models examples and provides structure. At the beginning of every school year, when I implement a mini-presentation, I always model one for students. This helps set expectations for the flow, the role of each student in the group, and how to deliver concise and useful information effectively. In addition, the employment of certain structural recommendations can greatly increase student efficacy and reduce student anxiety. First, break the presentation into chunks. For me, I chunk these sorts of presentations into:

- An introduction to the source (sourcing and contextualization)
- A summary of what the source says
- Identification of the factor(s) that impacted the legalization of same-sex marriage

- How that factor impacted the legalization of same-sex marriage
- Whether the source supports the claim that cultural change, political activism, and/or government action had more influence on the legalization of same-sex marriage

Finally, the remaining students in the group presenting must answer any questions generated by classmates or the teacher. This helps students to divide the work so that groups (no more than 4–6) can make an effective presentation. This is not foolproof and takes time and practice, but if it is utilized frequently, enough students will become confident and effective presenters.

At the conclusion of the first group presentation, students are provided signs with the terms *cultural change, political activism,* and *government action.* Students are asked to manipulate these signs to represent the relationship between the factors and which one they feel is having the largest impact on the success of the fight for marriage equality. The individual factors can be ranked, tied, or moved up or down in importance after each subsequent presentation. After students adjust their thinking as represented with the signs, I randomly allow a few to explain their reasoning and why they made any changes in the order or why they did not. This process continues after each source is presented.

Initial student responses indicated that they thought government was the most significant policy lever in the movement toward same-sex marriage. Subsequent to the presentations, students broke into small groups to reevaluate the evidence presented. The resulting discussion broke down into the rule of thirds. One-third of the students argued that cultural change led to activism, which in turn led to governmental action. People need to support an idea first, in this case the legality of same-sex marriage. Once support coalesced around an idea, then activism indicates to government that there has been a shift in policy. For these students, Sources A and C were the most significant. Another third of students made the claim that activism led to cultural change, which in turn led to government action. They saw the work of Sources B and G as decisive. Finally, a third of students stuck with their initial argument that government action was the most significant policy lever. For this cohort, it was the simple fact that cultural change and political activism cannot and did not alter the legal status for same- sex marriage. It was the Supreme Court, a governmental body. Ultimately, as designed, the overarching question and the evidence employed to support competing student claims leads to robust discussion. Students gain insight into the many factors that influence the development of public policy and understand how the LGBTQ+ movement serves as a great example of Americans using the democratic process to secure rights. The lesson serves as a great conclusion to this three-lesson arc. Although the progression aligns with a more "history is progressive" vibe because it ends in relatively modern times, it allows for students to make connections to events that are supporting or undermining the right for LGBTQ+ people to marry. Second, it centers on agency and success and not discrimination and persecution. Finally, it adheres to the advice that LGBTQ+ history should not be an extra, but instead woven into the narrative so that students see it as part of the overall history they are studying.

"WHAT'S THE BIG DEAL?"

At the conclusion of the Stonewall lesson, Nicole reflected on a conversation she overheard. Two of her students, athletes, were talking about the lesson. From their perspective, the lessons on LGBTQ+ history were not a "big deal." "This is just the way the world is and it's not a big deal learning about this," stated one student. "I do not understand why adults get so freaked out about this," stated the other. The LGBTQ+ fight for social, political, and economic rights is a story that I am glad is moving into the broader narrative of American history. When done with forethought and planning regarding the investigative questions selected, the resources utilized to frame the inquiry, and the techniques employed to investigate the topic, as well as attention to building a classroom community that is safe for student discussion, the teaching of this important story can be successful. The work done by Nicole and Adam speaks clearly to the importance of not avoiding hard histories but instead embracing them. As the conversation that Nicole overheard above clearly demonstrates, the LGBTQ+ story is a history that aligns with the world that students understand and in which they will function as adults.

Nevertheless, this is still a hard history topic, and there is some naivete to the students' response. Teaching LGBTQ+ history, sadly, still holds the potential for pushback from segments of the school community. I recognize that the publication of this book hits at a fraught time for teaching hard histories. No teacher should be put in a position where their job is in danger for teaching about the histories of the LGBTQ+ struggle for rights, the overthrow of the regime of Jim Crow, or how the confluence of redlining, blockbusting, and housing discrimination impacted the distribution of health and wealth outcomes. Sadly, this is the moment some teachers are facing. Although I have not provided professional learning yet on this set of lessons during this period of political, legal, and cultural circumstances, teachers are teaching these subjects, as well they should. As Brensilver (2021) reminds us, "It is impossible for students to understand the present when the version of the history they learn is incomplete. Omitting entire groups from history curricula establishes and perpetuates those groups invisibility." We cannot reject the humanity embedded in our collective history, both its ugliness and its beauty. Fear never wins, so these stories must be investigated. History is always on the side of freedom, so I hope that the freedom to teach these subjects returns to our brethren currently strangled by repressive laws.

CHAPTER 7

Avoiding the Shame of the Scantron Machine

Assessing Historical Thinking

While teachers . . . overwhelmingly claimed that their goals fit snugly with "inquiry methods" and "hands-on learning" their tests told a different story, requiring little more than the recall of names and dates and memorized information.

—John Goodlad, *A Place Called School*

The goal is for teachers to disentangle the various threads that comprise historical thinking in order to better target instruction and assessment.

—Abby Reisman

One of the scariest moments for a teacher occurs when you walk into the faculty lounge, turn on the Scantron machine, and start to run your multiple-choice answer sheets through the device. Many teachers will intentionally avoid completing this task until late in the day or early in the morning. Why? Well, if you have to ask, you have never been a teacher, or your career has benefited from the advent of the new optical readers that can be utilized right in the classroom!

The reason for this avoidance is simple: When the scans go through the machine, they make an audible clicking noise every time a wrong answer is marked. Tests where the student has done well go through quietly. Tests where the student has done poorly can sound like gunfire on the front line of a war. Teachers cringe when they hear that rapid gunfire. They fear the judgment of their peers; they fear the reality that perhaps they did not teach a particular subject as well as they had hoped; they fear that their kids did not step up to the plate and study as they should have. Be it the cacophony of an overactive Scantron machine or the arduous slog through mediocre essays, teachers have always found both solace and angst when they assess student learning. Nevertheless, assessing student understanding is as important a component of instruction as a well-designed lesson, engaging motivation, or the incorporation of technology.

The question that drives this chapter is, how can preservice and practicing teachers who have embraced the investigative approach to history instruction assess the skills that are central to this instructional methodology? It is between the sad reality illuminated by Goodlad above and the insightful words of Riesman that I try to fit my argument about the assessment of historical thinking. Assessment in history was, and continues to be, dominated by multiple-choice questions that at best measure low-level recall. The reality is that historical thinking is much more complex than simply knowing that the Battle of Gettysburg happened in 1863 and selecting from four answer choices to illustrate that knowledge. This chapter aims to illustrate and assuage doubts that teachers have about assessing historical thinking, we have a growing body of tools to assess this kind of thinking. The examples I illustrate within are designed to point our assessment ship toward a new North Star. Assessments are a reality and cannot be avoided, but my argument is that opportunity has knocked and there are now the occasion and tools necessary to focus more on instructionally embedded assessments that aid learning.

SOCIAL STUDIES ASSESSMENTS

There is some good news. Several trends regarding social studies assessments have emerged in the past 10 years, and those trends harbor opportunities for better assessment of history teaching and learning. First, social studies exams still dominate the Advanced Placement (AP) options and total numbers of test-takers. From Psychology to United States History and soon African American History, more students are taking more social studies–focused AP exams each year ("AP Program Results," 2021). Outside of the realm of AP, the trend in statewide summative assessments has gone in a different direction. Since the passage of the No Child Left Behind Act and subsequently the Every Student Succeeds Act, social studies has been outside of the assessments required by the federal government. Science, English, and mathematics are required to be administered to all students and thus have become part of the accountability programs within all 50 states, but without the force of law behind social studies, fewer states assess the subject and fewer still align those assessments with graduation requirements. In 2022, only 13 states assessed social studies, and only three tie passing the exams to graduation. As states have eliminated or scaled back statewide assessment in social studies, a vacuum has been created for politicians and advocacy groups. This has resulted in eight states requiring students to take and pass the citizenship test that is administered to prospective citizens (Mullen & Rowland-Woods, 2018). The fact that students have both the questions and the answers to these and that all they do is memorize undermines any value of these tools to measure teaching or learning, but nonetheless they have become the newest tool in the social studies wars (Petrilli & Finn, 2020). The vacuum created by the decline in state testing of social studies is ripe with opportunity.

For some, the decline of state assessments in social studies means the diminution of the discipline, the shifting of fiscal and human resources away from the subject, and less emphasis on the important skills and content taught and learned in social studies classrooms. On the other hand, the decline in state-mandated summative assessments opens the door for teachers to again claim the ownership of student assessment in history. My choice here is to recognize the opportunities created by the shift away from statewide social studies assessments. This is not to ignore the deleterious effects that the shift has created—they are real and problematic—but instead to highlight how the shift away from statewide assessments is an opportunity that has encouraged some innovative efforts to shift away from multiple-choice and document-based questions as the sole tools to assess teaching and learning.

I TOOK TESTS; WEREN'T THEY ASSESSING MY HISTORICAL THINKING?

At this point I am sure you are thinking: Haven't history teachers always assessed historical thinking? No, we have not. Even in the dark ages of the 1980s, I took tests, wrote essays, conducted research projects, and even once made a film strip (if you do not know what a film strip is, Google it!), but these instruments were not designed or scored to gain an understanding of my facility with historical thinking.

I was never once assessed on my ability to source a document, contrast the arguments made by two historical sources, or build an argument from a variety of historical sources. I was asked a lifetime of factual recall questions; I filled in the blanks, matched the terms, colored in the map, and distinguished true from false; I even marshaled facts to make an argument in a five-paragraph essay, but these were not measurements of historical thinking. These tests were simply iterations of the same task: assessments of content retention. There is nothing wrong with assessing content, but a singular focus on measuring just content limits our ability as teachers of history to measure the full range of students' historical understanding. Most importantly, the reduction of history to memorization in turn severely limits the type of instruction that can be used in the classroom. If a teacher is required to prepare students for an end-of-course assessment, and that assessment is a measurement of low-level content retention, then the teacher will only seek out instructional methods that promote memorization.

INSTRUCTION AND ASSESSMENT DISCONNECT

The first time I really recognized that there was a disconnect between my instruction and assessment was through the yearly class evaluations I gave every June. Several students indicated that they felt the tests did not measure what they had been doing in class. This was a point of pride for me. I always wanted to make sure that students were being assessed on the content they wrestled with in class. I hated the statement by teachers of my youth that "you should be ready for anything you might have read to be on the test." Really, so learning is knowing everything, no matter how prominent a focus it had in class! That attitude drove me nuts as a student, and I thought I had successfully accommodated that as a teacher.

As I probed deeper, I found that it was not the content that was the issue with my students, but the skills embedded within the history lab approach. Students had been spending time every unit immersed in a History Lab, wrestling with motivating and cognitively challenging historical questions and interrogating historical sources with an eye toward building a historical argument, and my tests were simply recall. Yes, there was an essay, but essays are recall of multiple facts where multiple-choice questions are recall of single facts. My students were right. They had bought into the doing of history, but I had not allowed them to use these skills on exams. For example, scanning some tests on the Incorporation of the American West unit from the late 19th and early 20th century, I discovered questions such as those in Figure 7.1.

My students generally did well on these recall questions, but I had no idea if they could think historically. That was the heart of the disconnect.

Figure 7.1. Wounded Knee Test Questions

A popular new faith among the Native American Plains tribes by the late 1880s was:

a. The Ghost Dance
b. The Sun Dance
c. Human sacrifice
d. Catholicism
e. The Great White Father

What happened at Wounded Knee, South Dakota, in 1890?

a. The Dawes Act was signed by representatives of the Sioux.
b. At least 150 Sioux men, women, and children were slaughtered.
c. Geronimo was captured after eluding the army for 2 years.
d. Red Cloud addressed his tribe for the final time.

Explain the significance/impact of any two of the following:

- Ghost Dance
- Sitting Bull
- Wounded Knee

As my instruction changed to one more focused on having students analyze evidence and apply it to a deep historical question, I realized that my approach to assessment had not evolved in a commensurate manner. I was giving greater emphasis instructionally to thinking historically, and yet when formative assessments at the end of lessons or unit tests rolled around, it was still overwhelmingly content that I looked to assess. As they always do when I make a mistake or they see something wrong with my teaching, it was students who pointed out this discrepancy. I would hear complaints that unit assessments or end-of-lesson assessments did not "cover what we did in class." These complaints rang true, and so again my students pushed me to adjust my approach to assessment, just as they had pushed my approach to instruction so many years ago when they queried: "Why won't you just tell us the answer?"

Assessing student understanding of historical thinking is different from measuring their understanding of historical content. Although the two are not mutually exclusive, traditionally the assessment of history has focused on the recall of factual information via multiple-choice, true-false, fill-in-the-blank, and matching questions, in addition to the explanation of factual information via short answers, identifications, essays, and the use of information from documents via document-based questions (Hamblin, 2020). This tight focus on content via multiple-choice questions is derived from issues of cost (it is cheaper to score multiple-choice questions than a written response), reliability (much easier to determine with multiple choice than with written responses), and convenience (most textbooks come with prepared question banks of multiple-choice and true-false questions).

Even the first few generations of the Advanced Placement exam in United States History rested solely on the measurement of historic content. When the Document-Based Question was added in the 1970s, it was in recognition that the exam did not measure students' thinking. The revision process for the DBQ in the 1980s recognized that students were neither utilizing background information when constructing the essays, nor critically considering the sources of information provided in the DBQ prompts Further complicating the DBQ was the fact that "Kids never drew on background knowledge, they simply summarized the sources" (Klein, 1983). In many ways, despite recent revisions by the College Board, similar concerns persist today. Bain reminds us, "When history assessments ask students to read historical documents and write substantial paragraphs, questions arise as to what extent the assessment is measuring historical thinking and to what extent general literacy skills" (Bain, 2006). So even the much-lauded, and now twice-reformed, DBQ is not the best measure of students' ability to think historically.

Measuring students' understanding of the content of history is an important component of what needs to be measured by teachers, but the essential word is *component.* What we have done since at least 1917 is use multiple-choice questions to measure students' recall of basic facts about the past. As VanSledright (2014) argues, "Testing as simple recall/recognition of a variety of historical names, dates, and events . . . fails to assess the full range of crucial forms of knowledge that enable historical thinking in the first place. . . ." This tendency to overemphasize the measurement of student understanding of factual information continues with the National Assessment of Educational Progress history exam and the soon-to-be-replaced version of the Advanced Placement United States History exam.

Still, I am not advocating throwing the content baby out with the bath water. Content is essential in the teaching of our discipline. Instead, I am arguing for finding a balance in our assessment regimen so that fact/recall can make room for the measurement of historical thinking. Abby Reisman argues that large scale assessment "designers cannot know what background knowledge students bring to the test, the classroom teacher can know whether students have sufficient background knowledge to interpret certain texts. A teacher who is interested in assessing historical reading might think about . . . assessing background knowledge . . . assessing students' ability to evaluate reliability and relevance of external evidence . . . and assessing student's ability to synthesize multiple documents into an account" (Reisman, 2015b).

NO DATES, NO NAMES—THEN WHAT DO I ASSESS?

The question becomes, what else besides names, dates, events, and vocabulary is worth measuring in a student's history education? In terms of what to assess beyond historical content, researchers in England and Canada have developed progression models around several historical thinking traits. Robust documents have been developed for causation and consequence, change and continuity, historical evidence, interpretation, significance, perspectives, and the ethical dimension of history (Ford, 2014a, 2014b, 2016; Fordham, 2012; Seixas & Morton, 2013). The Big Six historical thinking concepts out of Canada depicted in Figure 7.2 are equally well-organized and serve as my launching point for assessing skills. Organized to assist students and teachers in developing a framework of interrelated concepts that can become the architecture for history course(s) and/or curriculum, the Bix Six adds the ethical dimension of history to its list of skills. For each concept, Seixas and Morton (2013) provide guideposts that illuminate aspects of each thinking skill. Particularly useful are the criteria they set to show student progression of understanding for each of the guideposts. For example, a student progression for "generating powerful understandings of historical significance" is depicted in Figure 7.2.

Figure 7.2. Powerful Understandings of Historical Significance

Guidepost 1 Events, people, or developments have historical significance if they **resulted in change.** That is, they had deep consequences, for many people, over a long period of time.

DEMONSTRATION OF LIMITED UNDERSTANDING	DEMONSTRATION OF POWERFUL UNDERSTANDING
Student shows an unexamined faith in the textbook or other authority as a basis for significance, or relies on simple personal preference as the basis for historical significance.	Student explains the historical significance of events, people, or developments by showing that they **resulted in change**.

Guidepost 2 Events, people, or developments have historical significance if they are **revealing.** That is, they shed light on enduring or emerging issues in history or contemporary life.

DEMONSTRATION OF LIMITED UNDERSTANDING	DEMONSTRATION OF POWERFUL UNDERSTANDING
Student limits their criteria for historical significance to the level of impact of an event, person, or development.	Student explains the historical significance of events, people, or developments by showing what they **reveal** about issues in history or contemporary life.

Guidepost 3 Historical significance is **constructed.** That is, events, people, and developments meet the criteria for historical significance only when they are shown to occupy a **meaningful place in a narrative.**

DEMONSTRATION OF LIMITED UNDERSTANDING	DEMONSTRATION OF POWERFUL UNDERSTANDING
Student is unable to identify how significance is constructed in textbooks or other historical accounts.	Student identifies how historical significance is **constructed through narrative** in textbooks or other historical accounts.

Guidepost 4 Historical significance **varies** over time and from group to group.

DEMONSTRATION OF LIMITED UNDERSTANDING	DEMONSTRATION OF POWERFUL UNDERSTANDING
Student assumes that significance is fixed and unchanging (i.e., is inherent in an event, person, or development).	Student shows how historical significance **varies** over time and from group to group.

Source: Reprinted from *The Big Six Historical Thinking Concepts*, by P. Seixas and T. Morton, 2013, Nelson Education. Copyright © 2013 Nelson Education Ltd. Reproduced by permission.

This progression and those provided for the other five historical thinking skills are very useful tools for developing and measuring student acquisition of a particular historical thinking skill. They will structure many of the assessments I model in the remainder of the chapter.

Despite the robust nature of the progression models, my definition of what is meant by historical thinking has become clearer over the past 10 years. Because content should continue to be assessed, I reduced the universe of possible skills that I embed into instruction and attempt to assess. My list, first introduced in Chapter 1, is illustrated again in Figure 7.3.

Having identified what types of skills need to be assessed when measuring students' proficiency with historical thinking, we are now required to find or develop useful tools to measure student facility with historical thinking. Thankfully, some very bright people have already blazed this path.

Figure 7.3. A Broader View of Historical Thinking

CONTENT

CONTENT

CONTENT

Historical Literacy Skills

- Sourcing
- Contextualizing
- Close Reading
- Corroboration

Historical Thinking Concepts

- Historical Perspectives
- Cause and Consequence
- Continuity and Change
- Historical Significance

Argumentation about History

- Claims
- Counterclaims
- Use of Evidence

CONTENT

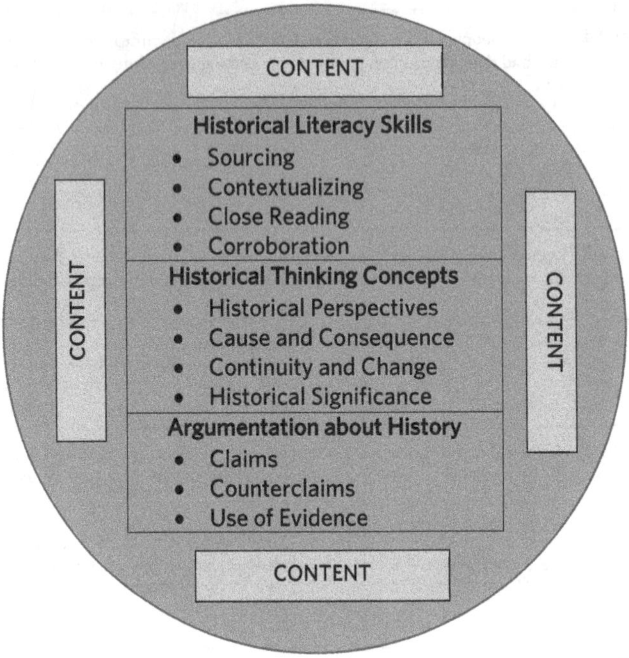

WHAT TOOLS ARE AVAILABLE FOR TEACHERS?

Specific tools have been developed. Bruce VanSledright argues for the use of Upside-Down, Weighted Multiple Choice Items (WMCI) (VanSledright, 2014.) These items literally tip a traditional multiple-choice item on its head. Instead of there being one correct answer out of four choices, VanSledright's WMCIs have three answers all varying in degrees of correctness and one that is completely incorrect. He structures them this way so that we can measure students' ability to understand the complexity of historical interpretation and the use of evidence. His work on assessment of historical thinking found concrete form in the Assessment Resource Center for History (ARCH), based out of the Center for History Education (CHE) at the University of Maryland, Baltimore County to develop assessment tools for historical thinking. The project developed entirely new assessment items that measure historical thinking skills rather than merely the retention of prior knowledge. ARCH is a repository of formative and summative assessment items in United States history that more closely match the demands of inquiry-based instruction. The site includes a selection of formative assessment items, including oral presentations, debates, and performance tasks. Examples of summative assessment items available on the website include constructed response items such as document-based questions, essays, and research projects, as well as selected response items in the form of traditional and weighted multiple-choice questions.

A more fleshed-out tool is the path-breaking collaboration between the Library of Congress (LOC) and Sam Wineburg, Joel Breakstone, and their colleagues at the Stanford History Education Group. Their Beyond the Bubble History Assessments website (https://sheg.stanford.edu/history-assessments) is a repository of items that are psychometrically calibrated to assess historical thinking. Just the title itself is fabulous—what teacher over the past 20 years has not railed against the constant and growing presence of standardized exams that ask students only to fill in the bubble on the answer sheet? What is intriguing about the site is that it provides assessments of historical thinking from soup to nuts. Visitors are provided with the task, sample student responses, a rubric, and an explanation of what historical thinking skills are being measured. Although the number of tasks available is limited relative to the holdings of the LOC, the Beyond the Bubble repository is still growing (Breakstone, 2013; Breakstone et al., 2013, 2015).

Wineburg and his colleagues describe their tasks as HATs: History Assessments of Thinking. Organized around one or two historical sources from the vast LOC collection, the tasks assess one or more of the following factors illustrated in Figure 7.4.

I have employed many of the tasks provided by *Beyond the Bubble* because they work and work well. One caveat is that the HATs serve more along the lines of summative test items rather than an organic element of instruction for a historical investigation I have designed and implemented with my students. I use HATs on unit tests, midterms, and final exams, but

Figure 7.4. Historical Assessments of Thinking (HATS)

Evaluation of Evidence: Involves the Critical Assessment of Historical Sources

- **Sourcing:** Asks students to consider who wrote a document as well as the circumstances of its creation.
- **Contextualization:** Asks students to locate a document in time and place and to understand how these factors shape its content.
- **Corroboration:** Asks students to consider details across multiple sources to determine points of agreement and disagreement.

Historical Knowledge: Encompasses various ways of knowing about the past, including:

- **Historical Information:** The recognition and recall of important factual data.
- **Significance:** Requires students to evaluate the importance of people or events.
- **Periodization:** Asks students to group ideas and events by era.
- **Narrative:** Deep knowledge of how the past unfolded over time.

Historical Argumentation: Requires the articulation of historical claims and the use of evidence to support them.

they often do not match well as an assessment at the end of an investigation. They do an excellent job of zeroing in on students' ability to apply the literacy skills of contextualization, sourcing, and corroboration, but they can at times feel disconnected from the content of the investigation.

Nonetheless, they are a tremendously important advancement in the assessment of historical thinking, and I would not be surprised to see some iteration of the HATs appear on a standardized exam such as Advanced Placement or statewide summative social studies assessments.

Although the *Beyond the Bubble* and ARCH tasks are a great starting point to develop assessments of historical thinking skills, I present a wider diversity of assessments so that students can neither game them nor get bored by seeing them after every lesson. The ones that I share in the remainder of the chapter do not have the psychometric reliability of the HATs. My items do not solely—in most instances—isolate the assessment of skills from content as precisely as the HATs do. Instead, they assess the spirit of specific historical thinking concepts and literacy skills while simultaneously assessing student content knowledge. Although each is torn from a specific lesson, they are easily adaptable to other topics, courses, and contents. The first set of assessments I discuss are envisioned as formative in nature and more focused on providing real-time information regarding student progress. The second set were utilized as summative assessments at the conclusion of a lesson or series of lessons.

FORMATIVE ASSESSMENT TOOLS FOR HISTORICAL THINKING

With formative assessment, instead of assessing students to determine what they learned as a result of a teacher's efforts, teachers are encouraged to assess students to understand where they are along the learning process and to help us make instructional decisions to aid student progress during the instructional process (William, 2011). What formative assessment was empowering me to do was to return to the classrooms of my school years, where assessment was teacher-based and facilitated a conversation between teacher and student about learning. By managing the transition to formative assessment correctly, I could reclaim from the summative assessments the ability to allow student work to be the catalyst that encourages the relationship between teacher and student.

As a classroom teacher, I can acquire more knowledge about my students' learning through well-structured assessments than I do from an external evaluation whose results come well after my students and I have parted company. Assessment measures should be rooted in a specific task, argue Geriant Brown and Sally Burnham (2014), because students learn most from using task-specific assessments. Further, they argue that the "purpose of assessment should be to improve student learning"(p. 10). Abby Reisman argues that when developing an assessment task, teachers need to be sure that the task captures the benefits and outcome of actual historical study and reflects the students' ability to interpret historical sources (Reisman, 2015b). The question for me was how to develop assessments that were tied to instruction. HATs and ARCH items provided some guidance, but the formality, especially of the HATs, pushed me to look at less prescribed tools. The samples I illustrate below are rooted within historical investigations. This is intentional so that the formative assessments can clue me in to what my students can do well regarding historical thinking and what they are struggling with.

"It's Like a DBQ and an Exit Ticket Had a Baby!"

My first example of a tool to formatively assess students' historical thinking is to engage students in focused *quick-writes*. A teacher who attended one of my professional development workshops emailed me to tell me that the quick write I was proposing was "like a DBQ and an exit ticket had a baby!" I took this as a great compliment, but a little background on this supposed procreation is in order.

A quick-write asks students to unpack their thinking in writing by responding to a short open-ended question. Responses should be done without the benefit of prewriting. I have often referred to it as cognitive vomit. Essentially, the student is unloading their thinking in a written format with more attention being paid to the content than the quality of the writing. Essentially, your brain vomits onto the paper: cognitive vomit! I decided to employ quick-writes as my assessment strategy because they:

- Are quick and easy to score/grade/provide feedback
- Isolate a specific literacy skill
- Are not an essay
- Are embedded within the content being studied
- Allow students to wrestle with the application of skills within the investigation in which they had just vested instructional time
- Empower students to write about something in which they are confident
- Can be used to track student growth with skill development over time

Rather than a closed task akin to the HATs or the more fully fleshed-out ARCH performance assessments, I find that my best and most telling results are generated by posing questions to students that require them to connect the evidence they examined to the overarching question that framed the History Lab. Structuring the task in this manner allows teachers to assess if students can connect the evidence to the overarching question or explain how the applied particular historical thinking skills connect to the evidence utilized in the investigation. The quick-write assessment enabled me to disentangle the student thinking Reisman mentioned and to aggregate it into something that helped guide my instructional decision in both the short and long term.

Quick Writing, but Deep Thinking

Conducting the quick-writes does not require much preparation time, and after some practice, scoring is also much less onerous than a five-paragraph essay or a full-blown DBQ. After completing a History Lab, I provide students with the writing prompts in Figure 7.5. A lesson on the events in Wounded Knee, South Dakota in 1890 serve as an example of using quick-writes as a formative assessment tool.

Assessing Student Learning

I employed the quick-writes in one of two locations during the Wounded Knee History Lab. Since I taught my students 45 minutes a day, every day, my labs were always split over 2 days. The quick-writes could be utilized at the conclusion of the first day to determine where they were with their understanding of the relationship between the evidence and the overarching

Figure 7.5. Quick-Write Prompts

Pick 1, and answer in 5–7 sentences. Be specific and use examples from our discussion and the evidence examined during the investigation.

- The context of ______________ source impacted the information gained from that source because . . .
- The subtext of ______________ source impacted the information gained from that source because . . .
- The two most important pieces of evidence were____because . . .
- The two least important pieces of evidence were____because . . .
- The two pieces of evidence that contradicted the most were____because . . .
- The two pieces of evidence that most complemented one another were____because . . .
- The two most important pieces of evidence were . . . because . . .
- The two pieces of evidence that presented the most difficulty were____because . . .
- The evidence whose subtext challenged the information provided in the text was____because . . .
- The least useful/reliable piece of evidence was___because . . .
- __________ provided the following challenges because . . .
- A useful piece of evidence to have would have been___because . . .

historical question. This was a perfect opportunity for gaining an (in)formative assessment of my students. I could review their writing at the end of the day and be set to adjust on the fly the next.

The quick-writes could also be utilized at the conclusion of the history lab on day 2. In this context, student responses would begin to build my understanding of how their ability to attack sources, corroborate sources, and connect sources to a central question was evolving over the course of the year. Either way, the students' responses were useful both to me and to them.

Discovering the American Past (Wheeler, 2007) and *Wounded Knee: Party Politics and the Road to an American Massacre* (Cox, 2011) provided the inspiration, documents, and question that drive the Wounded Knee investigation. What was amazing to me was the fact that at the time of the massacre, many Americans were asking if what occurred on the American Plains was a necessary battle or an avoidable massacre. At first blush, I thought this was a modern question asking students to judge the events of the past by the morals of today, but I quickly discovered that the question of inevitability hung over the actions of the American military from the time the shooting commenced. I knew that this question would be compelling for my students, so I designed the investigation around the question: Were the events at Wounded Knee in 1890 necessary, or an avoidable massacre?

The evidence trail blazed by these sources indicates that immediately after the event, perceptions regarding the events at Wounded Knee depended greatly on who was telling the story. Many of the Indian agents were sent to the reservations as patronage for generating voters in the previous presidential election. Their lack of familiarity with Native culture and the realities of life in the West quickly colored their view of events. Most telling was that D. F. Royer was nicknamed "man afraid of Indians" by the Sioux because of his timidity in the face of their concerns. In addition, the evidence trail is complicated by the congressional investigation that quickly followed the events. The sources originating from the generals and the report of the commissioner of Indian Affairs are colored by the self-preservation instinct that often accompanies such post hoc examinations of tragic events.

Important in selecting the sources was to genuinely challenge students to apply their understanding of how the context (when a source was created) and subtext (who created the source) impacted the information provided by the source. In many instances the information provided by the sources only makes historical sense when students understand who is saying it and why. For instance, one of the sources is a telegram sent by General Nelson A. Miles, commander of the Pine Ridge Reservation. It is very clear to students that he was opposed to the use of military force to put down the Ghost Dancers. He makes the argument that "cutting rations," "crop failures," and "compelled to live on half and two-thirds rations" led to the events of December 1890. That is a straightforward reading of the text of the source. What should complicate matters for students is the context that is provided, because the attack on the Ghost Dancers had already occurred and Miles was being questioned about his leadership after the events transpired. How do students make this connection?

To make this connection, students need to connect information from the background section of the source to the actual source itself. By understanding the context in which Miles sent the telegram, it helps students to understand partially why he is making that argument. In the box below is the background information about Miles that my students confront PRIOR to reading the actual source.

Background Information: Maj. Gen. Nelson A. Miles, commander of the military division where the reservations were located, was swayed by his own political ambitions, his (and the army's) long-standing efforts to wrest oversight of Indian affairs from the Interior Department, and his desire to preserve the Army's relevance in the face of growing interest in the Navy rather than the Army as the most important branch of the military. Miles feared for his own political future and was infuriated by the administration's criticisms of his handling of Indian affairs.

Students should take away that Miles was:

1. Angry about the decline in support for the army.
2. Frustrated that he was being criticized.
3. Writing information that is included in a report on the events that occurred in the recent PAST.

By understanding the author's background and the context for the source, students now have a better understanding that the information provided in the source cannot simply be taken at face value. Just because General Miles states that "cutting rations" and "crop failures" were important factors to consider does not mean he possessed a full view of the events occurring, nor that his testimony after the fact was not colored by a desire to protect himself.

With six sources, conflicting viewpoints, debating students, and thoughtful building of evidence-based historical arguments, the Wounded Knee investigation is one of my favorites. The problem was that how I assessed student learning was divorced from the complicated nature of the skills they were employing during the lesson. It was this realization, articulated by my students, of course, that helped me to realize that there was a serious disconnect between my instructional approach and my assessments.

The two student responses in Figures 7.6 and 7.7 highlight some of the ways in which (in)formative assessments via quick-writes could inform

Figure 7.6. Student Quick Write Response #1

The subtext of Source F by E.B Reynolds impacted the information gained from the source because Reynolds had no qualifications or prior experiences on a Reservation before he became an Indian Agent at a Reservation in South Dakota. Also Reynolds was only put in the position as a reward for his alliance to the Republican Party. This made Reynolds more judgemental of the Indians actions because he had never seen them before. Also he was a bad leader so he tried to blame everything on the Indians by saying that he felt threatened by the

practice. In Figure 7.6, the student has decided to illustrate how he or she dealt with the subtext of the source. This was administered at the conclusion of the first day of the lab.

Clearly the student understands how to examine information about the author of a document. When the student states, ". . . Reynolds had no qualifications or prior experiences on a reservation," and that he was "put in the position as a reward for his alliance to the Republican Party," they are showing a clear connection to the author's background, but the student goes further, to argue that the author's background could impact the author's argument in the source. Students convey this understanding by stating, "This [his lack of knowledge about and exposure to Indians] made him more judgmental of the Indians actions because he had never seen them before." Awesome, but, unfortunately, due to time constraints, lack of understanding of good writing, or deference to the spirit of a quick write, the student does not reinforce the contention about the author's background and his attitude toward the Indians by pulling evidence from the source. My takeaway from Figure 7.7 is that the student is about three-quarters of the way toward being able to effectively source a document and connect the author to the argument they are making.

The quick-writes became my go-to for (in)formative assessment for my History Labs. In addition, they can also be used as the basis for a summative assessment. Utilizing a modified rubric from the ARCH website displayed in Figure 7.8, I can score it if it is used in a summative manner, or use it to generate feedback if employed in a formative way. Ultimately, the quick-writes are more than just a grade for me. The "data" help me to see what my students understand and feel confident about when it comes to thinking historically and where they struggle. In addition, I can measure some of their

Figure 7.7. Student Quick Write Response #2

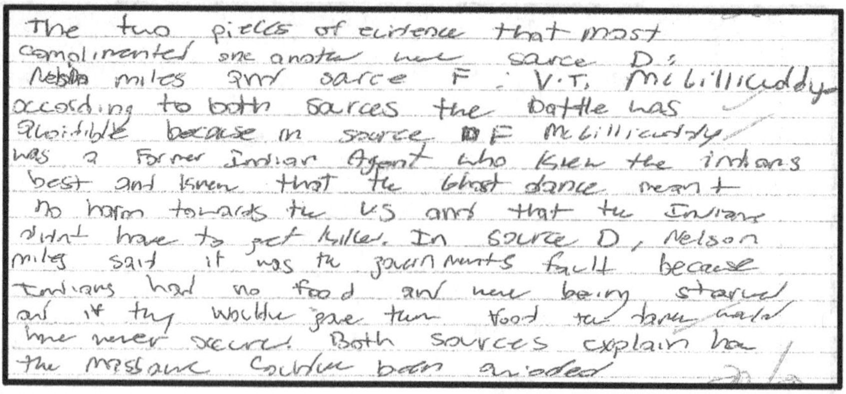

The two pieces of evidence that most complimented one another were source D: Nelson miles and source F: V.T. McGillicuddy according to both sources the battle was avoidible because in source F McGillicuddy was a Former Indian Agent who knew the indians best and knew that the Ghost dance meant no harm towards the US and that the Indians didnt have to get killed. In source D, Nelson miles said it was the governments fault because Indians had no food and were being starved and if they wouldve gave them food the tragedy would have never occured. Both sources explain how the massacre couldve been avoided

understanding of basic content. What is most effective about assessing students' historical thinking in this manner is that I can track students' growth over time. A quick-write in September can be compared to ones in December, March, and June, and it quickly becomes apparent if a student is growing in their understanding and application of various historical thinking skills.

In addition to tracking growth, the assessments help me get a quick and clear picture of whether students have spent their time examining the historical question at hand and linking the evidence to that question, or if they have simply been, well, out to lunch, let's say!

"NOT ANOTHER ESSAY!": EXPLORING ALTERNATIVE SUMMATIVE ASSESSMENTS

Assessment of historical thinking and content are important components of any rigorous history class. Unfortunately, many assessments take the form of five-paragraph essays. In either argumentative or narrative structure, content is central to the five-paragraph essay. Scoring essays usually focuses on the quality of the argument and the efficacy of the student's application of content to either support the argument or populate the narrative. Essays are not traditionally designed to measure all aspects of historical thinking because outside of claim and evidence, it is difficult to tease out the historical thinking from an essay. According to Smith et al. (2018), "Broad essays like the DBQ require the orchestration of so many skills that it is difficult to draw inferences about proficiency in any aspect of the domain. . . . It can be difficult to untangle these factors [evaluating documents, compositional fluency, background knowledge, etc.] when so many cognitive processes are implicated at once." Essays, then, are great for some things but fall short of

Figure 7.8. Adapted Historical Thinking Skills Rubric

Historical Thinking Skills Quick-Writes			
Criteria	Sourcing (Subtext)	Contextualizing (Context)	Corroboration (Contradictions and Compliments)
4	*Identification:* Fully understands the meaning and content of sources. *Attribution:* Cites all authors and all original dates of primary and secondary sources. *Perspective:* Evaluates the reliability of sources based on the author's perspective and when and why they were produced.	Connects the historical setting of sources to the author's argument. Uses that setting to interpret the sources within the historical context as opposed to a present-day mindset.	Constructs an interpretation of events using information and perspectives in the required number of sources. Identifies consistencies and inconsistencies among various accounts.
3	*Identification:* Mostly understands the meaning and content of sources. *Attribution:* Cites most authors and most original dates of primary and secondary sources. *Perspective:* Examines the reliability of sources based on the author's perspective and when and why they were produced.	Connects the historical setting of sources to the author's argument. Uses that setting to interpret the sources within the historical context as opposed to a present-day mindset. May attempt an interpretation of some sources with a present-day mindset or with a limited application to the historical context.	Explains similarities and differences by comparing information and perspectives in the required number of sources.
2	*Identification:* Understands the meaning and content of sources with appropriate scaffolding and support.	Attempts to determine the historical setting of sources without fully understanding the historical context.	Identifies similarities and differences in information in the required number of sources.

(continued)

Figure 7.8. (continued)

Historical Thinking Skills Quick-Writes			
Criteria	Sourcing (Subtext)	Contextualizing (Context)	Corroboration (Contradictions and Compliments)
	Attribution: Cites some authors and some original dates of primary and secondary sources. *Perspective:* Attempts to evaluate the reliability of sources.		
1	*Identification:* Attempts to understand the meaning and content of sources with the appropriate scaffolding and support. *Attribution:* Cites few authors and few original dates of primary and secondary sources. *Perspective:* Does not adequately examine reliability.	Demonstrates no attempt to understand the historical setting of sources.	Demonstrates little to no attempt to examine sources for corroborating or conflicting evidence.

Note: Adapted from materials developed by the UMBC Center for History Education and from the work of the Stanford History Education Group and VanSledright (2014).

being the complete assessment tool. The issues that the Advanced Placement History assessments have had provide visibility to this conundrum.

I do not say all of this to argue for throwing the five-paragraph essay overboard. I think writing is an essential skill and that longer writing should be a key component to any social studies course. My argument is for diversity in approach. There are 140 instructional days in a 180-day school year. If you assessed even one-quarter of your lessons with a five-paragraph essay, you would have 35 essays times the number of students to grade every year. For a teacher with a five-class load, with each class populated with 30 students, this would mean over 5,000 essays to grade a year!

There are assessment options other than the five-paragraph essay. Although many of them do incorporate writing, they do so in a focused manner. They are shorter to grade and increase the likelihood that a teacher can focus on historical thinking as well as content acquisition. Although the following examples are not as pure as the HATs offered by the Stanford History Education Group, they are intended to offer some diversity in formatting and provide alternatives to the five-paragraph essay format. In the examples that follow, the intent is for the assessment to function as a summative tool to be implemented at the end of a lesson. In each instance, the assessment was designed to require students to demonstrate both content knowledge and understanding through the lens of the particular historical thinking skills of historical perspectives, cause and consequence, continuity and change, and/or historical significance. These assessments differ from the quick-write in that they are not pure measures of the skills but instead intentionally blend the two. Work in England and Canada provides some consensus on how to focus summative and formative assessments in history (Ford, 2014b, 2016: Seixas & Morton, 2013). This is not a rubric for the assessment items that follow.

To provide a diverse set of examples, I have decided not to highlight one lesson but instead provide the examples with some narration. An important caveat is that often these thinking skills overlap. To assess significance, students need to consider continuity and change as well. In these examples, although I argue that they may be best to measure one skill over another, they are not exclusively tied to one skill.

Assessing Historical Perspectives

Students must not conflate their modern notions with those of the historical actors. Avoiding presentism and fully engaging the concept of historical perspectives is an essential building block for the development of a full understanding of history. When students "become aware that people in the past held beliefs, values, and knowledge different from their own," they become more adept at evaluating and understanding the past (Huijgen & Holthuis, 2018). That said, getting them to do so is tricky at best, and assessing it is even more difficult. Because developmentally students are more immersed in the present, and have a very parochial view of the present at that, it is difficult to strip them of that view and generate an understanding of the past on its own terms. Teenagers are judgmental and lack a significant pool of context in which to examine past actors and actions. To overcome these barriers, teachers must be intentional about drawing clear lines between now and the past. The guidelines shown in Figure 7.9, adapted from the work of Seixas and Morton (2013), aid me in generating that intentionality and structuring assessments intended to measure historical perspective. I do not share them with students, but use them as an internal check when aligning an inquiry and assessment with a particular historical thinking skill.

The John D. Rockefeller Facebook Page assessment in Figure 7.11 is the first example of an alternative assessment that focuses on historical

Figure 7.9. Historical Perspectives Progression

Elements of Historical Perspectives	Demonstration of Limited Understanding	Demonstration of Powerful Understanding
Past Is a Foreign Country. An ocean of difference can lie between current beliefs, values, and motivations and those of the past.	Student assumes that the beliefs, values, and motivations of people in the past were the same as those of people today.	Student identifies examples of the vast differences between the beliefs, values, and motivations prevalent today and those prevalent in the past.
No, They Were Not Stupid! It is important to avoid presentism—the imposition of present ideas on actors in the past. Nonetheless, cautious reference to universal human experience can help us relate to the experiences of historical actors.	Student assumes that people in the past had the same ideals, values, and motivations that we have today, which makes it difficult to understand the reasons for their actions.	Students exercise caution when drawing on universal human experiences to understand historical actors.
Put It in Context. The perspectives of historical actors are best understood by considering their historical context.	Student judges people in the past as dull-witted or weird because they ignore the historical context.	Student explains or illustrates perspectives of people in their historical context.
Evidence-Based, Please. Taking the perspective of historical actors means inferring how people felt and thought about the past. Valid inferences are those based on evidence.	Student equates perspective-taking as flights of imagination, failing to consider evidence to support their interpretations.	Student makes factually accurate, evidence-based inferences about the beliefs, values, and motivations of a historical actor, while recognizing the limitations of our understanding.
Diversity. Different actors have diverse perspectives on the events in which they are involved.	Student fails to recognize differences among the perspectives of various peoples in the past.	Student distinguishes a variety of perspectives among historical actors participating in a given event.

Adapted from *The Big Six Historical Thinking Concepts*, by P. Seixas and T. Morton, 2013, Nelson Education.

perspectives. In the assessment, students are asked to apply what they know about the growth of industrial America and monopolization through the lens of John D. Rockefeller. The lesson allows students to debate: **How should history remember the industrialists of the turn of the 20th Century?** After contrasting sources on Rockefeller and establishing him as the case study, students gather data on the context of the rise of the industrial empires of the late 19th century via cartoons, data, the interpretations of historians, and contemporary critics and supporters of the industrialists. The assessment targets how John D. Rockefeller would understand the request by various groups to friend him. The construct of Facebook is certainly anachronistic, but by placing students in the shoes of the historical actor at the center of the lesson, students are forced to consider the friend requests from a certain perspective. Specifically, students must address the elements of historical perspectives illustrated in Figure 7.10.

The content that students apply can only be applied if they understand and can consider things through the perspective of one of America's most controversial industrialists.

The Nixon's hollow head assessment in Figure 7.13 requires students to apply what they understand about Nixon's motivations and actions during the Watergate scandal. Students have investigated Watergate through the lens of the question: **What motivated President Nixon's decisions to form the Plumbers, support the break-ins, and use the office of the President to cover up his actions: paranoia or necessity?** After exploring a source trail that includes transcripts of White House tapes and debating the question, students are assessed on their understanding of Watergate though the perspective of the President. The three elements of historical perspectives that I am targeting are listed in Figure 7.12.

Because students are required to link the "thoughts in the President's head" to specific evidence, this assessment is more complex than the one in the Facebook example with Rockefeller.

Figure 7.10. Historical Perspectives Assessment: Assessment Checklist

Put It in Context

The perspectives of historical actors are best understood by considering their historical context.

Evidence-Based, Please

Taking the perspective of historical actors means inferring how people felt and thought about the past. Valid inferences are those based on evidence.

Diversity

Different actors have diverse perspectives on the events in which they are involved.

Figure 7.11. Historical Perspectives Assessment: Rockefeller's Facebook Page

John D. Rockefeller and Titans of Industry

John D. Rockefeller has set up a page on Facebook (yeah, I know, 100 years too early, but just go with it). The following people have asked Rockefeller to be his friend and allow him access to his page. Determine if he would allow each person access and then defend your answer. When formulating your responses, be sure to consider:

- Techniques used by Rockefeller to create Standard Oil
- Positive and negative impacts of Standard Oil on America
- Viewpoints provided by various sources examined in class

1. Newspaper journalist Ida M. Tarbell would like to be your friend:
YES or NO, *because . . .*

2. The owner of a former oil competitor would like to be your friend:
YES or NO, *because . . .*

3. Beneficiaries of John D. Rockefeller's philanthropy would like to be your friend: **YES or NO, *because . . .***

4. Political cartoonists from the time period would like to be your friend:
YES or NO, *because . . .*

5. A worker at one of your oil refineries would like to be your friend:
YES or NO, *because . . .*

Figure 7.12. Historical Perspectives Assessment: Nixon's Hollow Head Checklist

No, They Were Not Stupid!

It is important to avoid presentism—the imposition of present ideas on actors in the past. Nonetheless, cautious reference to universal human experience can help us relate to the experiences of historical actors.

Put It in Context

The perspectives of historical actors are best understood by considering their historical context.

Evidence-Based, Please

Taking the perspective of historical actors means inferring how people felt and thought about the past. Valid inferences are those based on evidence.

The final exemplar provided in Figure 7.15, like Figure 7.13, is also from a lesson in my industrialization unit. The lesson itself investigates workplace conditions within the industrialized economy. Students confront a source-based question derived from viewing a short clip from Charlie Chaplin's classic 1936 film *Modern Times*. The clip establishes an industrial workplace that eventually turns humans into machines by deskilling their labor and mechanizing the production process. The question students wrestle with is: **How accurate was the depiction of the industrial workplace in *Modern Times*?** The assessment continues the slight exaggeration of the workplace by asking students to apply the realities of the Taylorized workplace to the creation of an "ideal worker." Taylorism was an effort to use science to determine the most efficient ways for workers to conduct their jobs. It often led to the micromanaging of all steps in a work process. In the assessment, students take on the perspective of the owner of a factory and attempt to satirize what is happening to workers. This walks a fine line when it comes to having students recognize that "the past is a foreign country," but the explanations can ensure that students contextualize the decision (see Figure 7.14).

The ultimate intent of these assessments is to meld content knowledge with the concept of historical perspective. With the emphasis on centering student responses within a specific historical perspective, I hope to avoid responses that are speculative. Student response should be measured, limited by the bounds of evidence, context, and an understanding that people in the past were different.

Assessing Causes and Consequences

For me, causes and consequences are the most frequently assessed historical thinking skills. This phenomenon has to do with the fact that standards tend

Figure 7.13. Historical Perspectives Assessment: Nixon's Hollow Head

"Do whatever has to be done to stop these leaks": President Richard Nixon, White House Secrecy, and Presidential Resignation

Below is President Richard Nixon's hollow head. What were the top four issues he was concerned with during the Watergate scandal? Fill in each box with one of the president's thoughts and why he was concerned with that item (5–7 sentences). When deciding, be sure to consider:

- Nixon's background before becoming President
- The factors that led to the Watergate scandal
- The major events of the scandal (Pentagon Papers, Supreme Court rulings, the Plumbers, etc.)
- The relationship between Vietnam and Watergate

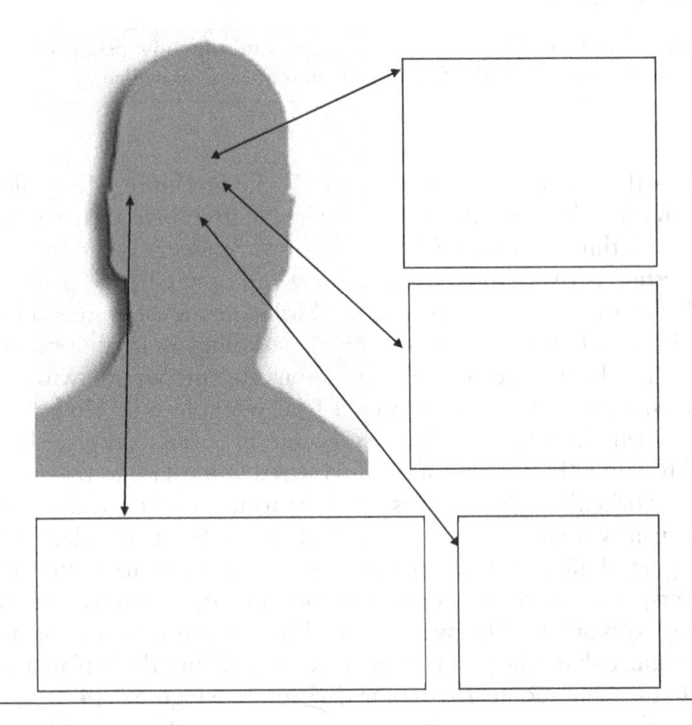

Figure 7.14. Historical Perspectives Assessment: Taylor Frankenworker Checklist

Past Is a Foreign Country

An ocean of difference can lie between current beliefs, values, and motivations and those of the past.

Put It in Context

The perspectives of historical actors are best understood by considering their historical context.

Figure 7.15. Historical Perspectives Assessment: Taylor Frankenworker

TAYLOR FRANKENWORKER!: LIFE IN THE INDUSTRIAL WORKPLACE

The businessmen of the 19th century are attempting to create their ideal worker. Complete the statements below from the perspective of an industrial worker by considering the following:

- Work conditions in a variety of industrial work settings
- Specific vocabulary about industrial conditions
- Deskilled workers and Taylorism

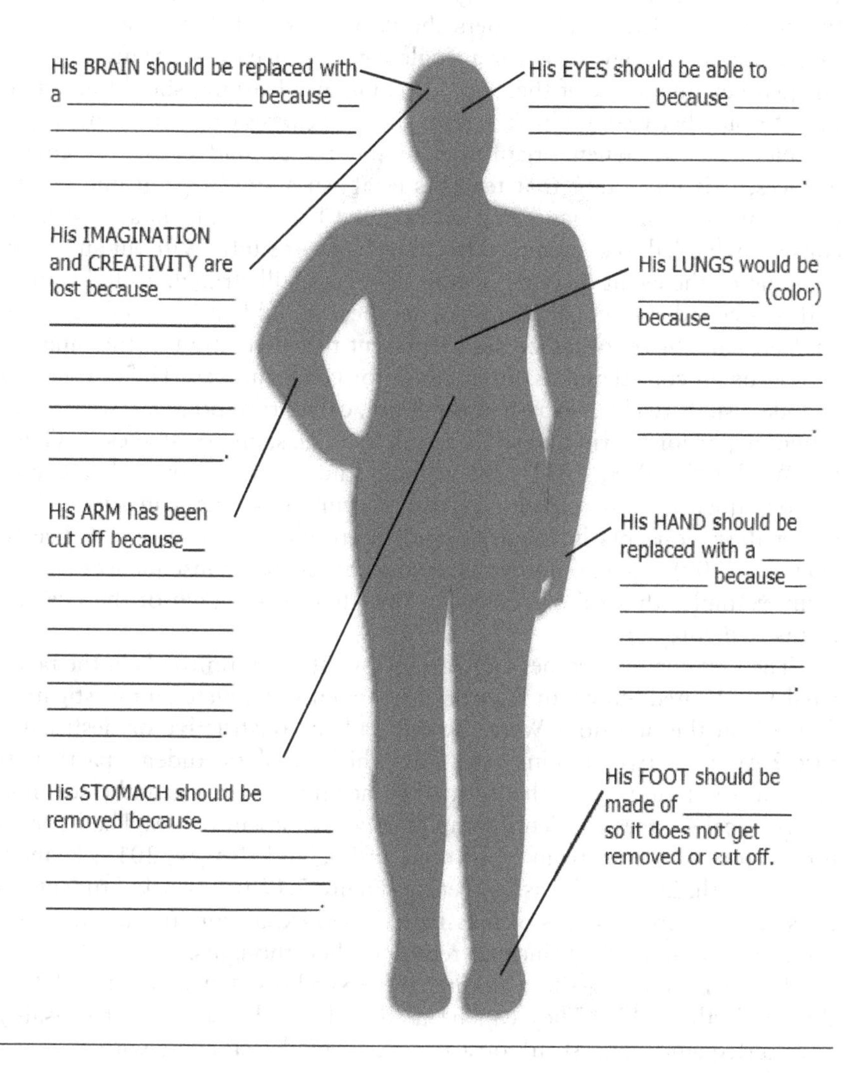

to emphasize cause and consequence more than the other skills, and thus lessons reflect that emphasis. In addition, the overrepresentation of causes and consequences in assessments arises from the fact that cause and consequence is one of the easier concepts for teachers to weave into their instruction, as it is comparatively easier to grasp than historical perspectives and requires an understanding of a narrower band of content than is demanded by continuity and change. Important to note is that despite significant overlap in how we consider both concepts, causes and consequences should be dealt with separately within an investigation. Building an inquiry that asks students to consider both causes and consequences reduces the complexity of both concepts, complicates the investigation, and generates student frustration. In addition, students and teachers should understand that an explanation that examines a single cause or a single consequence does not make for an adequate examination of the past. Teaching and learning should highlight the interplay between multiple factors, be they causes or consequences.

Nevertheless, when organizing an inquiry around causes or consequences, it is important that teachers establish a solid background about the event, person, or idea being investigated before students are asked to consider what led to or stemmed from the focus of study. Without an understanding of the event, person, or idea, students will struggle to link causes and associated consequences. Also, teachers should utilize tools to help students categorize, organize, and represent the interaction of the multiple factors being considered as either causal or consequences. These tools can include visuals (webs, hexagonal thinking), categories (political, social, and economic, or long-term and short-term), analogies, and/or shapes ("What's the Wisdom," 2019, 2021). By helping students focus on either causes or consequences and scaffolding their examination, they can successfully center these concepts in inquiries, and the results can be assessed (Lee & Shemilt, 2009). As you contemplate the causes and consequences assessment examples that follow, consider how they reflect each of the five elements in Figure 7.16.

The first example comes from an investigation of railroads in the post–Civil War United States. In Figure 7.17, students complete an investigation focused on the question: **Were the railroads a constructive or destructive force?** After the two-step investigation, which involves students participating in a simulation called the railroad game and an analysis and discussion of historical sources, students complete the assessment below. The impetus for the images comes from work done in England (Navey, 2018; Pennell, 2014; Worth, 2017). The assessment in Figure 7.17 below asks students to consider the consequences of massive railroad expansion and use the contrasting symbols as the vehicle to represent their thoughts.

I take no credit for developing these symbols, but absolutely I love them (Worth, 2017). They can be used in both the context of causality and consequence, and their consistent use provides students with a deeper

Figure 7.16 Causes and Consequences Progression

Elements of Causes and Consequences	Limited Understanding	Powerful Understanding
Causes and Consequences Are Webs Change is driven by multiple causes and results in multiple consequences. These create a complex web of interrelated short-term and long-term causes and consequences.	Student attributes events to a single cause, often a short-term one. Alternatively, student lists causes and consequences provided by others without understanding the interrelationships.	Student identifies multiple short-term and long-term causes and/or consequences and recognizes the complex interrelationship.
Ranking Causes and Consequences The causes that lead to a particular historical event vary in their influence, with some being more important than others.	Student does not differentiate between the influences of various causes.	Student analyzes the causes of an historic event and ranks them in comparison to one another.
Not Just People Events are caused by and result from the interplay of two types of factors: historical actors who take actions and the social, political, economic, and cultural conditions within which the actors operate.	Student personalizes all historical causes whether as great leaders or as abstractions with human attributes whose intentions cause events to take place.	Student identifies the interplay between the actions of historical actors and the conditions of the time.
No Crystal Balls Historical actors cannot predict the effect, conditions, opposing actions, and unforeseen reactions. These have the effect of generating unintended consequences.	Students think of past events as the expected results of plans and actions.	Student differentiates between intended and unintended consequences.
Not Inevitable The events of history were not inevitable, any more than those of the future are. Alter a single action or condition and an event might have turned out differently.	Student thinks of past events as inevitable by failing to consider human choice, intention, and decision-making.	Student demonstrates that an event in history was not inevitable.

Adapted from *The Big Six Historical Thinking Concepts*, by P. Seixas and T. Morton, 2013, Nelson Education.

Figure 7.17. Historical Causes and Consequences Assessment: The Iron Horse

"The Iron Horse" or Frankenstein: The Impacts of the Railroads on 19th-Century America

Between 1860 and 1930, the social, economic, and political changes wrought by the growth of the railroads dramatically changed the United States. Complete the assessment by:

- Selecting one size or shape that you think BEST represents the changes wrought by the expansion of railroads after the Civil War.
- Explain your decision in the space provided (be sure to reference specifics about the railroads).

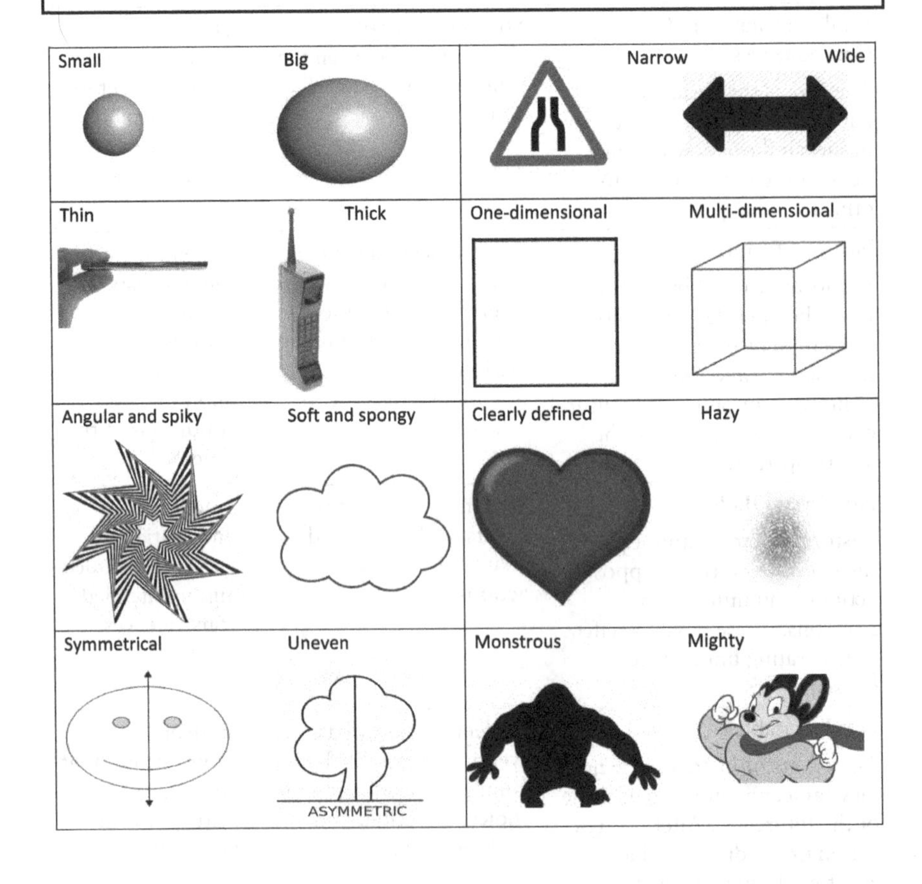

____

____

____

____

____

____

understanding of the interrelated nature of both. Student responses allow me to determine whether students recognize that change results in multiple consequences and that those consequences are interrelated. In addition, responses should illuminate if students are recognizing both actors and conditions. Students are always amazed at the power of the railroad to both create and destroy, and this assessment allows them the latitude to examine the multiple consequences of their rise. The assessment targets are outlined in Figure 7.18.

A similar example is found in Figure 7.19 in the Reconstruction Pie Chart. This assessment emphasizes the causes of the end of Reconstruction and asks students to make judgments on the relative impacts of a variety of factors as they debate the question: **Why did Reconstruction end?** The pie chart serves as both a pre-writing/thinking activity and a way to represent students' arguments visually. Unfortunately, I always have to explain to students that a pie chart adds up to 100% while a circle is comprised of 360 degrees—I guess we are all math teachers!

In the justification portion, students need to consider not only each individual cause, but also the relationships between the causes. Quality student responses interlink their factors rather than just summarizing each factor and arguing that the reasons for the end of Reconstruction function siloed from one another rather than working together. The assessment provides flexibility in that you could decrease it to three factors or increase it to five or six if time allows. Similar to the railroad assessment, student responses allow for insight into their ability to recognize that change is driven by multiple causes, both short- and long-term, and that some causes have more influence than others.

Figure 7.18. Historical Causes and Consequences Assessment: The Iron Horse Checklist

Causes and Consequences Are Webs

Change is driven by multiple causes and results in multiple consequences. These create a complex web of interrelated short-term and long-term causes and consequences.

Ranking Causes and Consequences

The causes that lead to a particular historical event vary in their influence, with some being more important than others.

Not Just People

Events are caused by and result from the interplay of two types of factors: historical actors who take actions and the social, political, economic, and cultural conditions within which the actors operate.

Figure 7.19. Historical Causes and Consequences Assessment: The Decline of Reconstruction Pie Graph

"The plain truth is that the North has got tired . . .": The Decline of Reconstruction

Complete the following pie graph by deciding the percentage that **at least 4 factors** played in the decline of Reconstruction. Be sure to consider:

- What percentage of credit do your 4 factors receive? Nope, 25% apiece is not acceptable!
- Be sure to consider the difference between events occurring in the South and the North
- Remember, pie graphs add up to 100%, not 360! ☺
- Finally, justify (**in at least two paragraphs of 5–7 sentences per paragraph**) how your factors combined to bring Reconstruction to an end. Be specific, give examples, and support with details. Be sure to explain your factors and how they linked to end Reconstruction.

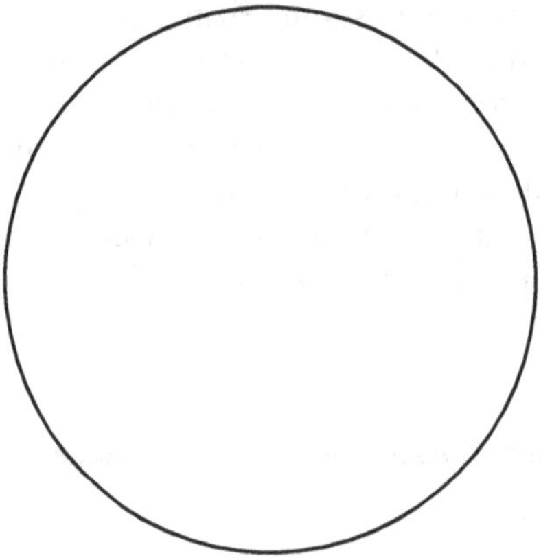

Key

☐ =

☐ =

☐ =

☐ =

Explanation

The Barbie assessment in Figure 7.21 is implemented at the conclusion of a lesson on the feminist movement of the 1970s and early 1980s. Students have gone through a series of lessons that look at the origins of the movement, the history of the Equal Rights Amendment, and how popular culture—particularly films and television—reflected the changes wrought by feminism. Students wrestle with the question: **How significant were the changes created by the postwar feminist movement?** Barbie was selected because the doll's objectification and stereotyping of women serves as an easy foil that allows students the creativity to apply what they know to her make over. In this instance, the assessment combines both causes and consequences, as the new accessories proposed by the student could address both. Briefcases, pantsuits, birth control pills, credit cards, advanced college degrees, and numerous other accoutrements are used to adorn Barbie and to represent the causes and consequences of second- wave feminism (see Figure 7.21). Figure 7.20 enumerates the factors that students' responses must address.

The tree in Figure 7.23, women's suffrage, was developed by a wonderful colleague, Beth Ann Haas. It is designed to represent visually the multiple factors that that gave birth to the suffrage movement in the United States and the short- and long-term consequences of the push for voting rights. A similar tool is also provided in Figure 7.24 via the bar graph example for my lesson on the end of the Cold War. These examples provide other formats for students to wrestle with and their understanding of the elements of cause and consequence outlines in Figure 7.22.

Figure 7.20 Historical Causes and Consequences Assessment: 1980s Barbie Checklist

Elements of Causes and Consequences

Causes and Consequences Are Webs

Change is driven by multiple causes and results in multiple consequences. These create a complex web of interrelated short-term and long-term causes and consequences.

Ranking Causes and Consequences

The causes that lead to a particular historical event vary in their influence, with some being more important than others.

Not Just People

Events are caused by and result from the interplay of two types of factors: historical actors who take actions and the social, political, economic, and cultural conditions within which the actors operate.

Figure 7.21. Historical Causes and Consequences Assessment: 1980s Barbie

1980s Barbie: Postwar Second-Wave Feminism Assessment

The Barbie of the 1980s desires to be outfitted with three accessories that will reflect the feminist movement and not the objectification of women that defined her initial release. Select three accessories that would represent the movement and explain **(5–7 sentences)** why you selected each. When making your decisions, be sure to consider:

- The factors that caused the feminist movement
- The debate over the Equal Rights Amendment (ERA)
- The changes that resulted from the feminist movement
- How these changes (positive and negative) were reflected in popular culture of the 1980s

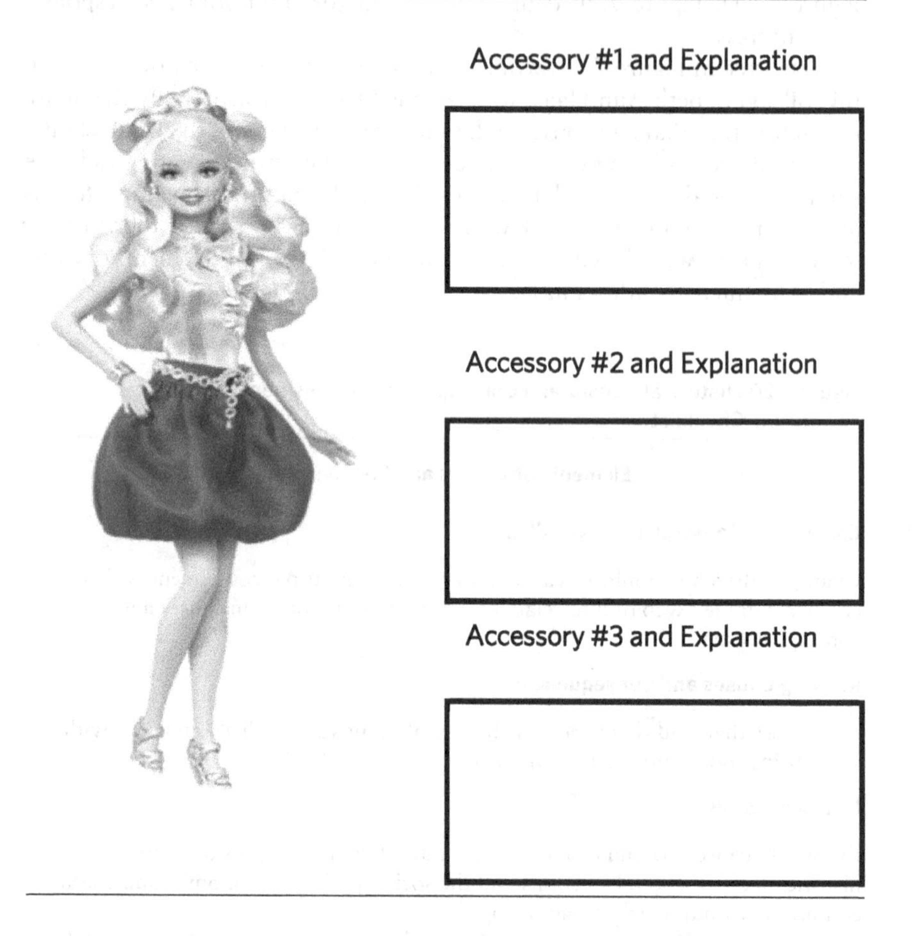

Figure 7.22. Historical Causes and Consequences Assessment: The Tree of Suffrage and Cold War Bar Graph Checklist

Causes and Consequences are Webs

Change is driven by multiple causes and results in multiple consequences. These create a complex web of interrelated short-term and long-term causes and consequences.

Ranking Causes and Consequences

The causes that lead to a particular historical event vary in their influence, with some being more important than others.

Not Just People

Events are caused by and result from the interplay of two types of factors: historical actors who take actions and the social, political, economic, and cultural conditions within which the actors operate.

No Crystal Balls

Historical actors cannot predict the effect, conditions, opposing actions, and unforeseen reactions. These have the effect of generating unintended consequences.

Figure 7.23. Historical Causes and Consequences Assessment: The Tree of Suffrage

"We women of America tell you that America is not a democracy": The Women's Suffrage Movement

Now that you have learned about the elements of the Suffrage Movement, it is time to branch out and show your knowledge. **Create a TREE** with the important information about the growth and efforts of the movement for women's suffrage. Like any tree, your **ROOTS are your foundation;** the most important ideas would be found in the roots. The **BRANCHES** show how your tree has expanded; the big ideas, leaders, and successes will go on the branches. The **LEAVES** represent your secondary ideas; remember, some leaves fall off.

Make sure the following information appears on/in your tree:

- ✓ Social Housekeeping
- ✓ Cult of Domesticity
- ✓ Major Women's Suffrage Organizations
- ✓ Alice Paul versus Carrie Chapman Catt
- ✓ 19th Amendment
- ✓ Tactics and Arguments of All Parts of the Suffrage Movement

Figure 7.24. Historical Causes and Consequences Assessment: End of the Cold War Bar Graph

"Tear down this wall": The End of the Cold War

Using your knowledge of the events that led to the events surrounding the conclusion of the Cold War, create a bar graph that represents what you believe to be the four most important reasons for the conclusion of the tensions between the United States and the Soviet Union. After selecting your causes and displaying them on the bar graph, justify your choices below. **Be sure to link each factor directly to the end of the Cold War and to relate the factors to one another.** Consider:

- The efforts of President Ronald Reagan
- The efforts of Soviet Premier Mikhail Gorbachev
- Events within the Soviet Union
- Events within the Soviet satellite states

100%

% OF RESPONSIBILITY

0%

Reasons for the end of the Cold War:

Explanation

Assessing Historical Significance

Kids think assessing historical significance is easy. They attribute the significance of an event to the authority from which they derive their knowledge: the teacher and or the textbook. The overwhelming centrality of these two resources in social studies instruction means that they become the default mechanisms by which students derive significance. "The book covered it," or "there are multiple paragraphs in the textbook," or "we saw a movie on it" become intellectual crutches students often use to prop up why they feel an event was significant. Unfortunately, this means that students are not actually developing or applying this historical thinking skill but instead are just mimicking what they hear. Their deference to the teacher or textbook as the gatekeeper of what is important to know dulls their ability to think historically.

Ultimately, if students are going to develop the skill of assigning and justifying historical significance, they must understand how to ask questions that lead them to draw thoughtful conclusions regarding what about the past retains significance today. "So what," and "why should we care" are the heart of questions that *students must ask to draw conclusions about what is significant from the past.* Both students and teachers pose questions about "so what" and "why should we care." Teachers pose them when they are considering what content to emphasize or what investigative questions to pose. Students are also always asking similar questions (sometimes out loud and sometimes under their breath!). They want to know how this information helps them to understand their world, human behavior, or current events. To ensure that students are not simply studying content so that there is something to cover, teachers need to make sure that there is a good answer to the "so what" and "why should we care" questions. If the answer to either is anything along the lines of "because I told you so," or because "it is on the exam," then the significance of what is being studied must be seriously questioned. To structure assessments that target historical significance, I have blended criteria, found in Figure 7.25, for the concept and its assessment from several sources (Barton, 2005; Bradshaw, 2006; Cercadillo, 2006; Counsell, 2004; Dawson, 2003; Lévesque, 2005; Partington, 1980; Seixas & Morton, 2013).

In each of the sample assessments provided, students need to consider an event, individual, or idea and draw some conclusions regarding what makes them significant.

In Figure 7.26 students have examined the immigration that occurred from the end of the American Civil War through the Johnson-Reed Immigration Act of 1924. The significance is communicated via the artifacts that students select for their museum. Tangentially, the assessment looks at causes and consequences, but rather than just saying, "a consequence of immigration was Nativism and therefore I have included an anti-immigrant

Figure 7.25. Historical Significance Progression

Elements of Historical Significance	Limited Understanding	Powerful Understanding
Events, people, or developments have historical significance if they resulted in change that has deep consequences for many people, over a long period of time, and over a large geographic area.	Student places faith in a textbook or other authority as a basis for significance or relies on personal preference without evidence as the basis for historical significance.	Student explains historical significance of events, people, or developments by showing they resulted in change.
What is historically significant varies over time and from group to group.	Student assumes that significance is fixed and unchanging.	Student shows how historical significance varies over time and from group to group.

Adapted from *The Big Six Historical Thinking Concepts*, by P. Seixas and T. Morton, 2013, Nelson Education.

cartoon," students need to extend their explanation to include why Nativism as a response to the new immigrants is still significant today. A strong student response links to how immigration "resulted in change that has deep consequences for many people, over a long period of time, and over a large geographic area." In addition, students need to focus on the full scope of immigration that occurred during this 60-year period. Significance should include a balance of both Asian and European immigration experiences. Students often prefer to draw the items rather than write a description, and that is a great way to allow students to pull in some artistic ability into the assessment.

In Figure 7.27, students consider the Articles of Confederation. The personification of the Articles through the lens of an obituary is a fun twist that results in some great work by students. I provide them with the Pillsbury Doughboy example not only for a giggle but also to help them envision the structure. Historical significance comes into play when they must determine the consequences that the document had on America in both the short and long terms.

Significance assessments allow students to consider how we commemorate events and people from the past. Statues, historical markers, inclusion in textbooks, stamps, and other tools of public history demand that students consider what is significant about these people and events. Figures 7.28 and 7.29 are examples of how students can consider an event through the lens of public history rather than just as an academic exercise.

Figure 7.26. Historical Significance Assessment: The Museum of American Immigration

THE MUSEUM OF AMERICAN IMMIGRATION

You have been invited to contribute to the new exhibit at the Museum of American Immigration. The museum is developing an exhibit on the New Immigrants of 1880–1925 that focuses on the reasons they came and their treatment in the United States. Your exhibit must include at least five items that would help a visitor to the museum understand the new immigrants. Exhibits may include artifacts, documents, maps, biographies, or other materials that help people understand the importance of the new immigrants. Consider the countries of origin for these immigrants, examples of them being accepted/rejected by American culture, legal barriers they faced, and other characteristics of their journey to or stay in the United States. **Your justification should not only explain the item and what it tells us about the time period but also why you decided to include it in the exhibit.**

Item Description	Justification for Inclusion in the Exhibit

CONCLUSION

Assessment, in both its formative and summative manifestations, must be an essential component of teaching and learning. For history and social studies, the questions are no longer should I assess or even when should I assess, but instead what I should assess and what tools I should use. Multiple-choice, true/false, and fill-in-the-blank questions can no longer be the staples of our

Figure 7.27. Historical Significance Assessment: The Article of Confederation Obituary

AN OBITUARY FOR A DEAD FRIEND . . . THE ARTICLES OF CONFEDERATION

We have examined the Articles of Confederation and how it attempted to organize the United States during and after the American Revolution. By 1787 it became apparent that the Articles were in desperate need of revision or perhaps replacement. Your task is to write an obituary for the recently deceased Articles. You will want to consider the Articles as a living being who has passed away. Be sure to include the following in your obituary:

- A description of two accomplishments of this document
- At least three specific problems that occurred during its life
- Why the document finally died
- Survivors
- Cause of death
- Date of birth/date of death
- How the Articles impacted United States History

PILLSBURY DOUGHBOY, 71

Veteran Pillsbury spokesperson the Pillsbury Doughboy died yesterday of a severe yeast infection and complications from repeated pokes to the belly. He was 71.

Doughboy was buried in a slightly greased coffin. Dozens of celebrities turned out, including Mrs. Butterworth, the California Raisins, Hungry Jack, Betty Crocker, the Hostess Twinkies, Captain Crunch, and many others.

The graveside was piled high with flours. Longtime friend Aunt Jemima delivered the eulogy, describing Doughboy as a man who "never knew how much he was kneaded."

Doughboy rose quickly in show business, but his later life was filled with many turnovers. He was not considered a very smart cookie, as he wasted much of his dough on half-baked schemes.

Despite being a little flaky at times, even as a crusty old man he was considered a role model for millions. Toward the end it was thought he'd rise once again, but he was no tart.

Doughboy is survived by his second wife, Play Dough. They have two children, one in the oven. The funeral was held at 3:50 for about 20 minutes.

Figure 7.28. Historical Significance Assessment: Evaluating an Historic Monument

ASSESSING A MONUMENT

Consider everything you know about the causes, course, and consequences of the events surrounding the Haymarket bombing and the police memorial statue, and respond to the following question in 7–8 sentences: Is this statue an effective/accurate/appropriate commemoration of the events at Haymarket? Should something else have been erected instead? Why/why not?

The following statue honoring the efforts of the police during the Haymarket Riot of 1884 was constructed in 1889 and placed adjacent to Haymarket Square. The statue itself honors the policemen's staunch assertion of authority in the face of anarchy. The inscription on the pedestal proclaims it to be dedicated by the grateful city "to her defenders in the riot of May 4, 1886." The honor at the dedication of the police monument went to the teenage son of Officer Matthias Degan, who had been killed by the Haymarket bomb and for whose death the eight anarchists were found guilty. Mayor DeWitt Cregier delivered the main address. With the support of the same businessmen who had helped arm the militia against civil disorder and had opposed clemency—including R. T. Crane, in front of whose factory the riot had taken place—the funds needed to complete the project were soon raised.

Figure 7.29. Historical Significance Assessment: Malcolm X Historic Stamp

"By Any Means Necessary": From Malcolm Little to Malcolm Shabazz

In 1990, the United States Postal Service issued a stamp (see below) commemorating the life of Malcolm X. Should the United States Government have issued such a stamp? Why or why not? As you compose your one paragraph response (4–6 sentences) be sure to consider:

- The beliefs, events, and actions that defined the various phases of Malcolm's life
- The role of Malcolm X and the Black Power/Black Nationalist Movement in the Civil Rights struggle
- The similarities and differences between Malcolm X and the efforts of Dr. Martin Luther King, Jr. and the non-violent wing of the Civil Rights Movement

assessment diet. By looking for alternatives that assess historical thinking and knowledge in history, we can diversify our instruction and gain more insight into student thinking than is traditionally achieved in the traditional history classroom. The essay is an important instrument, and writing is an essential and a much-neglected skill, but teachers should diversify the assessment tools within their instructional tool kit and seek alternatives to a five-paragraph essay. Clear, focused, and evidence-based written responses are central to all the examples I modeled in this chapter, but they intentionally attempt to give insight into student ability to operationalize various historical thinking skills, in addition to measuring student knowledge of key historical content. Assessment must "disentangle the various threads that comprise historical thinking" (Reisman, 2015b), and I hope these examples will serve as a stepping-off point for achieving this recalibration of how you assess students.

Conclusion

"I Don't Always Mention Those Words": The Power of Partnerships

Let's start where we began: Philadelphia, in the summer. As I relayed in the opening, a disgruntled teacher stormed out of a professional development session when new content did not square with his understanding. In many ways, this is emblematic of the problems with the professional learning we provide all teachers generally, and history teachers specifically. In, usually, one drive-by session, or at best a few scattered sessions, the expectation behind most professional development is that teacher practice can change instantaneously. A few well-delivered, research-based, practical applications of new pedagogy, and teachers will return to their classrooms and change their practice. Nope.

The efficacy of any instructional reform hinges on its ability to be implemented without stressing the already overburdened professional life of a classroom teacher. A variety of factors, including the culture of a particular school, district-wide expectations, accountability demands, teacher confidence, and student needs, can affect the ability of a new instructional practice to take root. Ultimately, a simple cost-benefit analysis determines if the practice will become habitual or die on the vine. Given these professional realities, this book concludes with an examination of my effort to address the lingering frustration felt at the end of every professional development session: Will this make a difference? Can the historical investigations model as a form of classroom instruction be successfully transferred from one teacher to another? I knew that the drive-by model in which I had engaged so frequently was not a path to success, but was there a more effective path?

It is my contention that an instructional approach that emphasizes the interrogation of historical sources to develop evidence-based interpretations in response to provocative historical questions can be achieved and indeed be transferred from one practitioner to another, but not by utilizing the normal approach to professional learning that dominates the field. Instead, my prescription is to facilitate long-term partnerships between experienced and new teachers to promote long-term instructional change. This prescription includes avoiding the drive-by model and instead seeking sustained, discipline-specific, professional learning that is content-focused, rooted in a common problem of practice, and focused on long-term growth and not short-term mimicry (Callahan et al., 2016; Gulamhussein, 2013; Neumann, 2012; van Boxtel et al., 2020; Yoon et al., 2007).

INITIATING THE PARTNERSHIP

Before the start of the 2010–2011 school year, I established a partnership with a colleague, Catherine. Looking for an opportunity to teach something other than World History and Advanced Placement European History, Catherine and I decided to split the school's honors United States History courses between us and to work collaboratively to integrate historical thinking and the historical investigations model into the course. We each came to the relationship with different motivations but with a common goal: to deepen students' abilities to think historically and to investigate the past.

The idea of a partnership was the by-product of having managed several teaching American History grants. In those grants, participating teachers were paired up to participate in a modified version of a lesson study (Halvorsen & Lund, 2013; Saye & Howell, 2016). They developed investigations in the summer, shared them with the members of their cohort for feedback, and then, when the investigation was being taught, they visited one another, observed instruction, and engaged in a postmortem conversation. These instructional intervisitations led to rich instructional dialogues that were centered on the pedagogical content knowledge needed to promote the investigation of meaty historical questions. Having worked with Catherine since her first year in the profession, I knew that her enthusiasm for teaching and work ethic would make her a great partner in this endeavor.

Is the history investigations model transferable as a form of instruction? What Catherine and I discovered is that the answer is yes, but the road to this destination is occupied by several important challenges.

THE PLANNING MEETING

The main forum for exposing Catherine to the historical investigations model was a weekly planning meeting at which transparency was the modus operandi. Through discussion of lessons, we hoped to lay bare the thought processes behind the elements of lessons and the manner in which the overarching question and the sources worked together to put students in a position of assessing and applying evidence. Our desire was to have the meetings be nonhierarchical, fluid discussions that forced both of us to make transparent our thoughts about instruction. The honesty and lucidity were designed to facilitate the transfer of the historical investigations approach from one teacher to another. These weekly meetings were often animated and ultimately very productive. Be it the wording of a question that would structure a student investigation, the selection of historical sources that would be examined, or how to best balance our desire to have students investigate the past rather than simply commit facts to memory, we debated constantly. Yet these open and honest dialogues during our boisterous planning sessions—a central component to our yearlong efforts—yielded substantial harvests as we attempted to transfer historical investigation as an instructional model.

INTERVISITATIONS

The second tool we employed was the use of intervisitations. When we were teaching an investigation, we watched each other teach the lesson and then discussed how it went. We examined student work and discussed the manner in which the sources impacted student thinking and the overall effectiveness of the investigation. This tool was tremendously beneficial, as it allowed us to explore how planning contrasted with implementation. It also enabled us to assess student work and allow it to serve as an indicator of what went well and what needed tweaking. For a full school year, Catherine and I employed the cycle of planning meetings, intervisitation, and feedback to move her instruction further into the historical investigations arena.

"I DON'T ALWAYS MENTION THOSE WORDS"

When interviewed at the end of the academic year, Catherine stated that:

> As I assess my first year of teaching historical investigations, what shocks me most is my unwillingness to use the language of the program as well as the intellectual commitment that this teaching strategy required of me. At the beginning of the school year, I agreed to embrace all parts of the program, yet I was unable to commit to the language—*text, subtext,* and *context.* Although I am confident that my students acquired the skills to identify the text, subtext, and context of a source, I repeatedly chose to describe the terms instead of teaching the students the vocabulary of historical investigations. There is no logical reason for my choice not to use the language of the program, since a bulletin board was mounted in my classroom with the terms on it as a reminder. My initial thought was that I became so focused on knowing the context and subtext of each historical investigation that I could not do it all, and therefore I chose to drop what I saw as less relevant—the vocabulary. After further thought, I concluded that since my academic studies in history did not use the language and since my

> colleagues do not use the terms, the terminology remained foreign and unfamiliar. To adopt the language, teachers must become more conscious in their decisions to use the terminology in their classroom as well as among themselves. The terms must become part of teaching history at all levels. In the end, the decision not to use the terminology did not have a major effect on student learning, but it required me to define the words repeatedly and may have meant that I lost some teaching time.

What Catherine did not say was that her students could not think historically. Instead, she identified a gap in her practice that inhibited students from being able to do so. This, I think, is one of the most significant benefits of providing the professional learning in a sustained and job embedded manner rather than as a drive-by. In a drive-by, teachers express concerns that their students "cannot do this." I push back, outline the research, model the instruction, and share student work, but then I leave. There is no sustained practice embedded into their daily instruction that addresses this elephant in the instructional room and allows them to develop the skills to make friends with the elephant and then alter instructional practice. For Catherine, there was, and I think that is the difference-maker.

As Sam Wineburg (2001) reminds us, historical thinking is an "unnatural act" for students. They do not come to the classroom already possessing the ability to deeply examine historical sources by questioning authorship and purpose, by placing sources within their historical context, or by connecting the text of a source to its subtext. Instead, students are better prepared to identify the main idea of a historical source than they are to question the source and apply the information to the formulation of an evidence-based answer to a guiding historical question. Catherine's challenge with using the vocabulary that exposes the underlying historical thinking is not an isolated phenomenon. When she says, "To adopt the language, teachers must become more conscious in their decisions to use the terminology in their classroom as well as among themselves," Catherine is recognizing the unnaturalness of thinking historically. Catherine frequently mentioned in our meetings toward the end of the year that she "always mention[s] those words," and this admission is consistent with the "unnatural" nature of historical thinking.

Jeffrey Nokes (2011) outlined several barriers that impede students' abilities to read historical sources like historians. One of the earliest barriers is that of the language that hamstrung Catherine. "Historical thinking," argues Nokes, "is cognitively challenging," and therefore requires that teachers make explicit how to read a historical document for more than just the main idea. Nokes, in addition to identifying the barriers, provides a number of useful "Instructional Interventions" for teachers to consider when attempting to overcome these barriers. The use of posters, bookmarks, graphic organizers, modeling, and repeated practice can help ease students into the cognitive challenges inherent in thinking historically. Nokes's work is a clear path any teacher can follow to incorporate historical thinking into their instructional program(381).

As Catherine recognizes, the literacy skills embodied within three simple vocabulary terms—*text, context,* and *subtext*—are a key hurdle to a successful transition to historical investigations. To cross the breach dividing historians from high school students, classroom instruction must make explicit the skills involved in historical literacy. Students must be taught the fact that historical sources are three-dimensional packages of information, created by someone, at some point, for some reason, and reflecting all of these elements in the information they provide. Once taught, these critical literacy skills must be practiced frequently to make the unnatural natural. Catherine's admission that she didn't "always mention those words" says clearly that in many ways this is the most difficult hurdle for teachers to overcome as they learn to incorporate historical investigations into their classrooms.

My own classroom practice and research demonstrate to me how difficult yet essential the infusion of historical thinking through a common vocabulary is to ensuring students' ability to investigate the past. What I have discovered is that students must see the language as part of how they "do" history. Just as in math students must understand order of operations, prime numbers, and what happens when two negative numbers encounter each other, students in history classes must understand how to read historical documents, assess the information derived from the evidence, and then associate concepts such as significance, chronology, and change over time when applying this evidence to the investigation of a historical question (Lesh, 2011).

In Catherine's second year teaching American History, she and I continued to work together and met regularly to revise and improve the curriculum. With Catherine's understanding of the methods of the historical investigations model and her ability to communicate historical thinking to her students effectively, her students' ability to develop evidence-based answers to deep historical questions bloomed.

While Catherine bloomed, I am left to wonder about the thousands of teachers I worked with in the drive-by model. Were they able to understand the research, modify materials, and make the instructional transition? How did they develop proficiency in identifying what happens between labs, promoting effective discussion strategies within investigations, navigating the investigation of hard histories, developing engaging questions, and utilizing formative and summative assessments that align with the investigation of the past? All these and other components of this instructional approach require much more than a simple 1-, 3-, or 5-day drive-by professional development experience. My goal with this book is to address the questions and concerns that were raised during my professional development sessions. I realize that this does not provide the kind of partnership that may be essential to making the transition from telling history to investigating it, but hopefully it at least aids that process.

Most importantly, I hope that the work assuages concerns that historical investigations are only for a small group of students. Yes, your students can do this!

References

Abrams v. United States, 250 U. S. 616 (1919). https://www.oyez.org/cases/1900-1940/250us616.

Adapting documents for the classroom: Equity and access. (n.d.). TeachingHistory.org https://teachinghistory.org/teaching-materials/teaching-guides/2356

AP program results: Class of 2021. (2021).The College Board. https://reports.collegeboard.org/ap-program-results/2021

AP United States History: Course and exam description. (2020). The College Board. https://apcentral.collegeboard.org/media/pdf/ap-us-history-course-and-exam-description.pdf

Alfieri, L., Brooks, P. J., Aldrich, N. J., & Tenenbaum, H. R. (2011). Does discovery-based instruction enhance learning? *Journal of Educational Psychology, 103*(1), 1–18. https://doi.org/10.1037/a0021017

Allen, J. (1999). *Without sanctuary: Lynching photography in America.* Twin Palms Publishers.

Almarza, D. J. (2001). Contexts shaping minority language students' perceptions of American history. *Journal of Social Studies Research, 25*(2), 4–22.

Andolina, M. M., Jenkins, K., Zukin, C., & Keeter, S. (2003). Habits from home, lessons from school: Influences on youth civic engagement. *Political Science and Politics, 36*(2), 275–280.

Asbury, N. (2021, December 19). D.C. third-graders were made to reenact episodes from the Holocaust. *The Washington Post.* https://www.washingtonpost.com/education/2021/12/19/holocaust-reenactment-watkins-school-dc/.

Ashby, R., Lee, P. J., & Shemilt, D. (2005). Putting principles into practice: Teaching and planning. In National Research Council, *How students learn: History in the classroom* (pp. 78–178). The National Academies Press.

Ashby, R., & Lee, P. (1987). Children's concepts of empathy and understanding in history. In C. Portal (Ed.), *The history curriculum for teachers* (pp. 62–88). Falmer.

Aulls, M. W. (2008). Developing students' inquiry strategies: A case study of teaching history in the middle grades. In B. M. Shore, M. W. Aulls, & M. A. B. Del-Court (Eds.), *Inquiry in education, vol. II: Overcoming barriers to successful implementation* (pp. 1–49). Lawrence Erlbaum Associates.

Avery, P. G. (2002a). Political socialization, tolerance, and sexual identity. *Theory & Research in Social Education, 30,* 190–197.

Avery, P. G. (2002b). Teaching tolerance: What research tells us. *Social Education, 66*(5), 270–275.

Avery, P. G., Levy, S. A., & Simmons, A. M. M. (2013). Deliberating controversial public issues as part of civic education. *The Social Studies, 104,* 105–114.

Bain, B. (2000). "They thought the world was flat?" Applying the principles of how people learn in teaching high school history. In M. S. Donovan & J. D. Bransford (Eds.), *How students learn: History in the classroom* (pp. 179–213). The National Academies Press.

Bain, B. (2006). Rounding up the usual suspects: Facing hidden authority in the history classroom. *Teachers College Record, 108*(10), 2080–2114.

Bain, B. (2015). Into the swampy lowlands of important problems. In K. Erikan & P. Seixas (Eds.), *New directions in assessing historical thinking* (pp. 64–72). Routledge.

Ball, M. (2015, July 1). How same sex marriage became a constitutional right. *The Atlantic.* https://www.theatlantic.com/politics/archive/2015/07/gay-marriage-supreme-court-politics-activism/397052/

Bartelds, H., Savenije, G. M., & van Boxtel, C. (2020). Students' and teachers' beliefs about historical empathy in secondary history education. *Theory and Research in Social Education, 48*(4), 529–551.

Barton, K. (1997a). "I just kinda know": Elementary students' ideas about historical evidence. *Theory and Research in Social Education, 25,* 407–430.

Barton, K. (1997b). "Bossed around by the Queen": Elementary students' understanding of individuals and institutions in history. *Journal of Curriculum and Supervision, 12,* 290–314.

Barton, K. (1997c). History—it can be elementary: An overview of elementary children's understanding of history. *Social Education, 61,* 13–16.

Barton, K. (2005). Best not to forget them: Secondary students' judgments of historical significance in Northern Ireland. *Theory & Research in Social Education, 33*(1), 9–44.

Barton, K. (2008). Students' ideas about history. In L. S. Levstik & C. A. Tyson (Eds.), *Handbook of research in social studies education* (pp. 239–258). Routledge.

Barton, K. (2018). Historical sources in the classroom: Purpose and use. *HSSE Online: Research and Practice in Humanities and Social Studies Education,* 7(2). http://www.hsseonline.edu.sg/journal/volume-7-issue-2-2018/historical-sources-classroom-purpose-and-use

Barton, K. (2019). Assessing historical discussion. *HSSE Online: Research and Practice in Humanities and Social Studies Education, 8*(1). http://www.hsseonline.edu.sg/journal/volume-8-issue-1-2019/ assessing-historical-discussion

Barton, K., & Levstik, L. (1998). "It wasn't a good part of history": National identity and students' explanations of historical significance. *Teachers College Record, 99*(3), 478–513.

Barton, K., & Levstik, L. (2003). Why don't more history teachers engage students in interpretation? *Social Education, 67*(6), 358–361.

Barton, K., & Levstik, L. (2004). *Teaching history for the common good.* Lawrence Erlbaum Associates.

Barton, K., & McCully, A. (2005). History, identity and the school curriculum in Northern Ireland: An empirical study of secondary students' ideas and perspectives. *Journal of Curriculum Studies, 37*(1), 85–116.

Beck, D., & Eno, J. (2012). Signature pedagogy: A literature review of social studies and technology research. *Computers in the Schools*, *29*, 70–94.

Bell, J. C., & McCollum, D. F. (1917). A study of the attainments of pupils in United States history. *Journal of Educational Psychology, 8*(5), 257–274.

Berger, W. (2014). *A more beautiful question: The power of inquiry to spark breakthrough ideas*. Bloomsbury Press.

Berman, S. B. (2022). *LGBTQ+ history in high school classes in the United States since 1990*. Bloomsbury Press.

Berti, A. E., Baldin, I., & Toneatti, L. (2009). Empathy in history: Understanding a past institution (ordeal) in children and young adults when description and rationale are provided. *Contemporary Educational Psychology*, *34,* 278–288.

Bickford, J. (2010a). Uncomplicated technologies and erstwhile aids: How PowerPoint, the internet, and political cartoons can elicit engagement and challenge thinking in new ways. *The History Teacher*, *44*(1), 51–66.

Bickford, J. (2010b). Complicating students' historical thinking through primary source reinvention. *Social Studies Research and Practice*, *5*(1), 47–60.

Bickford, J. (2011). Students' original political cartoons as teaching and learning tools. *Social Studies Research and Practice, 6*(2), 47–59.

Bolinger, K., & Warren, W. (2007). Methods practiced in social studies instruction: A review of public-school teachers' strategies. *International Journal of Social Education*, *22,* 68–84.

Bondie, R. (2010). *Crop it.* TeachingHistory.org. https://teachinghistory.org/teaching-materials/teaching-guides/25697

Booth, M. (1978). Ages and concepts: A critique of the Piagetian approach to history teaching. In C. Portal (Ed.), *The history curriculum for teachers* (pp. 22–38). Falmer.

Bradshaw, M. (2006). Creating controversy in the classroom: Making progress with historical significance. *Teaching History*, *125*, 18–25.

Bransford, J., Brown, A., & Cocking, R. (2000). *How people learn: Brain, mind, experience, and school.* National Research Council National Academies Press.

Breakstone, J. (2013). *History assessments of thinking: Design, interpretation and implementation* [Doctoral dissertation]. http://purl.stanford.edu/nt301xp3169

Breakstone, J., Smith, M., & Wineburg, S. (2013). Beyond the bubble in history/social studies assessments. *Kappan Magazine*, *94*(5), 43–57.

Breakstone, J., Wineburg, S., & Smith, M. (2015) Formative assessment using Library of Congress documents. *Social Education*, *79*(4), 177–180.

Brensilver, S. (2021). *LGBTQ+ history in high school classes in the United States since 1990.* Bloomsbury Press.

Brooks, S. (2011). Historical empathy as perspective recognition and care in one secondary social studies classroom. *Theory & Research in Social Education, 39*(2), 166–202.

Brow, R., & Schell, S. (2016, May). Not your grandfather's U.S. History class: Abandoning chronology and teaching thematically. *The American Historian*, May, 10–15.

Brown, A., & Brown, K. (2010). Strange fruit indeed: Interrogating contemporary textbook representations of racial violence toward African Americans. *Teacher's College Record*, *112*(1), 31–67.

Brown, G., & Burnham, S. (2014). Assessment after levels. *Teaching History, 157*, 8–22.

Brown, S. D., & Hughes, R. L. (2018). It's not something we thought about: Teachers' perception of historiography and narratives. *Social Studies Research and Practice, 13*(1), 16–30.

Bruner, J. (1978). The role of dialogue in language acquisition. In A. Sinclair, R. J. Jarvelle, & W. J. M. Levelt (Eds.), *The child's concept of language*. Springer-Verlag.

Brush, T., & Saye, J. (2014). An instructional model to support problem-based historical inquiry: The persistent issues in History Network. *Interdisciplinary Journal of Problem-Based Learning, 8*(1).

Bulgren, J., Sampson, P., & Deshler, D. (2013). Literacy challenges and opportunities for students with learning disabilities in social studies and history. *Learning Disabilities Research and Practice, 28*(1), 17–27.

Burack, J. (2010). *Interpreting political cartoons in the history classroom*. Teaching History.org, the National History Education Clearinghouse. https://teachinghistory.org/teaching-materials/teaching-guOk, ides/21733

Burkholder, P., & Schaffer, D. (2021). *History, the past, and public culture: Results from a national survey*. American Historical Association.

Byford, J., Lennon, S., & Russell, W. (2009). Teaching controversial issues in the social studies: A research study for high school teachers. *Cleaning House: A Journal of Educational Strategies, Issues, and Ideas, 84*(4), 65–170.

Calder, L. (2013). The stories we tell. *OAH Magazine of History, 27*(3), 5–8. https://doi.org/10.1093/oahmag/oat017.

Callahan, C., Howell, J., & Maddox, L. (2019). Selecting and designing visual curriculum materials for inquiry-based instruction. *Social Studies Research and Practice, 14*(3), 321–334.

Callahan, C., Saye, J., & Brush, T. (2016). Interactive and collaborative professional development for in-service history teachers. *The Social Studies, 107*(6), 2 227–243.

Camicia, S.(2008). Deciding what is a controversial issue: A case study of social studies curriculum controversy. *Theory and Research in Social Education, 36*(4), 98–316.

Caron, E. J. (2005). What leads to the fall of a great empire? Using central questions to design issues-based history units. *The Social Studies, 96*(2), 51–60

Cazden, C. (2001). *Classroom discourse: The language of teaching and learning* (2nd ed.). Heinemann.

Cercadillo, L. (2006). Maybe they haven't decided yet what is right: English and Spanish perspectives on teaching historical significance. *Teaching History, 125*, 18–26.

Chaplin, C. (Director). (1936). *Modern times*. United Artists.

Chapman, A. (2003). Camels, diamonds, and counterfactuals: A model for teaching causal reasoning. *Teaching History, 112*, 46–53.

Chenowith, K. (2009). *How it's being done: Urgent lessons from unexpected schools*. Harvard Education Press.

Claravall, E., & Irey, R. (2022). Fostering historical thinking: The use of document-based instruction for students with learning differences. *The Journal of Social Studies Research, 46*(3), 249–264.

Cohen, E., & Lotan, R. (2014). *Designing groupwork: Strategies for the heterogenous classroom* (3rd ed.). Teachers College Press.
Cole, P. (2011). *American labor in U.S. History textbooks: How labor's story is distorted in high school history textbooks*. The Albert Shanker Institute.
Collins, C., & Ehrenhalt, J. (n.d.). *Best practices for serving LGBTQ students: A Teaching Tolerance guide*. Southern Poverty Law Center. https://www.learningforjustice.org/sites/default/files/2018-10/TT-Best-Practices-for-Serving-LGBTQ-Students-Guide.pdf.
Coltham, J. (1971). *The development of thinking and learning in history*. Historical Association.
Counsell, C. (2000). Historical knowledge and historical skills: A distracting dichotomy. In J. Arthur & R. Phillips (Eds.), *Issues in history teaching* (pp. 54–71). Routledge.
Counsell, C. (2004). Looking through a Josephine Butler shaped window: Focusing pupils' thinking on historical significance. *Teaching History, 114,* 30–36.
Cox, H. R. (2011). *Wounded Knee: Party politics and the road to an American* massacre. Basic Books.
Crew, S. (2010). *From field to factory: Voices of the Great Migration*. Smithsonian Folkways.
Cuban, L. (1982). Persistent instruction: The high school classroom, 1900–1980. *Phi Delta Kappan, 64,* 113–118.
Cuban, L. (1993). *How teachers taught: Constancy and change in American classrooms, 1890–1980*. Teachers College Press.
Cuban, L. (2009, April 27). Hugging the middle. *Education Week*. https://www.edweek.org/teaching-learning/opinion-hugging-the-middle/2009/04
Cuban, L. (2012). Standards vs. customization: Finding the balance. *Educational Leadership*, *69*(5), 10–15.
Curwin, R. (2012, July 31). How to beat "teacher proof" programs. *Edutopia*. https://www.edutopia.org/blog/beating-teacher-proof-programs-richard-curwin.
Davis, S., Sumara, D. J., & Luce-Kapler, R. (2000). *Engaging minds: Learning and teaching in a complex world*. Routledge.
Dawson, I. (2003). *What is history: Y7 pupil's book*. Holder Murray.
Dawson, I. (2009). What time does that tune start? From thinking about "sense of period" to modelling history at key stage 3. *Teaching History*, *135*, 50–57.
Debs v. United States, 249 U. S. 211 (1919). https://www.oyez.org/cases/1900-1940/249us211.
Department of Justice. (2012). *Confronting discrimination in the post-9/11 era: Challenges and opportunities ten years later: A report on the Civil Rights Division's post-9/11 civil rights summit hosted by George Washington University Law School October 19, 2011*. https://www.justice.gov/sites/default/files/crt/legacy/2012/04/16/post911summit report 2012-04.pdf
D'Emilio, J. (1983). *Sexual politics, sexual communities: The making of a homosexual minority in the United States*. The University of Chicago Press.
De La Paz, S. (2005). Effects of historical reasoning instruction and writing strategy mastery in culturally and academically diverse middle school classrooms. *Journal of Educational Psychology*, *97*(2), 139–156.
De La Paz, S. (2012). Effective instruction for history and the social studies: What works forstudents with learning disabilities. In B.Y.L. Wong & D. L.

Butler (Eds.), *Learning about learning disabilities* (4th ed., pp. 325–353). Elsevier.

De La Paz, S. (2013). Teaching and learning in history: Effective and reform-based practices for students with learning disabilities. *Learning Disabilities: A Contemporary Journal, 11*(1), 89–105.

Dickson, T. (2002). The road to United States involvement in World War I: A simulation. *OAH Magazine of History, 17*(1), 48–56.

Dillon, J. (1994). *Using discussion in classrooms*. Open University Press.

Dobbs, M. (2008, July 7). Myths of the missile crisis. *BBC News Today*. http://news.bbc.co.uk/today/hi/today/newsid_7492000/7492678.stm

Dobbs, M. (2009). *One minute to midnight: Kennedy, Khrushchev, and Castro on the brink of nuclear war*. Vintage.

Donovan, S., & Bransford, J. (2005). *How students learn: History, mathematics, and science in the classroom*. The National Academies Press.

Doppen, F. (2000) Teaching and learning multiple perspectives: The atomic bomb. *The Social Studies, 91*(4), 159–169.

Dow, P. (2019). Inquiry in the social studies: Reflections of an octogenarian. *Social Education, 83*(2), 77–80.

Downey, M., & Long, K. (2016). *Teaching for historical literacy: Building knowledge in the history classroom*. Routledge.

Drake, I. (2008). Classroom simulations: Proceed with caution. *Learning for Justice, 33*(Spring). https://www.learningforjustice.org/magazine/spring-2008/classroom-simulations-proceed-with-caution.

Dulberg, N. (2005). The theory behind how students learn: Applying developmental theory to research on children's historical thinking. *Theory and Research in Social Education, 33*(4), 508–531.

Endacott, J. (2011). Power and liberty: A long-term course planning strategy to encourage the contextualization of events in American history. *The Social Studies, 10*(2), 73–79.

Endacott, J., & Brooks, S. (2013). An updated theoretical and practical model for promoting historical empathy. *Social Studies Research and Practice, 8*, 41–58.

Engle, R., & Conant, F. (2002). Guiding principles for fostering productive disciplinary engagement: Explaining an emergent argument in a community of learner's classroom. *Cognition and Instruction, 20*(4), 399–483.

Epstein, T. (2012). Preparing history teachers to develop young people's historical thinking. *Perspectives on History*. https://www.historians.org/publications-and-directories/perspectives-on-history/may-2012/preparing-history-teachers-to-develop-young-peoples-historical-thinking.

Epstein, T. (2000). Adolescents' perspectives on racial diversity in U.S. history: Case studies from an urban classroom. *American Educational Research Journal, 37*(1), 185–214.

Epstein, T. (2009). *Interpreting national history: Race, identity, and pedagogy in classrooms*. Abingdon, Routledge, Taylor, and Francis.

Fallace, T., & Neem, J. (2005). Historiographical thinking: Towards a new approach to preparing history teachers. *Theory and Research in Social Education, 33*(3), 329–346.

Fenton, E. (1990). Reflections on the New Social Studies. *Social Studies, 82*(3), 84–91.

Ferretti, R., MacArthur, C. D., & Okolo, C. M. (2001). Teaching for historical understanding in inclusive classrooms. *Learning Disabilities Quarterly, 24*, 59–71.

Finn, C., & Ravitch, D. (1987). *What do our 17-year-olds know?: A report on the First National Assessment of History and Literature*. Harper & Row.

Fischer, F. (2022). Teaching Trump in the history classroom. *The Journal of American History, 108*(4), 772–778.

Fisher, D., & Frey, N. (2021). *Better learning through structured teaching: A framework for the gradual release of responsibility* (3rd ed.). ASCD.

Fisher, D., & Frey, N. (2010). *Guided instruction: How to develop confident and successful learners*. ASCD.

Flanders, N. (1970). *Analyzing teacher behavior*. Addison-Wesley.

Fleming, T., Darrow, R., & Oculto, R. (2019). *Teaching LGBTQ history: An educator's guide*. https://www.lgbtqhistory.org/wp-content/uploads/2019/05/TeachingLGBTHistoryEducatorsGuide_14Feb2019.pdf.

Ford, A. (2014a). "Setting us free?: Building meaningful models of progression for a 'post-levels' world. *Teaching History, 157*, 28–41.

Ford, A. (2014b). *Progression in historical thinking: An overview of key aspects of the mastery of historical thinking and practice*. https://www.academia.edu/26175928/Progression_in_historical_thinking_an_overview.

Ford, A. (2016). *Progress & progression in history*. And All That. http://www.andallthat.co.uk/uploads/2/3/8/9/2389220/apf_-_progression_pack.pdf

Fordham, M. (2012). *But have you not thought about the consequences?: Using causation's forgotten sibling in the history classroom*. Paper presented at the Annual Conference of the Historical Association, Reading, England.

Foster (Eds.), *Historical empathy and perspective taking in the social studies* (pp. 69–96). Rowman & Littlefield.

Foster, R. (2016). Historical change: In search of argument. In C. Counsell, K. Burn, & A. Chapman (Eds.), *Master class in history education: Transforming teaching and learning* (pp. 5–22). Bloomsbury.

Foster, S., & Yeager, E. (2001). The role of empathy in the development of historical understanding. In O. L. Davis, E. A. Yeager, & S. J. Foster (Eds.), *Historical empathy and perspective taking in the social studies* (pp. 13–21). Rowman and Littlefield.

Foster, S., & Padgett, C. (1999). Authentic historical inquiry in the social studies classroom. *The Clearing House, 72*(6), 357–363.

Fowler, D., & LaBoiunty, S. (2019). *Contextualizing LGBT+ history within the social studies curriculum* (NCSS Position Statement). National Council for the Social Studies. https://www.socialstudies.org/position-statements/contextualizing-lgbt-history-within-social-studies-curriculum

Gamoran, A., & Nystrand, M. (1992). Taking students seriously. In F. Newmann (Ed.), *Student engagement and achievement in American schools* (pp. 40–61). Teachers College Press.

Geraci, J., Palmerini, M., Cirilo, P., & McDougald, V. (2017). *What teens want from their schools: A national survey of high school student engagement*. Thomas B. Fordham Foundation.

Gerwin, D., & Zevin, J. (2010). *Teaching United States history as mystery*. Routledge.

GLSEN. (2019). *The 2019 national school climate survey: The experiences of lesbian, gay, bisexual, transgender, and queer youth in our nation's schools*.

https://www.glsen.org/sites/default/files/2021-04/NSCS19-FullReport-032421-Web_0.pdf.

Goldberg, T., & Savenije, G. (2018). Teaching controversial historical issues. In S. A. Metzger & L. M. Harris (Eds.), *The Wiley International Handbook of History Teaching and Learning* (pp. 503–526). Wiley.

Gonzalez, J. (2019). *Think twice before doing another historical simulation.* Cult of Pedagogy. https://www.cultofpedagogy.com/classroom-simulations/.

Good, A. (2009). Framing American Indians as the "first Americans": Using critical multiculturalism to trouble the normative American story. *Social Studies Research and Practice*, *4*(2), 49–66.

Good, R. (2013). Using *E Pluribus Unum* as a narrative framework for the U.S. History survey. *OAH Magazine of History*, *27*(3), 11–15.

Goodwin, B. (2016). Research matters: Novice teachers benefit from lesson plans. *Educational Leadership*, *74*(2), 75–76.

Gorman, M. (1998). The structured inquiry is not a contradiction in terms: Focused teaching for independent learning. *Teaching History*, *92*, 20–25.

Gradwell, J. (2006). Teaching in spite of, rather than because of, the test: A case of ambitious teaching in New York state. In S. G. Grant (Eds.), *Measuring history: Cases of high stakes testing across the United States* (pp. 157–176). Information Age Publishing.

Grant, S. G. (2003). *History lessons: Teaching, learning, and testing in U. S. high school classrooms.* Lawrence Erlbaum Associates.

Grant, S. G. (Ed.). (2006). *Measuring history: Cases of state-level testing across the United States.* Information Age Publishing.

Grant, S. G. (2018). Teaching practices in history education. In A. Metzger & L. H. McArthur (Eds.), *The Wiley international handbook of history teaching and learning* (pp. 419–448). John Wiley and Sons.

Grant, S. G., & Gradwell, J. (2010). *Teaching history with big ideas: Cases of ambitious teachers.* Rowman & Littlefield.

Grant, S. G., Gradwell, J., & Cimbricz, S. (2004). A question of authenticity: The document-based question as an assessment of student's knowledge of history. *Journal of Curriculum and Supervision*, *19*, 309–337

Grant, S. G., Swann, K., & Lee, J. (2017). *Inquiry-based practice in social studies education: Understanding the inquiry design model* (1st ed.) Routledge.

Grant, S. G., Swann, K., & Lee, J. (2018). *Inquiry design model: Building inquiries in social studies.* National Council for the Social Studies.

Grant, S. G., & VanSledright, B. A. (2014). *Elementary social studies: Constructing a powerful approach to teaching and learning* (3rd ed.). Routledge.

Greer, C. (2006). *Primary source strategies.* The College Board. https://secure-media.collegeboard.org/apc/ap05_ushist_greer_2_p_50286.pdf

Gruber, M., Gelman, B., & Ranganath, C. (2014). States of curiosity modulate hippocampus-dependent learning via the dopaminergic circuit. *Neuron*, *84*(2), 486–496.

Guidelines for teaching about the Holocaust. (n.d.). United States Holocaust Memorial Museum. https://www.ushmm.org/teach/fundamentals/guidelines-for-teaching-the-holocaust.

Gulamhussein, A. (2013). *Teaching the teachers: Effective professional development in the era of high stakes accountability.* National School Board Association, Center for Public Education. http://conference.ohioschoolboards.org/2017/wp-%20content/uploads/sites/17/2016/07/1pm111317A114Job-embedPD.pdf.

Haas, J. D. (1977). *The era of the new social studies*. Boulder: ERIC Clearinghouse for Social Studies/Social Science Education and Social Science Education Consortium.

Hallam, R. N. (1970). Piaget and thinking in history. In M. Ballard (Ed.), *New movements in the study and teaching of history* (pp. 162–178). Indiana University Press.

Hallam, R. N. (1971). Thinking and learning in history. *Teaching History, 2,* 337–346.

Halvorsen, A., & Lund, A. K. (2013). Lesson study and history education. *The Social Studies, 104,* 123–129.

Hamblin, T. (2020). The current state of assessing historical thinking: A literature review. *The Nebraska Educator: A Student-Led Journal, 5*, 148–176.

Hardwicke, C. (Director). (2003). *Thirteen days*. Fox Searchlight Pictures.

Harris, L. M., & Girard, B. (2014). Instructional significance for teaching history: A preliminary framework. *The Journal of Social Studies Research, 38*(4), 215–225.

Harris, L. M. A., Endacott, J., & Brooks, S. (2018). Historical empathy: Perspectives and responding to the past. In *The Wiley international handbook of history teaching and learning* (pp. 203–226). Wiley-Blackwell.

Harris, L. M., Sheppard, M., & Levy, S. (2022). *Teaching difficult histories in difficult times: Stories of practice*. Teachers College Press.

Harris, R., & Hayden, T. (2006) Pupils' enjoyment of history: What lessons can teachers learn from their pupils? *The Curriculum Journal, 17*(4), 315–333.

Harris, L. M., Archambault, L., & Shelton, C. (2021). Getting serious about sourcing information: Considerations for teachers and teacherpreneurs. *Social Education, 85*(5), 260–266.

Hartmann, U., & Hasselhorn, M. (2008). Historical perspective taking: A standardized measure for an aspect of students' historical thinking. *Learning and Individual Differences, 18,* 264–270.

Hattie, J. (2009). *Visible learning: A synthesis of over 800 meta-analyses relating to achievement*. Routledge.

Hattie, J. (2012). *Visible learning for teachers: Maximizing impact on learning*. Routledge.

Hattie, J., Stern, J., Fisher, D., & Frey, N. (2020). *Visible learning for social studies, grades K–12: Designing student learning for conceptual understanding*. Corwin.

Havekes, H., Coppen, P-A, & van Boxtel, C. (2012). Knowing and doing history: A conceptual framework and pedagogy for teaching historical contextualization. *International Journal of History Teaching Learning and Research, 11*(1), 72–93.

Havekes, H., van Boxtel, C., Coppen, P-A., & Luttenberg, J. (2017). Stimulating historical thinking in a classroom discussion: The role of the teacher. *Historical Encounters: A Journal of Historical Consciousness, Historical Cultures, and History Education, 4*(2), 71–93.

Heitzman, W. R. (1998). *The power of political cartoons in teaching history*. National Council for History Education Occasional Paper.

Henry, M. S. (1986). The intellectual origins and impact of the document-based question. *Perspectives, 24*(2), 14–16.

Hess, D. (2009a). Teaching about same-sex marriage as a policy and constitutional issues. *Social Education 73*(7), 344–349.

Hess, D. (2009b). *Controversy in the classroom: The democratic power of discussion*. Routledge

Hess, D. (2004a). Discussion in the classroom: Is it worth the trouble? *Social Education, 68*(2), 151–155.

Hess, D. (2004b). Controversies about controversial issues in democratic education. *PSOnline,* April, 257–261.

Hess, D., & Posselt, J. (2002). How high school students experience and learn from the discussion of controversial public issues. *Journal of Curriculum and Supervision, 17*(4), 283–314.

Heumann, J. (2020). *Being Heumann: An unrepentant memoir of a disability rights activist.* Beacon Press.

Hillis, P. (2005). Assessing investigative skills in history: A case study from Scotland. *History Teacher, 38*(3), 341–360.

Hirsch, E. D. (1987). *Cultural literacy: What every American needs to know.* Houghton Mifflin.

Ho, L., McAvoy, P., Hess, D., & Gibbs, B. (2017). Teaching and learning about controversial issues and topics in the social studies. In M. Manfra & C. Bolick (Eds.), *The Wiley Handbook of Social Studies Research* (pp. 319–335). Wiley-Blackwell.

Holt, T. (1990). *Thinking historically: Narrative, imagination, and understanding.* The College Board.

Howells, G. (2007). Life by sources A to F: Really using sources to teach AS history. *Teaching History, 128*, 30–37.

Huggins, N (Ed.). (1986). *W. E. B. Du Bois: Writings*. Library of America.

Husbands, C., & Kitson, A., Steward, S. (2011). *Teaching history 11–18: Understanding the past.* McGraw-Hill Education.

Huijgen, T., & Holthuis, P. (2018). Man, people in the past were indeed stupid. *Teaching History, 172*, 30–38.

Hynd, C. (1999). Teaching students to think critically using multiple texts in history. *Journal of Adolescent and Adult Literacy, 6*(42), 428–436.

Interview with David K. Johnson. (2004). The University of Chicago Press. https://press.uchicago.edu/Misc/Chicago/404811in.html

Jadallah, M., Anderson, R. C., Nguyen-Jahiel, K., Miller, B. W., Kim, I.-H., Kuo, L.-J., Dong, T., & Wu, X. (2011). Influence of a teacher's scaffolding moves during child-led small-group discussion, *American Educational Research Journal, 48*(1), 194–230.

Jennings, K. (2006). Out in the classroom: Addressing lesbian, gay, bi-sexual, and transgender (LGBT) issues in the social studies curriculum. In E. W. Ross (Ed.), *The social studies curriculum: Purposes, problems, and possibilities* (3rd ed., pp. 255–264). SUNY Press.

Jensen, E. (2005). *Teaching with the brain in mind* (2nd ed.). ASCD.

Johnson, D. (2006). *The Lavender Scare: The Cold War persecution of gays and lesbians in the federal government.* University of Chicago Press.

Johnson, D. W., & Johnson, R. T. (1988). *Critical thinking through controversy. Educational Leadership, 45*(8), 58–64.

Jones, S. (2020). Ending curriculum violence: Yes, curriculum can be violent—whether you intend it or not. Here's what it looks like and how you can avoid it. *Teaching Tolerance*, 64. https://www.learningforjustice.org/magazine/spring-2020/ending-curriculum-violence.

Journell, W. (2011). Teachers' controversial issue decisions related to race, gender, and religion during the 2008 presidential election. *Theory and Research in Social Education, 14*(2), 113–138.

Journell, W. (2020). Controversial decisions within teaching controversial issues. *Annals of Social Studies Education Research for Teachers, 1*(1), 5–9.

Kaufman, S. (2015). High school history teacher forced into early retirement for showing anti-gay film from the 1950s. *Salon.* https://www.salon.com/2015/05/07/high_school_history_teacher_forced_into_early_retirement_for_showing_anti_gay_film_from_the_1950s/.

Kennedy, D. A. (2001). *Freedom from fear: The American people in depression and war*, 1929–1945. Oxford University Press.

Kerr, S., & Adams, E. (2017). What do you see? Visual(izing) social studies for all students. *The Oregon Journal of the Social Studies, 5*(1), 30–41.

Kidd, C., & Hayden, B. (2015). The psychology and neuroscience of curiosity. *Neuron, 88*(3), 449–460.

Kitson, A., & McCully, A. (2005). "You hear about it for real in school." Avoiding, containing, and risk-taking in the history classroom. *Teaching History, 120,* 32–37.

Klein, S. F., (1983). The genesis of shorter document-based questions in the Advanced Placement American History examination. *Perspectives, 21*(5), 22–24.

Knowles, R., & McCafferty-Wright, J. (2015). Connecting open classroom climate to social movement citizenship: A study of 8th grades in Europe using the IEA ICCS data. *The Journal of Social Studies Research, 39,* 255–269.

Larson, B. (2000). Influences on social studies teachers' use of classroom discussion. *The Clearing House: A Journal of Educational Strategies, Issues, and Ideas, 73*(3), 174–181.

Larson, B. E. (2022). Guiding principles for using classroom discussion. In J. Lo (Ed.), *Making classroom discussions work: Methods for quality dialogue in the social studies* (pp. 11–26). Teachers College Press.

Lattimer, H. (2008). Challenging history: Essential questions in the social studies classroom. *Social Education, 72*(6), 326–329.

Lawrence v. Texas, 539 U. S. 558 (2003). https://www.oyez.org/cases/2002/02-102.

Lawrence, J., & Meyers, W. D. (1995). *The great migration: An American story.* Perfection Learning.

Lee, P. (2005). Putting principles into practice: Understanding history. In M. S. Donovan & J. D. Bransford (Eds.), *How students learn: History in the classroom* (pp. 61–65). The National Academies Press.

Lee, P., & Ashby, R. (2001). Empathy, perspective taking, and rational understanding. In O. L. Davis, E. A. Yeager, & S. J. Foster (Eds.), *Historical empathy and perspective taking in the social studies* (pp. 21–50). Rowman & Littlefield.

Lee, P., Dickinson, A., & Ashby, R. (1997). Just another emperor: Understanding action in the past. *International Journal of Educational Research, 27,* 233–244.

Lee, P., & Howson, J. (2009). Two of five did not know that Henry VIII had six wives. In L. Symcox & A. Wilschut (Eds.), *History education, historical literacy, and historical consciousness. National history standards: The problem of the canon and the future of history teaching* (pp. 211–261). Information Age Publishing.

Lee, P., & Shemilt, D. (2003). A scaffold, not a cage: Progression and progression models in history. *Teaching History, 113,* 13–23.

Lee, P., & Shemilt, D. (2004). "I just wish we could go back in the past and find out what really happened": Progression in understanding about historical accounts. *Teaching History, 117,* 25–31.

Lee, P., & Shemilt, D. (2009). Is any explanation better than none?: Overdetermined narratives, senseless agencies, and one-way streets in students' learning about cause and consequence in history. *Teaching History, 137,* 42–49.

Lee, P., & Shemilt, D. (2011). The concept that dares not speak its name: Should empathy come out of the closet? *Teaching History, 143,* 39–49.

Lei, H., Cui, Y., & Zhou, W. (2018). Relationships between student engagement and\academic achievement: A meta-analysis. *Social Behavior and Personality: An International Journal*, *46*, 517–528.

Leming, J., Ellington, L., Schug, M. & Dieterle, D. (2009). *Social studies in our nation's high schools: National random survey of high school social studies teachers' professional opinions, values, and classroom practices.* Center for Survey Research and Analysis, University of Connecticut.

Lesh, B. (2011). "*Why won't you just tell us the answer?" Teaching historical thinking in grades 7–12*. Stenhouse.

Lévesque, S. (2005). Teaching second-order concepts in Canadian history: The importance of "historical significance." *Canadian Social Studies, 39*(2).

Lévesque, S. (2009). *Thinking historically: Educating students for the 21st century.* University of Toronto Press.

Levinson, M. (2012). *No citizen left behind* (Vol. 13). Harvard University Press.

Levstik, L. (2001). Crossing the empty spaces: New Zealand adolescents' understanding of perspective-taking and historical significance. In O. L. Davis, E. A. Yeager, & S. J.

Levstik, L., & Barton, K. (2023). *Doing history: Investigation with children in elementary and middle school* (6th ed.). Routledge.

Lingard, B., Hayes, D., & Mills, M. (2003) Teachers and productive pedagogies: Contextualizing, conceptualizing, utilizing. *Pedagogy, Culture & Society, 11*(3), 399–424.

Linter, T. (2018). The controversy over controversy in the social studies classroom. *Southeastern Regional Association of Teacher Educators Journal*, *27*(1), 14–21.

Lowenthal, D. (1985). *The past is a foreign country.* Cambridge University Press.

Luff, I. (2001). Beyond 'I speak, you listen, boy!' Exploring diversity of attitudes and experiences through speaking and listening. *Teaching History, 105,* 10–18.

MacKenzie, T. (2019). *Dive into inquiry: Amplify learning and empower students.* Elevate Books.

Maguth, B., & Taylor, N. (2004). Bringing LGBTQ topics into the social studies classroom. *The Social Studies, 105,* 23–28.

Mandel, N., & Malone, B. (2008). *Thinking like an historian: Rethinking history instruction: A framework to enhance and improve teaching and learning.* Wisconsin Historical Society Press.

Map: Where critical race theory is under attack. (2021, June 11). *Education Week.* http://www.edweek.org/leadership/map-where-critical-race-theory-is-under-attack/2021/06

Marino, M. (2022). Rethinking historical thinking: How historians use unreliable evidence. *The History Teacher*, *55*(2), 270–304.

Mayer, R. (2008). Applying the science of learning: Evidence-based principles for the design of multi-media instruction. *American Psychologist, 63*(8), 76–769.

Mayo, J. B. (2017). Sexuality and queer theory in the social studies. In M. M. Manfra & C. M. Bolick (Eds.), *The Wiley Handbook of Social Studies Research* (1st ed., pp. 54–269). Wiley-Blackwell.

Mayo, J. B. (2011). GLBT issues in the social studies: An essential reader. In W. B. Russell III (Ed.), *Contemporary social studies: An essential reader* (pp. 243–260). Information Age Publishing.

McAvoy, P., & Hess, D. (2014). Debates and conversations from the ground up. *Educational Leadership, 72*(3), 48–53.

McAvoy, P., & Ho, L. (2020). Professional judgement and deciding what to teach as controversial. *Annals of Social Studies Education Research for Teachers, 1*(1), 27–31.

McGirr, L. (2016). *The war on alcohol: Prohibition and the rise of the American state.* Norton.

McKeown, M., & Beck, I. (1990). The assessment and characterization of young learners' knowledge of a topic in history. *American Education Research Journal, 27*(4), 688–726.

McTighe, J., & Wiggins, G. (2013). *Essential questions: Opening doors to student understanding.* ASCD.

McTighe, J., & Wiggins, G. (2011). *Understanding by design guide.* ASCD.

Melville, A., & Minigan, A. P. (2018). Using the question formulation technique to guide primary source learning. *Library Resources* https://www.ebsco.com/blog/article/using-the-question-formulation-technique-to-guide-primary-source-learning.

Michaels, S., O'Connor, C. & Resnick, L. (2008). Deliberative discourse idealized and realized: Accountable talk in the classroom and in civic life. *Studies in Philosophy and Education*, 27, 283–297.

Michaels, S., & O'Connor, C. (2012). *Talk science primer.* TERC. https://inquiryproject.terc.edu/shared/pd/TalkScience_Primer.pdf

Minigan, A. P., & Beer, J. (2017). Inquiring minds: Using the question formulation technique to activate student curiosity. *The New England Journal of History, 74*(1), 114–136.

Minigan, A., Westbrook, S., Rothstein, D., & Santana, L. (2017). Stimulating and sustaining inquiry with students' questions. *Social Education, 8*(15), 268–272.

Minor v. Happersett, 88 U.S. 162 (1874). https://www.law.cornell.edu/supremecourt/text/88/162

Michaels, S., O'Connor, C, & Resnick, L. (2008). Deliberative discourse idealized and realized: Accountable talk in the classroom and in civic life. *Studies in Philosophy and Education, 27*, 283–297.

Mitchell, C. (2021, January 20). The violent history of white supremacy is rarely taught in schools. It should be. *Education Week.* https://www.edweek.org/teaching-learning/insurgency-refocuses-need-for-history-of-white-mob-violence-to-be-taught-in-classroom/2021/01

Mohamud, A., & Whitburn, R. (2019). Anatomy of an enquiry: Deconstructing an approach to history curriculum planning. *Teaching History*, *177*, 28–39.

Monte-Sano, C. (2008). Qualities of historical writing instruction: A comparative case study of two teachers' practices. *American Educational Research Journal, 45*(4), 1045–1079.

Monte-Sano, C., De La Paz, S., & Felton, M. (2014). *Reading, thinking, and writing about history: Teaching argument writing to diverse learners in the Common Core classroom, grades 6–12*. Teachers College Press.

Mueller, R. (2016). Making them fit: Examining teacher support for student questioning. *Social Studies Research and Practice, 11*(1), 40–55.

Mueller, R. (2017a). From potential to practice: Compelling questions as an impetus for curricular and instructional change. *Journal of Social Studies Research 42(3)*, 1–2.

Mueller, R. (2017b). Calibrating your compelling compass: Teacher-constructed prompts to assist question development. *Social Education, 81*(6), 343–354.

Mueller, R. (2017c). Episode 72: Compelling questions with Rebecca Mueller. *Visions of Education Podcast*. https://visionsofed.com/2017/12/19/episode-72-compelling-questions-with-rebecca-mueller/.

Mueller, R. (2018). Examining teachers' development and implementation of compelling questions. *Social Studies Research and Practice, 13*(1), 1–15.

Mullen, J., & Rowland-Woods, J. (2018). 50 state comparison: State summative assessments, social studies. *Education Commission of the States*, https://www.ecs.org/50-state-comparison-state-summative-assessments/.

Nash, G., & Crabtree, C. (1996). *National standards for history, basic edition*. National Center for History in the Schools, University of California Los Angeles.

National Assessment of Educational Progress. (n.d.). *U.S. History*. https://nces.ed.gov/nationsreportcard/ushistory/

National Center for Technology Innovation & Center for Implementing Technology in Education (n.d.). *Teaching history to support diverse learners*. LD Online. https://www.ldonline.org/ld-topics/educational-technology/teaching-history-support-diverse-learners

National Council for the Social Studies. (2015). *The college, career, and civic life (C3) framework for social studies state standards: Guidance for enhancing the rigor of K–12 civics, economics, geography, and history*. https://www.socialstudies.org/sites/default/files/2017/Jun/c3-framework-for-social-studies-rev0617.pdf

National Research Council. (2005). *How students learn: History in the classroom*. The National Academies Press.

Navey, M-A. (2018). Dealing with consequences: What do we want to do with consequence in history? *Teaching History*, 172(September), 40–49.

Neumann, D. (2012). Training teachers to think historically: Applying recent research to professional development. *The History Teacher*, 45(4), 383–403.

Neumann, D. (2021). Presenting historical content: The inquiry connections of a neglected practice. *The Social Studies*, 112(5), 231–246.

Neumann, D., Gilbertson, N., & Hutton, L. (2014). Context: The foundation of close reading of primary source texts. *Social Studies Research and Practice*, 9(2), 68–76.

Newmann, F. (1992). *Student engagement and achievement in American secondary schools*. Teachers College Press.

Newmann, F., Bryk, A. S., & Nagaoka, J. K. (2001). *Authentic intellectual work and standardized tests: Conflict or coexistence? Improving Chicago's Schools*. Consortium on Chicago School Research.

Niemi, R. G., Sanders, M. S., & Whittington, D. (2005). Civic knowledge of elementary and secondary school students, 1933–1998. *Theory and Research on Social Education, 33*(2), 172–199.

Nokes, J. D. (2010). Observing literacy practices in history classrooms. *Theory and Research in Social Education, 38*(4), 515–544.

Nokes, J. D. (2011). Recognizing and addressing the barriers to adolescents' "reading like historians." *History Teacher, 44*(3), 379–404.

Nokes, J. D. (2013). *Building students' historical literacies: Learning to read and reason with historical texts and evidence.* Routledge.

Nokes, J. D. (2019). *Teaching history, learning citizenship.* Teachers College Press.

Nokes, J. D., Dole, J., & Hacker, D. (2007). Teaching high school students to use heuristics while reading historical texts. *Journal of Educational Psychology, 99*(3), 492–504.

Novak, K. (2016). *UDL Now! A teacher's guide to applying Universal Design for Learning in today's classroom.* CAST Publishing.

Nystrand, M., Gamoran, A., & Carbonaro, W. (1998). *Towards an ecology of learning: The case of classroom discourse and its effects on writing in high school English and social studies.* Center on English Learning and Achievement.

Nystrand, M., Gamoran, A., Kachur, R., & Prendergast, C. (1997). *Opening dialogue.* Teachers College Press.

Nystrand, M., Wu, L., Gamoran, A., Zeiser, S., & Long, D. (2003). Questions in time: Investigating the structure and dynamics of unfolding classroom discourse. *Discourse Processes, 35*(2), 135–198.

Obenchain, K., Orr, A., & Davis, S. (2011). The past as a puzzle: How essential questions can piece together a meaningful investigation of history. *The Social Studies, 102*(5), 190–199.

Obergefell v. Hodges, 576 U. S. 644 (2015). https://www.oyez.org/cases/2014/14-556

O'Connor, C., Anderson, N.C., & Chapin, S. (2013). *Classroom discussions in math.* Math Solutions Publications.

Okrent, D. (2010). *Last call: The rise and fall of Prohibition.* Scribner.

Parker, W., & Hess, D. (2001). Teaching with and for discussion. *Teaching and Teacher Education, 17,* 273–289.

Partington, G. (1980). What history should we teach? *Oxford Review of Education, 6*(2), 157–176.

Pawling, K. (2011). Universal design for learning in social studies classrooms. T. Lintern & W. Scheder (Eds.), *Practical strategies for teaching K–12 social studies in inclusive classrooms* (pp. 19–28). Information Age Publishing.

Paxton, R. J. (2003). Don't know much about history—never did. *Phi Delta Kappan, 85*(4), 264–273.

Paxton, R., & Marcus, A. (2018). Film media in history teaching and learning. In S. A. Metzger & L. M. Harris (Eds.), *The Wiley International Handbook of History Teaching and Learning* (pp. 579–602). John Wiley & Sons, Inc.

Pegram, T. (1998). *Battling demon rum: The struggle for a dry America, 1800–1933.* Ivan R. Dee.

Pennell, C. (2014). On the frontlines of teaching the history of the First World War. *Teaching History, 155: First World War Edition,* 34–40.

Perlman, M. (2019). How the word "queer" was adopted by the LGBTQ community. *Columbia Journalism Review*, January. https://www.cjr.org/language_corner/queer.php.

Petrilli, M., & Finn, C. (2020). *How to educate an American: The conservative vision for tomorrow's schools*. Templeton Press.

Phillips, R. (2006). Historical significance—The forgotten key element? *Teaching History, 106*, 65–70.

Philpott, S., Clabough, J., McConkey, L., & Turner, T. (2010). Controversial issues; to teach or not to teach? That is the question! *The Georgia Social Studies Journal*, 9(1), 32–44.

Polikoff, M., Silver, D., Rapaport, A., Saavedra, A., & Garland, M. (2022, October). *A House divided? What Americans really think about controversial topics in schools*. University of Southern California. http://uasdata.usc.edu/education

Popp, J., & Hoard, J. (2018). Supporting elementary students' sourcing of historical texts. *The Reading Teacher*, 72(3), 301–311.

Potash, B. (2020). Hexagonal thinking: A colorful tool for discussion. *Cult of Pedagogy*. https://www.cultofpedagogy.com/hexagonal-thinking/.

Ray, R., & Gibbons, A. (2021). Why are states banning critical race theory. *FIXGOV Blog*. https://www.brookings.edu/blog/fixgov/2021/07/02/why-are-states-banning-critical-race-theory/.

Reinhart, S. (2000). Never say anything that a kid can say: Mathematics teaching in the middle school. *National Council of Teachers of Mathematics, 5*(8), 478–483.

Reisman, A. (2011). *Reading like an historian: A document-based history curriculum intervention in urban high schools*. Dissertation, Stanford University, https://stacks.stanford.edu/file/druid:vv771bw4976/Reisman_Dissertation_ReadinglikeaHistorian-augmented.pdf.

Reisman, A. (2015a). Entering the historical problem space: Whole-class, text-based discussion in history class. *Teachers College Record, 117*(2), 1–44.

Reisman, A. (2015b). The difficulty of assessing disciplinary historical reading. In K. Erikan & P. Seixas (Eds.), *New directions in assessing historical thinking* (pp. 29–39). Rutledge Press.

Reisman, A. (2017). How to facilitate discussions in history. *Educational Leadership*, 74(5), 30–34.

Reisman, A., Cipparone, P., Jay, L., Monte-Sano, C., Schneider Kavanagh, S., McGrew, S., & Fogo, B. (2019). Evidence of emergent practice: Teacher candidates facilitating historical discussions in their field placements. *Teaching and Teacher Education, 80,* 145–156.

Reisman, A., Enumah, L., & Lightning, J. (2020). Interpretive frames for responding to racially stressful moments in history discussions. *Theory and Research in Social Education, 48*(3), 321–345.

Reisman, A., & McGrew, S. (2018). Reading in history education text, sources, and evidence. In S. Metzger & L. McArthur (Eds.), *The Wiley International Handbook of History Teaching and Learning* (529–550*)*. Wiley-Blackwell.

Reisman, A., & Wineburg, S. (2008) Teaching the skill of contextualizing in history, *The Social Studies*, 99(5), 202–220.

Reitman, I. (Director). (1990). *Kindergarten cop*. Universal Studios.

Riley, M. (2000). Intro to key stage 3 history: Choosing and planning your enquiry question. *Teaching History*, *99*, 8–13.

Robinson, K., & Meyer, A. (2012). Doing history the universal design way. In T. Hall, A. Meyer, & D. Rose (Eds.), *Universal design for learning in the classroom: Practical applications* (pp. 90–105). The Guilford Press.

Rogers, P. (1987). The past as a frame of reference. In C. Portal (Ed.), *The history of curriculum for teachers* (pp. 3–21). Falmer Press.

Romano, A. (2011, March 20). How dumb are we? *Newsweek*, pp. 56–60.

Rorabaugh, W. J. (1979). *The alcoholic republic: An American tradition*. Oxford University Press.

Rosenzweig, R., & Thelen, D. (1998). *The presence of the past: Popular uses of history in American life*. Columbia University Press.

Rothschild, E. (2000). The impact of the document-based question on the teaching of United States history. *The History Teacher*, *33*(4), 495–500.

Rothstein, D., & Santana, L. (2012). *Make just one change: Teach students to ask their own questions*. Harvard Education Press.

Rosado, A., Cohen-Postar, G., & Eisen, M. (2022). *Erasing the Black freedom struggle: How state standards fail to teach the truth about Reconstruction*. The Zinn Education Project. https://www.teachreconstructionreport.org/

Russell, W., & Byford, J. (2009). Fostering discussion through case studies in the history classroom: A case study of high school students. *History Education Research Journal*, *8*(92), 133–139.

Sabataso, J. (2020, February 17). Feeling 'everything and nothing': Understanding curriculum violence in schools. *Rutland Herald*. https://www.rutlandherald.com/news/local/feeling-everything-and-nothing-understanding-curriculum-violence-in-schools/article_f0638c15-11fc-50f7-aa17-a92bc527f460.html

Sawchuk, S. (2022, January 19). Revising America's racist past. *Education Week*. https://www.edweek.org/teaching-learning/revising-americas-racist-past/2022/01

Saye, J., & Howell, J. (2016). Using lesson study to develop a shared professional teaching knowledge culture among 4th grade social studies teachers. *The Journal of Social Studies Research*, *40*, 25–37.

Saye, J., & Social Studies Inquiry Research Collaborative (SSIRC). (2013). Authentic pedagogy: Its presence in social studies classrooms and relationship to student performance on state-mandated tests. *Theory and Research in Social Education*, *41*(1), 89–132.

Schenck v. United States, 249 U. S. 47 (1919). https://www.oyez.org/cases/1900-1940/249us47.

Schmidt, J., & Pinkney, N. (2022). *Civil discourse: Classroom conversations for stronger communities*. Corwin Press.

Schwartz, S. (2019, May 27). Mock auctions. Pretending to flee captors. Do simulations have a place in lessons on slavery? *Education Week*. https://www.edweek.org/teaching-learning/mock-auctions-pretending-to-flee-captors-do-simulations-have-a-place-in-lessons-on-slavery/2019/03

See, think, wonder: A routine for exploring works of art and other interesting things. (2019). Visible Thinking Project. https://pz.harvard.edu/sites/default/files/See%20Think%20Wonder_2.pdf

Segall, A., Crocco, M., Halverson, A-L., & Jacobsen, R. (2018). Lessons learned about challenges of classroom deliberations. *Social Education*, *82*(6), 336–342.

Seixas, P. (1996). Conceptualizing the growth of historical understanding. In D. Olsen & N. Torrance (Eds.), *Handbook of education and human development: New models of learning, teaching, and schooling* (pp. 765–783). Blackwell.

Seixas, P., & Morton, T. (2013). *The big six historical thinking concepts*. Nelson Education.

Seixas, P., & Peck, C. (2004). Teaching historical thinking. In A. Sears & I. Wright (Eds.), *Challenges and prospects for Canadian social studies* (pp. 109–117). Pacific Educational Press.

Shemilt, D. (1980). *History 13–16 evaluation study*. Holmes McDougall.

Shemilt, D. (1987). Adolescent ideas about evidence and methodology in history. In C. Portal (Ed.), *The history curriculum for teachers* (pp. 36–61). The Falmer Press.

Shemilt, D. (2009). Drinking an ocean and pissing a cupful: How adolescents make sense of history. In L. Symcox & A. Wilschut (Eds.), *National history standards: The problem of the canon and the future of teaching history. International Review of History Education, Vol. 5* (pp. 141–210). Information Age Publishing.

Shernoff, D., & Csikszentmihalyi, M. (2014). Flow in schools: Cultivating engaged learners and optimal environments. In M. J. Furlong, R. Gilman, E. S. Huebner (Eds.), *Handbook of positive psychology in schools* (2nd ed., pp. 211–226). Routledge.

Shilts, R. (2007). *And the band played on* (20th anniv. ed.). St Martin's Press. (Original work published 1987)

Shuster, K. (2018). *Teaching hard history*. Southern Poverty Law Center. https://www.splcenter.org/20180131/teaching-hard-history

Simon, K. G. (2001). *Moral questions in the classroom: How to get kids to think deeply about real life and their schoolwork*. Yale University Press.

Sipress, J. (2004). Why students don't get evidence and what we can do about it. *History Teacher, 37*(3), 351–364.

Sismondo, C. (2011). *America walks into a bar: A spirited history of taverns, saloons, speakeasies, and grog shops*. Oxford University Press.

Smit, J., Van Eerde, H., & Bakker, A. (2013). A conceptualization of whole-class scaffolding. *British Education Research Journal, 39*(5), 817–834.

Smith, J., & Niemi, R. (2001). Learning history in school: The impact of coursework and instructional practice on achievement. *Theory and Research in Social Education, 29*(1), 18–42.

Smith, M., Breakstone, J., & Wineburg, S. (2018). History assessments of thinking: A validity study. *Cognition and Instruction, 37*(1), 118–144.

Smith, M. (2016). Reading like a historian: Using document-based lessons to teach historical thinking skills to students with specific learning disabilities [Master's thesis, California State University, Dominguez Hills]. https://scholarworks.calstate.edu/concern/theses/pr76f402c

Smith, P. (2001). Why Gerry now likes evidential work. *Teaching History, 201*, 8–13.

Snapp, S., Burdge, H., Licona, A., Moody, R., & Russell, S. (2015). Students' perspectives on LGBTQ-inclusive curriculum. *Equity and Excellence in Education, 48*(2), 249–265.

Sousa, D. (2017). *How the brain learns* (5th ed.). Corwin Press.

Sousa, D., & Tomlinson, C. (2018). *Differentiation and the brain: How neuroscience supports the learner-friendly classroom (*2nd Ed.). Solution Tree Press.

Styles, E. (1996). Curriculum as window and mirror. *Social Science Record,* Fall. http://www.nationalseedproject.org/images/documents/Curriculum_As_Window_and_Mirror.pdf.

Swafford, E. (2022, March 24). Teaching historiography in the K–12 classroom: *An AHA2022 Online Recap. Perspectives on History.* https://www.historians.org/publications-and-directories/perspectives-on-history/march-2022/teaching-historiography-in-the-k-12-classroom-an-aha22-online-recap

Swann, K., Crowley, R., Stamoulacatos, N., Lewis, B., & Stringer, G. (2022). Countering the past of least resistance: A hard history inquiry-based curriculum. *Social Education, 86*(1), 34–39.

Swann, K., Lee, J., & Grant, S. G. (2018a). *Inquiry design model: Building inquiries in social studies.* National Council for the Social Studies and C3 Teachers.

Swann, K., Lee, J., & Grant, S. G. (2018b). *Teaching about American slavery through inquiry.* Teaching Tolerance. https://www.learningforjustice.org/sites/default/files/2018-02/TT-Teaching-Hard-History-C3-Report-WEB-February2018.pdf

Sylvester, D. (1994). Change and continuity in history teaching, 1900–1993. In H. Bourdillian (Ed.), *Teaching history: A reader* (pp. 9–25). Routledge.

Teaching Tolerance. (2019). *Let's talk: Facilitating critical conversations with students.* The Southern Poverty Law Center.

Thomas, S. (2004). Teaching America's GAPE (or any other period) with political cartoons: A systematic approach to primary source analysis. *The History Teacher, 37*(4), 425–446.

Thornton, S. (2002). Does Everybody Count as Human?. *Theory & Research in Social Education, 30*(2), 178–189.

Thornton, S. (2003). Silence on gays and lesbians in social studies curriculum. *Social Education, 67*(4), 226–230.

Thornton, S. (1991). Teacher as curricular-instructional gatekeeper in social studies. In J. Shaver (Ed.), *Handbook of research on social studies teaching and learning* (pp. 237–248). Macmillian Library Reference.

Tomlinson, C. (2017). *How to differentiate instruction in academically diverse classrooms.* ASCD.

Traille, K. (2007). 'You should be proud about your history. They make you feel ashamed': Teaching history hurts. *Teaching History, 121,* 31–37.

van Boxtel, C., & van Drie, J. (2012). That's in the time of the Romans! Knowledge and strategies students use to contextualize historical images and documents. *Cognition and Instruction, 30,* 113–145.

van Boxtel, C., & van Drie, J. (2018). Historical reasoning: Conceptualizations and educational applications. In S. A. Metzger & L. M. Harris (Eds.), *The Wiley International Handbook of History Teaching and Learning* (pp. 49–176). Wiley-Blackwell.

van Boxtel, C., van Drie, J., & Stoel, G. (2020). Improving teachers' proficiency in teaching historical thinking. In C. W. Berg & T. M. Christou (Eds.), *The Palgrave handbook of history and social studies education* (pp. 97–117). Palgrave MacMillan.

Van de Pol, J., Volman, M., & Beishuizen, J. (2010) Scaffolding in teacher–student interaction: A decade of research. *Educational Psychology Review, 22*(3), 271–297.

van der Leeuw-Roord, J. (2009). Yearning for yesterday: Efforts of history professionals in Europe at designing meaningful and effective school history curricula. In L. Symcox & A. Wischult (Eds.), *National History Standards: The problem of the canon and the future of history teaching* (pp. 73–94). Information Age Publishing.

VanSledright, B. (2001). From empathic regard to self-understanding: Im/positionality, empathy, and historical contextualization. In O. L. Davis, E. A. Yeager Jr., & S. J. Foster (Eds.), *Historical empathy and perspective taking in the social studies* (pp. 51–68). Rowman & Littlefield.

VanSledright, B. (2002). *In search of America's past: Learning to read history in elementary school.* Teachers College Press.

VanSledright, B. (2011). *The challenge of rethinking history education: On practices, theories, and new policy.* Routledge

VanSledright, B. (2014). *Assessing historical thinking and understanding: Innovative designs for new standards.* Routledge.

VanSledright, B., & Frankes, L. (2000). Concept and strategic knowledge development in historical study: A comparative exploration in two fourth grade classrooms. *Cognition and Instruction, 18*(2), 239–283.

Viator, M. (2012). Developing historical thinking through questions. *Social Studies, 103*(5), 198–200.

Voelker, D., & Armstrong, A. (2013). Designing a question-driven U.S. history course. *OAH Magazine of History, 27*(3), 19–24

von Garnier, K. (Director). (2004) *Iron jawed angels.* HBO Video.

Voss, J., & Wiley, J. (1997). Developing understanding while writing essays in history. *International Journal of Educational Research, 27*(3), 255–265.

Wanzek, J., Shawn C. Kent, S. C., & Stillman-Spisak, S. J. (2015). Student perceptions of instruction in middle and secondary U.S. history classes. *Theory and Research in Social Education, 43*(4), 469–498.

Waring, S., & Hartshorne, R. (2020). *Conducting authentic historical inquiry: Engaging learners with SOURCES and emerging technologies.* Teachers College Press.

Wassermann, S. (2010). Effective classroom discussions: Five guidelines can build students' higher-order thinking skills. *Educational Leadership, 67*(5).

Weibe, G. (2016, November 18). Crop it: Hands on primary source analysis strategy. *History Tech.* https://historytech.wordpress.com/2016/11/18/crop-it-hands-on-primary-source-analysis-strategy/

Weibe, G. (2017, March 9). Tip of the week: The perfect mashup-PSSAs and evidence analysis window frames. *History Tech.* https://historytech.wordpress.com/2017/03/09/tip-of-the-week-the-perfect-mashup-pssas-and-evidence-analysis-window-frames/

Weibe, G. (2020, December 2). I'm still loving hexagonal thinking. And so should you. *History Tech.* https://historytech.wordpress.com/2020/12/02/im-still-loving-hexagonal-thinking-and-so-should-you/

Wexler, N. (2019). *The knowledge gap: The hidden cause of America's broken education system—and how to fix it.* Avery.

What's the wisdom on . . . evidence and sources. (2019). *Teaching History, 176,* 22–25.

What's the wisdom on . . . enquiry questions. (2020). *Teaching History, 176,* 16–19.

What's the wisdom on . . . consequence. (2021). *Teaching History, 182,* 50–53.

Wheeler, W. (2007). *Discovering the American past: A look at the evidence, Volume 2.* Cengage Learning.

Whittington, D. (1991). What have seventeen-year-olds known in the past? *American Educational Research Journal, 28,* 759–80.

Why simulation activities should not be used. (2018). ADL. https://www.adl.org/education/resources/tools-and-strategies/why-simulation-activities-should-not-be-used

Wilen, W. (2004). Refuting misconceptions about classroom discussion. *The Social Studies, 95*(1), 33–39.

Wiley, J., & Voss, J. (1999). Constructing arguments from multiple sources: Tasks that promote understanding and not just memory for text. *Journal of Educational Psychology, 91*(2), 301–311.

William, D. (2011). *Embedded formative assessment.* Solution Tree Press.

Willingham, D. (2010). *Why don't students like school? A cognitive scientist answers questions about how the mind works and what it means for the classroom.* Wiley.

Willingham, D. (2017). *The reading mind: A cognitive approach to understanding how the mind reads.* Jossey-Bass.

Wilschut, A. (2012). *Images of time: The role of a historical consciousness of time in learning history.* Information Age.

Wilschut, A., & Schiphorst, K. (2019). "One has to take leave as much as possible of one's own standards and values": Improving and measuring historical empathy and perspective reconstruction. *History Education Research Journal, 16*(1), 74–87.

Wilson, H. (1928). Cartoons as an aid in the teaching of history. *The School Review, 36*(3), 192–198.

Wineburg, S. (1991). On the reading of historical texts: Notes on the breach between school and the academy. *American Educational Research Journal, 28*(3), 495–519.

Wineburg, S. (2001). *Historical thinking and other unnatural acts: Charting the future of teaching the past.* Temple University Press.

Wineburg, S., & Martin, D. (2009). Tampering with History: Adapting Primary Sources for Struggling Readers. *Social Education, 73*(5), 212–216.

Wineburg, S., Martin, D., & Monte-Sano, C. (2011). *Reading like a historian: Teaching literacy in middle and high school classrooms.* Teachers College Press.

Wineburg, S., Mosborg, S., Porat, D., & Duncan, A. (2007). Forrest Gump and the future of teaching the past. *Phi Delta Kappan, 89*(3), 168–177.

Woodson, A. (2015). "What you supposed to know": Urban Black students' perspectives on history textbooks. *Journal of Urban Learning Teaching and Research, 11,* 57–65

Woodward, A., & Elliott, D. (1990). *Textbook use and teacher professionalism: Textbooks and school in the United States.* National Society for the Study of Education.

Worth, P. (2017). 'It's like this big, black hole, Miss, that's dragging everything into it.' Year 9 consider the impact of World War I on Russia by playing with the idea of consequence 'shapes.' *lobworth.* lobworth.com/2017/09/24/its-like-this-big

-black-hole-missthats-dragging-verything-into-it-year-9-consider-the-impact-of-world-war-ion-russia-by-playing-with-the-idea-of-consequence-shapes/

Yazzie-Mintz, E. (2010). *Charting the path from engagement to achievement: A report on the 2009 high school survey of student engagement.* Indiana University Center for Evaluation and Education Policy.

Yoon, K., Duncan, T., Lee, S., Scarloss, B., & Shapley, K. (2007). *Reviewing the evidence on how teacher professional development affects student achievement.* U.S. Department of Education, Institute of Educational Sciences, National Center for Education Evaluation and Regional Assistance, Regional Educational Laboratory Southwest.

Young, K., & Leinhardt, G. (1998). Writing from primary documents: A way of knowing history. *Written Communication, 15,* 25–68.

Zimmerman, J., & Robertson, E. (2017). *The case for contention: Teaching controversial issues in American schools.* University of Chicago Press.

Index

The letter *f* following a page number refers to a figure.

About the Author

Bruce A. Lesh was a high school teacher and social studies department chair for 22 years in the Baltimore County Public Schools in Maryland, where he taught United States history, world history, and Advanced Placement United States Politics and Government. From 2015 to 2022, he worked as the coordinator of social studies and then as a curriculum director at the Maryland State Department of Education, where he provided support to 24 Local Education Agencies' (LEA) supervisors and teachers for social studies, science, STEM, environmental literacy, and disciplinary literacy standards and frameworks.

In Maryland, Bruce co-founded and served as a member of the board of directors for the Center for History Education at the University of Maryland, Baltimore County, and was elected president of the Maryland Council for the Social Studies and vice-chair of the National Council for History Education. In 2008 he was named the national Teacher of the Year by the Organization of American Historians, and in 2013 the Maryland Secondary Social Studies Teacher of the Year by the Maryland Council for the Social Studies. From 2001 to 2011, Bruce served as a master teacher on 41 federally funded Teaching American History grants and has provided professional development in 38 states. In 2011, his book *"Why Won't You Just Tell Us the Answer?" Teaching Historical Thinking in Grades 7–12* was published.

About the Author